Violence and the Oedipal Unconscious

Violence and the Oedipal Unconscious

VOLUME 1

THE CATHARSIS HYPOTHESIS

Nidesh Lawtoo

Michigan State University Press · *East Lansing*

Michigan State University Press
East Lansing, Michigan 48823-5245

This project has received funding from the European Research Council (ERC) under the European
Union's Horizon 2020 research and innovation programme (grant agreement n°716181).

Library of Congress Cataloging-in-Publication Data is available
ISBN 978-1-61186-448-9 (paperback)
ISBN 978-1-60917-724-9 (PDF)
ISBN 978-1-62895-491-3 (ePub)
ISBN 978-1-62896-485-1 (Kindle)

Cover design by David Drummond, Salamander Design, www.salamanderhill.com.
Cover art is *Color-Dream*, by Michaela Lawtoo.

Visit Michigan State University Press at *www.msupress.org*

To Kim
explorer of many myths

Through the arousal of pity and fear [tragedy] effect[s] the *katharsis* of such emotions.
—Aristotle, *Poetics*

Under the treatment, therefore, "catharsis" came about when the path to consciousness was opened and there was a normal discharge of affect.
—Sigmund Freud, "Two Encyclopedia Articles"

"You'd think, that if people could commit any crime they could think of, they'd get it out of their system."
—Detective Tedeschi, *Vice*

Contents

Acknowledgments

Violence is not an abstract subject that can be captured via a totalizing, universal theory; rather, it emerges from specific historical contexts that consciously and often unconsciously inform cultural theory—including mimetic theory. It is thus not indifferent that the genealogical starting point of this Janus-faced study goes back to a visiting appointment I held at Johns Hopkins University from 2013 to 2016. At Hopkins, I had the privilege of working at the legendary Humanities Center that played such a major role in the birth of (French) theory back in 1966—including poststructuralism and mimetic theory. Baltimore also provided the less privileged experience of living in a city plagued by segregation, violence, and racist oppression. Freddie Gray was murdered during my stay; so was a four-year-old African American child in my son's primary school in West Baltimore. If the first context provided the logos to reopen the ancient dossier on the relation between representations of violence and the unconscious, the latter provided the contemporary pathos that urged me to start writing in the first place.

I would like to thank my former colleagues Paola Marrati, Hent de Vries, Michael Fried, Ruth Leys, Paul Delnero, Yi-Ping Ong, Leonardo (Leo) Lisi, Evelyn Ender, Gabrielle (Gaby) Spiegel, and the members of the Mellon seminar for providing a stimulating intellectual context during my stay, and Richard (Dick) Macksey for sharing stories about Derrida, Girard, and other suspects in his legendary library. On the side of politics, warm thanks go to William (Bill) Connolly, Jane Bennett, and our "nameless" reading group for vibrant summer-night discussions that turned into friendships. Bill deserves double thanks for always fostering exemplary intellectual explorations over professional territorializations. And Mikkel Borch-Jacobsen I thank for continuing conversations started long ago confirming that the *bistouri* of the philosophical physician cuts deep in the pathologies of the modern soul.

Most of this study was written thanks to the generous support of the European Research Council (ERC) under Horizon 2020, which single-handedly funded the *Homo Mimeticus* (HOM) project from 2016 to 2022 at the Institute of Philosophy and the Faculty of Arts, KU Leuven, Belgium. Interdisciplinary bridges tend to be promoted in theory, but the reality is that they are dependent on external funding to be constructed in practice— and on friendly collaborations. Many joined in the bricolage of a new theory of mimesis by participating in the HOM seminar (2017–), workshops, and international conferences. First in line is my HOM team, now redoubled by the Gendered Mimesis team—including Niki Hadikoesoemo, Daniel Villegas Vélez, Wojciech Kaftanski, María Ortega Máñez, Marina García-Granero, Giulia Rignano, Willow Verkerk, and Isabell Dahms—all contributing to shifting the focus of mimesis from simple realism to complex forms of dramatic, affective, and performative practices.

Along the journey, I benefited from a host of invitations and transdisciplinary collaborations that helped the dissemination of homo mimeticus. Names of supporters include, in rough chronological order, Henry Staten, Christian Borch, Pierpaolo Antonello, Patricia Pisters, Jean-Luc Nancy, Adriana Cavarero, Jean-Michel Rabaté, Bill Connolly, Jane Bennett, Esa Kirkkopelto, Hélio Rebello, Ortwin de Graef, Tom Toremans, Sascha Bru, Anke Gilleir (and the MDRN Team), Roland Breeur, Julia Jansen, the LMU Mimesis Team, Carlo Brentari, James Corby, Ivan Callus, Deborah Jenson, Andrea (Mubi) Brighenti, Wolfgang Palaver, Dietmar Regensburger and the Colloquium on Violence & Religion, Alessandra Campo, Hans Alma, Agnieszka Soltysik Monnet, Rafael Sànchez, Fabrizio Deriu, Sandor (Sandy)

Goodhart, Silvia Benso, Herman Siemens, Susanna Lindberg, Kieran Keo-
hane, and many others still joining as I write.

And over the years, a number of influential thinkers and friends from
both sides of the Atlantic have joined forces in productive dialogues and
encounters now part of HOM Videos. Each encounter is always singularly
unique; each dialogue flourished in unforgettable locations—from Baltimore to Deer Isle, Paris to Verona, Strasbourg to Leuven, among other
inspiring places—that provide not simply a background but an atmosphere
for the ancient but always new practice of *dia-logos*. In different tonalities
of voices, they all contribute to the *mimetic turn*, or *re*-turn to mimesis,
in different areas of critical theory. Singular-plural voices and perspectives
on film include J. Hillis Miller (literary theory), Bill Connolly (political
theory), Edgar Morin (complexity theory), Jean-Luc Nancy (philosophy),
Adriana Cavarero (feminist philosophy), Christoph Wulf (anthropology),
Marco Iacoboni (neuroscience), Kevin Warwick and Katherine Hayles
(posthuman studies), Gunter Gebauer (philosophy), and Mikkel Borch-
Jacobsen (history of psychology).[1] I could not have hoped for a more
inspiring, stimulating, and life-affirmative chorus to give a pluralist voice
to homo mimeticus.

And then, after a long journey, every author needs a home attentive to
both the rigor of logos and the lived experience of pathos. Special thanks
go to my editor, William (Bill) Johnsen, for capturing my first phantom
book early on, whispering to a sailor on a stormy passage, "Why not write
another?" and, in a last affirmative push, encouraging a nomadic theorist to
launch homo mimeticus toward new hypermimetic territories.

Last but not least, this journey would never have started in the first
place without the *sympatheia* of my nomadic family: Kim I thank for never
tiring of navigating the *Odyssey*, whose passage home (*nostos*) provides
HOM with a *stella maris*; Nia, for echoing Athena's wisdom and confirming that "violence is very dangerous"—a blue-eyed beacon for this dark
subject; and Michi Lawtoo, for sharing the helm and keeping it steady over
numerous high-risk sea passages. I find it only adequate that her inimitable *techne* in the end, captured the artistic auras of both the Oedipal and
mimetic unconscious—now on the surface to see and feel.

Portions of volumes 1 and 2 have appeared in modified form in the following journals and collections. I am grateful they could be reproduced and expanded to form a broader argument.

"Violence and the Mimetic Unconscious (Part One). The Cathartic Hypothesis: Aristotle, Freud, Girard," *Contagion* 25 (2018): 159–91.

"Violence and the Mimetic Unconscious (Part Two). The Contagious Hypothesis: Plato, Affect, Mirror Neurons," *Contagion* 26 (2019): 123–60.

"The Mimetic Unconscious: A Mirror for Genealogical Reflections," in *Imitation, Contagion, Suggestion: On Mimesis and Society*, ed. Christian Borch, 37–53. London: Routledge, 2019.

"The Double Meanings of Violence: *Catharsis* and *Mimesis*," in *Violence and Meaning*, ed. Lode Lauwaert, Laura Katherine Smith, and Christian Sternad, 137–65. London: Palgrave Macmillan, 2019.

"The Insurrection Moment: Intoxication, Conspiracy Assault," *Theory & Event* (2023).

Prologue

This is a Janus-faced study about the affective power of violent images
that cannot simply be contemplated from a safe visual distance. Instead,
they tend to break through the screen of representation, affecting and
infecting us in our daily lives—if not consciously, at least unconsciously so.
I say "us," rather than "humans" or "them," because a degree of first-person,
affective, and perhaps even embodied participation coming from a plurality
of—gendered, ethnic, sexual, social, national, etc.—perspectives, is called for
to come to terms with the all too human relation between violence and the
unconscious. My wager is, in fact, that it is necessary to initially experience the
connection with the pathos of violence from an affective proximity in order to
better theorize it from a critical distance.

Perhaps, then, to involve you from the outset as an active participant in
this diagnostic investigation, let me start by asking you a few questions. If
you picked up this book, you are already interested in the relation between
violence and the unconscious. But let me start closer to home, by inverting

perspectives, and asking you something more personal, maybe too personal, but also more experientially felt. After all, these feelings may have been accentuated by the prolonged period of lockdown caused by the coronavirus pandemic across the world since 2020—a pandemic that, at the moment I write, is still ongoing and is quite likely to return in the near future.

So, here come my questions: Does your unconscious want something that is beyond your reach? Now imagine a place where there are no laws, no rules, no consequences. Imagine it in detail. Relax, immerse yourself in an imaginary scene of your own choice, and give free rein to your most secret fantasies. . . . You would like to travel to exotic locations? Why not rent a luxurious bungalow on a deserted island surrounded by turquoise water? You want money and a rush of excitement? Enact a bank robbery modeled on legendary cinematic classics. You dream of a more active nightlife? Imagine no restrictions and go out clubbing with stunning models dancing to the beat of intoxicating music, from dusk till dawn. Or perhaps you are in the mood for a little adventure, some romance, or maybe even uncensored eroticism? Transgress a few taboos with the same models who respond to intimate embraces with pathos and sex appeal—or anything else you ever dreamed of. And since there are no laws, and thus no consequences, you can go far, very far, to the limit of transgressive experiences where sex turns into violence—and death.

Cut! Rewind. Now replay the scene in slow motion.

Is the pathos triggered by these imaginary fantasies revisited from a critical distance already making you uncomfortable? That is indeed part of the point. But please rest assured. In a superficial sense, there should be no cause for concern. After all, I have just welcomed you to join a fictional, rather than real, scenario—an imaginary scenario that sets the critical, but also affective and conceptual, stage for an ancient yet also modern and, as we shall see, still contemporary riddle on the cathartic and/or contagious effects of representations of violence on the unconscious in the digital age.

A Fictional Scene

"Welcome to *Vice*!" says Bruce Willis at the opening of a trailer for a science-fiction (sf) film titled *Vice* (2015), directed by Brian A. Miller. With his

Julian Michaels (Bruce Willis) and VICE Resort in *Vice* (dir. Brian Miller, 2015)

inimitable sarcastic smile, Willis appears against the very background of the cinematic fantasies I have just echoed at one remove, on the page; the film originally projects these fantasies on the digitized screen of your own choice, redoubling the actor's suggestive power to trigger viewers' transgressive imagination.

Elegantly dressed, radiating confidence, success, and a prestige amplified by his status as a cinematic star, Bruce Willis plays the role of a fictional character named Julian Michaels, the CEO of an "adult entertainment" company who welcomes spectators—both within the film and, at one remove, outside the screen—into a futuristic world of leisure, pleasure, sex, and violence. Staring straight into the camera, the actor voluntarily breaks the fourth wall and asks: "Have you ever wanted something that is beyond your reach? Now imagine a place where there are no laws, no rules, no consequences." And by saying so, "he," Bruce Willis, that is, Julian Michaels, invites spectators to join him, if only for a few hours, on his side of the screen to vicariously participate in a futuristic and quite exclusive resort called VICE, which he sells as nothing less than "a utopian paradise where you can have or do *anything* you want." Not only luxurious hotels, robberies, clubbing, and uncensored eroticism, but also physical assault, rape, and murder are fair game in the world of VICE—precisely because it is "just" a game. Or rather, it is a cinematic fiction that reflects, and urges critically inclined viewers to reflect on, contemporary forms of entertainment that include film as well as TV series, online platforms, pornographic websites, and video games that, on our side of the screen, already simulate violent, often misogynistic, and racist fantasies that, as *Vice* suggests, are, nolens volens, constitutive of the digital age. "No laws," we are assured, are limiting this world of pure entertainment. And so, for the duration of the film, Michaels encourages spectators to suspend disbelief, relax, lower the critical guard, and accept the welcome to VICE and, by extension, the welcome to the digitized world of violent simulations it alludes to.

The Riddle Reloaded

Reflecting on a specific case study that already belongs to a "traditional" twentieth-century medium such as film, allows us to reevaluate the pros and cons of an ancient riddle on the psychic effects of representations of violence that are no longer limited to cinema but are constitutive of a plurality of new digital media in the twenty-first century. With respect to the traditional defenses of aesthetic representations of violence, the pros are familiar; they are not deprived of convincing arguments, which are implicit in the very genre of fiction (from Latin, *fingere*, "to shape or form" but also "to feign").

   After all, *Vice*, just like the violent online simulations the film alludes to, dramatizes an entertaining illusion that should not be confused with reality, if only because as a sf film, it is not even based on a transparently realistic representation of reality. As we decide to go to the cinema, watch a film on our flat screen, or, more likely, stream it directly from Netflix on a computer, tablet, or smartphone, we are clearly invited into a fictional world of make-believe that few in the digital age would mistake for reality itself. Actors like Bruce Willis are lavishly paid to impersonate roles; no real transgressions are normally committed on the set—though unintentional killings are not unheard of. Above all, as we watch the movie from an aesthetic distance, we certainly are not breaking any laws—at least not in a free, democratic, and pluralist world not plagued by censorship. If spectators feel like imaginatively partaking in scenes of violence whose origins are as old as the dawn of aesthetics, which films like *Vice* invite us to contemplate, and video games like *Cyberpunk 2077* allow us to actively simulate, there should indeed be no consequences, as the film's trailer promises. Perhaps, then, what was true for tragic spectacles in the past remains true for the violence internal to contemporary films and games in the present: the fictional images on-screen are but shadows or phantoms that a minimally alert spectator has learned since childhood not to confuse with the real world—if only because they are mere copies, appearances, or simulacra that should not be mistaken for reality itself.

And yet, as the ancient Greeks were the first to suspect at the dawn of philosophy, representations of violence, no matter how false in appearance, call for careful diagnostics of their affective powers to generate effects in spectators nonetheless—be they good or bad, therapeutic or pathological. Thus, the counterargument goes, if the trailer stages violent cinematic actions that are fictional, illusory, and, in this epistemological sense, not real, that is, false, and far removed from reality, the powers of fictions can also trigger affective impressions on spectators that are clearly felt, experienced, and, in this psychological sense, have real embodied effects, again—for both good and ill. In revisiting the ancient riddle of the effects of violent representations, or simulations, from a contemporary perspective, my focus will thus not be moral, let alone moralistic, but instead diagnostic and interpretative.

Media change historically, generating new forms of simulation, but the philosophical problem is far from new. We will thus be in good intellectual company in the pages that follow. A respectable genealogy of thinkers engaged with the heterogeneous problematic of *mimesis* (imitation and representation, but also impersonation, identification, influence, reproduction, simulation, among other meanings) has been diagnostically attentive to what we call (new) media violence. Already Plato, for instance, critiqued representations of violence in literary classics like the *Iliad* for dramatizing models of behavior that promote violent affects and sexual transgressions. He did so not only because these mythic tales did not tell what he considered to be the truth about the gods (moral and epistemic reasons), but also because he worried such spectacles generate contagious effects on the irrational part of the soul (psychological and pedagogical reasons). Conversely, Plato's most influential student, Aristotle, in an agonistic inversion of perspective that is not deprived of mirroring continuities with his teacher, defended tragedies like *Oedipus Rex* that stage an exemplary case of violent actions and sexual transgressions that reach into the present. Aristotle defended tragedy not only for encouraging rational, cognitive, perhaps even philosophical thoughts; he also considered that the pathos tragic violence generates has purifying effects he grouped under the concept of "catharsis," an enigmatic concept that will inform a number of subsequent theories and methods—including the "cathartic method" that gave birth to psychoanalytical theories predicated on an Oedipal myth.

Over two millennia later, due to genealogical vicissitudes we shall have to trace in some detail, such myths are still with us, giving us interpretative keys that inform, or misinform, contemporary perspectives. For instance, the fantasies the *Vice* trailer represents in the illusory sphere of cinematic fiction seem specifically constructed to trigger in the audience what René Girard would call "mimetic desires." The desire to see the movie in the first place and get a taste of such lawless, utopian, and transgressive representations of vice—albeit at two removes; but perhaps also the desire to be in the prestigious position Julian Michaels dramatizes as a fictional character, and Bruce Willis impersonates as an actor qua cinematic star in reality—an imaginary identification that, the trailer assures, allows you to "have anything you want."

Once such perspectives are considered in the company of a long genealogy of thinkers of violence and mimesis that goes from antiquity to modernity reaching into the present, an affective and conceptual Pandora's box is reopened and a plurality of more insidious diagnostic questions that go beyond good and evil evaluations naturally emerge. For instance: Who is the "you" that is the subject of this "want"? And if Michaels addressing "you" clearly intends to include all viewers of the film, do *you* really want it? After all, films like *Vice*, and the kinds of entertainment the images in the background refer to (robberies, dance, sex, etc.), target a specifically male, often white, privileged, and digitally connected audience. Consequently, the mimetic mechanisms surreptitiously at play in the film's trailer already structure viewers' desires, beginning, middle, and end, on prescribed cinematic (male/white) models that designate other (female) subjects as privileged "objects" of desire.

Do *we*, then, consciously—that is, intentionally—want to be affectively involved in a patriarchal, misogynistic, and phallocentric transgressive utopia that, as the film will soon confirm, can quickly turn into a violent dystopia? Or should we consider such forms of entertainment (film, internet websites, video games) as legitimate virtual resorts that allow for transgressive experiences that can be put to social, progressive, and perhaps even emphatic or therapeutic social use? More generally, are we the conscious subjects of the desires these (new) media intentionally elicit in the sphere of fiction? Or are we rather being unconsciously subjected to fictional actions that trigger deeply felt, embodied reactions that threaten to blur the line dividing fiction and reality, online and offline behavior? Above all, and to echo diagnostic preoccupations that are already internal to the plot of *Vice*: Do simulations of violence serve a therapeutic, medical, or, to use this ancient concept, cathartic function that gets violence out of people's systems? Or, alternatively, do these simulations have the potential to bleed across the screen dividing the world of entertainment from "this world" via a pathological form of affective contagion?

An Ancient Quarrel

As these questions indicate, this cinematic fiction brings us very quickly to the heart of an ancient yet also modern and still contemporary quarrel over the effects of aesthetic representations of violence on spectators. This quarrel, like all good quarrels worth revisiting, is Janus-faced, for it looks in opposed directions. On one side, it looks back to the origins of western aesthetics and reopens an ancient contest, or agon, that posits Plato's hypothesis on the contagious effects of representations of violence (or affective hypothesis) contra Aristotle's hypothesis on their cathartic effects (or catharsis hypothesis); on the other side, it looks ahead to contemporary quarrels on network-based (new) media violence that, despite the numerous innovations in the media that allow for increasing degrees of immersive participation—or perhaps because of it—continue, to this day, to oscillate, pendulum-like, between these competing hypotheses. If my linguistic reproduction of *Vice*'s cinematic welcome was far removed indeed from the original cinematic fiction, it may at least have succeeded in subliminally foregrounding one point that, despite the oscillations of perspectives, will remain central throughout this study on violence and the unconscious: namely that, for good and ill, fictional representations or simulations of violence may not always remain confined within the autonomous sphere of fiction; they can also generate affective, embodied, and unconscious effects on viewers and users that call for new diagnostic investigations in the digital age.

Confronted with this Janus-faced quarrel, my mimetic hypothesis will thus also be double; and this doubleness is already reflected in the two-part structure of this study that form a diptych on violence and the unconscious. My argument will unfold in two separate but related volumes that both mirror and invert perspectives on the double problematic of violence and the unconscious. The mirroring titles of these volumes reflect two competing conceptions of the unconscious that offer different perspectives on the effects of representations of violence throughout the ages. The first is titled *Violence and the Oedipal Unconscious*, volume 1, *The Catharsis Hypothesis*; it establishes a genealogical connection between a conception of catharsis that originates in classical antiquity in Aristotle's thought and, via a series of genealogical vicissitudes I shall consider in detail, provides a key to the so-called Freudian "discovery" of the unconscious that finds in *Oedipus Rex* a paradigmatic and universal case study that continues to cast a shadow on contemporary culture. The second is titled *Violence and the Mimetic Unconscious*, volume 2, *The Affective Hypothesis*, and its starting point is equally ancient: it originates in Plato's critique of mimesis and, via a series of equally complex genealogical turns, finds its contemporary version in recent discoveries in the neurosciences that contribute to a return of attention to a relational, embodied, and performative conception of mimesis internal to homo mimeticus. The competing genealogical perspectives on the relation between violence and the unconscious differ significantly and will eventually lead to antithetical conclusions. And yet, like all mirroring confrontations, the advocates of each tradition know their respective counterparts, reflect on one another, and will help us reevaluate the value of their hypotheses on catharsis and contagion. Hence the need to tell both sides of a Janus-faced story of violence and the unconscious via a diptych on catharsis and contagion before coming to any rushed diagnostic conclusion.

At the level of method, both volumes share two general mimetic principles that inform both the catharsis and the affective hypothesis and give intellectual unity to this double argument. On one side, I draw on a long-standing tradition of transdisciplinary theorists of mimesis in order to take some genealogical distance from the still controversial topic of media violence. This genealogical distance will allow me to trace the theoretical

vicissitudes of two antagonistic but related concepts (catharsis and contagion) that, while fundamental to the debate on (new) media violence, have
rarely, if ever, been reevaluated from a *longue durée*, genealogical perspective. This perspective is long for it considers major thinkers of violence and
mimesis that go from antiquity (Plato and Aristotle) to modern(ist) theories
of the unconscious (Bernays to Nietzsche, Freud to Bataille) to contemporary theories of violence (Girard to Lacoue-Labarthe, Arendt to Cavarero),
among others.

At the same time, theoretical reflections on contagion and catharsis will
be shadowed by specific examples of (new) media violence involving genres
as diverse as theater, film, reality TV, and video games (like *Cyberpunk 2077*),
stretching to include (new) fascist insurrections triggered by conspiracy
theories and anticipated by TV series (like *Black Mirror*). On the other
side, we will articulate a genealogy of the contagion and catharsis hypothesis internal to disciplines as diverse as continental philosophy, psychology,
psychoanalysis, aesthetics, literary theory, media studies, digital humanities,
cultural studies, literary theory, and political theory. Together, these perspectives stretch to include recent turns to affect, embodiment, and mirroring
reflexes constitutive of what I call the mimetic turn or *re*-turn; they will also
open up two related but competing conceptions of the unconscious—the
Oedipal and the mimetic unconscious—on which contemporary debates on
media violence often rest, if not explicitly at least implicitly so. Once joined,
we shall see that these two cathartic/affective hypotheses on violence and the
unconscious provide broader, not always completely new, but nonetheless
revealing, illuminating, and perhaps even original genealogical foundations
to account for the riddle of (new) media violence *Vice* invites us to revisit.
A methodological point should be clear from the outset. As my subjective
opening, interpretative case study, and imaginary and rather unorthodox
questionnaire already implicitly suggested, this study is not intended as an
empirical, quantifiable, sociological contribution to what is an already widely
discussed and still controversial topic in the social and empirical sciences.
While the debate on the effects of impersonations, representations, and
simulations of violence is still ongoing and difficult to answer unilaterally
given the protean diversity of new media, the different forms of violence at
play in the digital age, and the methodological difficulty in proving direct
causal effects between (new) media violence and behavioral violence, at least

one point looks increasingly certain: the line dividing fiction and reality, violent representations online and violent insurrections offline, imaginary actions and embodied reactions in a world increasingly immersed in simulations of violence that are also violent simulations, is becoming increasingly porous, generating heterogeneous affective continuities that might spill over and beyond the screen of digital representations that connect and disconnect digital users hooked on a plurality of digital screens. Disturbing homologies can potentially emerge as the heterogeneous violence we *see* from an exterior aesthetic distance generates a violent pathos already at play in the real world. Sometimes this violence can even be lethal for actors on cinematic sets, as real guns can still be legally used in the United States to simulate fictional scenes with all too real effects—already an alarming indication that the line dividing fiction and reality can be thin and porous at best. More regularly, however, the pathos of fictional violence might contribute, if not to directly trigger, cause, or determine, at least to partially influence, normalize, or even numb viewers and gamers, to violent models of behavior that increasingly affect new generations in the digital age.

Furthering a modernist theory of mimesis inaugurated in a trilogy of books started in *The Phantom of the Ego* (2013), subsequently developed in *Conrad's Shadow* (2016), and brought to bear onto the present in *(New) Fascism* (2019), in this diptych on *Violence and the Unconscious* I shall step farther back to the origins of theories of *mimēsis* in classical antiquity to leap ahead and provide steps toward a new theory of imitation for the future. In order to do so, new concepts will have to be created that expand the reaches of our modernist mimetic theory to a generalized theory of homo mimeticus. For instance, while desires remain imitative, a future-oriented theory cannot be restricted to mimetic desire alone. Instead, I propose the concept of *mimetic pathos* to indicate that all affects are mimetic, for both good and ill. Thus, I rely on a double perspective attentive to both the infectious and experiential power of affect or pathos to generate what I call *pathologies*, on one side, and a critical account or logos on this pathos considered from a genealogical distance I group under the rubric of *patho-logies*, on the other. Catharsis and contagion will thus serve as the conceptual links that both connect and disconnect pathologies from patho-*logies*. In the process, the catharsis hypothesis and the infective, contagious or, as I shall call it, affective hypothesis also set the stage for a theoretical contest, or *agon*, that traverses the history of western aesthetics and organizes this book in two related, sometimes competing, and ultimately symmetric and mirroring arguments. Since the mirroring continuities between the cathartic and affective hypotheses are as significant as the inversion of perspectives that mirroring reflections usually entail, I shall qualify this agon in terms of *mimetic agonism*. Catharsis contra contagion: this is the genuine mirroring antagonism I will be struggling with in the diptych that follows. The ambition? Contribute to a new theory of homo mimeticus that is already facing some of the main challenges of the twenty-first century.[1]

Last but not least, this genealogy of violence and the unconscious will lead me to go repeatedly beyond fictional representations. I shall thus investigate scenes of crimes that increasingly blur the line between representations of violence and real violence via classical but also modern and contemporary examples, or case studies, some of which are quite recent, that continue to emerge as I write these prefatory lines. We live in a hypermimetic world haunted by new and heterogeneous forms of violence that may metastasize online before bleeding offline; or, vice versa, they might start offline before being disseminated online and subsequently retroacting offline, generating spiraling feedback loops that call for new diagnostic operations.

This mimetic or, better, hypermimetic spiral includes the much-discussed issue of media violence and the mass shootings that continue to plague countries deprived of basic gun regulations but are not limited to them. In the age of progressive movements like Black Lives Matter (BLM) and #MeToo, on one side, and violent insurrections constitutive of (new) fascism and authoritarian wars on the other, it is crucial for new generations of theorists of mimesis to broaden the scope of investigation and include emerging phenomena that are not limited to (new) media violence but cast a revealing light on the relation between violence and the unconscious more generally. As this Janus-faced argument unfolds, I shall thus take care to look back, genealogically, to the foundations of theories of catharsis and contagion from antiquity to modernity while also keeping an eye on the present. Especially in the second volume, I shall increasingly put genealogical lenses to use to propose close readings of police murders of ethnic minority populations, especially African Americans; sexual assaults on women; conspiracy theories online that give rise to (new) fascist insurrections offline; and role-playing video games, among other recent manifestations of violent pathologies that cast a long shadow on the contemporary world.

As an introductory gesture, let me thus step into the detective's shoes, so to speak. My aim is to supplement the fictional diagnostic internal to the plot of *Vice* from a broader genealogical perspective attentive to the enigmatic relation between violence and the unconscious from antiquity to the present.

Introduction

Homo Mimeticus

The riddle of the effects of media violence that *Vice* stages cinematically is not original and has already received much attention in recent years; yet this does not mean that the riddle has been adequately solved, or that the subject of investigation has lost any of its originality in the digital age. Quite the contrary, the proliferation of digital media in a network-based society continues to make this ancient subject new, bringing it regularly, insistently, and perhaps even obsessively to the forefront of the daily news, while also encouraging new generations of theorists to take critical distance from the pathos that mediatized violence generates.

In the wake of steady numbers of mass shootings that routinely plague the United States but are increasingly frequent in other parts of the world as well, terrorist attacks that often seem to be modeled on previous attacks, including fictional or cinematic attacks, wars that start in cyberspace and now bleed over into territorial invasions, not to speak of the contagious spread of conspiracy theories that are epistemologically false yet generate all too real, and often violent and deadly, effects, both traditional and new media tend to give the impression that violence is everywhere: in the news and in the streets, in films and in schools, in TV series and in the office space, in reality

TV shows and in fictional political shows, on social media and video games, at home and on the way home, among other venues, which, as anti-violence transnational movements like #MeToo and BLM have made clear, continue to disproportionally affect women and ethnic minorities across the globe.

In a hyperconnected world, it is indeed difficult to spend one day without falling under the shadow of the protean manifestations of violence, be it real or fictional, represented or simulated, played out in video games or suffered in daily life. Consequently, especially (but not only) when it comes to mass shootings, it is not surprising that journalists might be prompted by the deeply felt pathos for the victims (often children) of what appear to be meaningless forms of violence to establish a direct causal connection between fictional crimes that perpetrators may have observed in films, or simulated in video games, and the horrifying crimes they reenacted in reality. This is an understandable emotional association. It can be intuitively felt and, in many cases, legitimately suspected. And yet, to this day, it remains very difficult to confirm empirically. If generalized and repeated uncritically, this simplistic billiard-ball causal view might even be contributing to generating conspiracy theories about (new) media violence online, in a spiraling regress that contributes to blurring the already tenuous line between reality and fiction, online theories and offline practices.

Establishing a correlation is one thing; proving direct causation is quite another. This, at least, is what the growing literature on media violence tends to agree upon, though a consensus on the effects of such a complex phenomenon is far from being reached—and naturally so, given the increasingly heterogeneous media environment characteristic of the digital age.[1] If I group this problematic under the rubric of "(new) media violence," it is thus not in an impossible aspiration to cover all the empirical manifestations of this protean and fast-evolving phenomenon, for my approach will be focused on two specific hypotheses that provide the theoretical foundations that launched the debate in the first place.

The parentheses around the "(new)" serve thus a double function: first, they indicate that the media may be new in the digital age but the debate on media violence is far from new and goes back to the origins of aesthetic theory—hence the need to familiarize ourselves with this tradition; second, they suggest that the line dividing traditional media (literature, film, TV) and network-based digital media (social media, internet websites, video games) is porous and permeable at best—hence the need of diagnostics attentive to both continuities and discontinuities between old and new media. If the effects of violent simulations at play in different forms of fictional entertainment continue to be the source of a proliferating number of empirical studies, this book takes a less traveled, more qualitative, theoretical, and interpretative route. It considers that the tension, contest, or, as I prefer to call it, *agon* between the contagion and catharsis hypotheses internal to films like *Vice* cannot be restricted to *fictional* scenes of violence alone. Rather, it rests on a long-standing genealogy in western thought that goes all the way back to classical antiquity, informs modern theories of the unconscious, and stretches beyond the sphere of aesthetic representations or simulations to inform contemporary discussions about the effects of (new) media violence on the psychic life of the ego—turning a fictional agon into a real and quite complex theoretical agon.

The Catharsis vs. Contagion Agon

The diagnostic that emerges from the fictional yet theoretically realistic scene of violence in *Vice* is double and provides this book with a Janus-faced perspective on the ancient but always contemporary quarrel that opposes defenders of the catharsis hypothesis to advocates of the contagion or affective hypothesis on (new) media violence. In guise of introduction, let us take a closer look at the agon internal to this cinematic fiction. It will serve as a springboard to cast a retrospective glance on the theories that inform these competing perspectives, from antiquity to modernity, reaching into the present as well. If this method may sound academically unorthodox, we shall repeatedly confirm that it is rather classical in inspiration. It rests on an influential genealogy that ultimately goes back to Plato and Aristotle, two towering figures who set the stage for the philosophical contest on media violence via conceptually and affective informed analyses based on close readings of specific fictions. On their shoulders, I start from a present fiction that may not be a classic but has the theoretical advantage of looking ahead to future forms of new media violence that are currently impressing new generations in the digital age, while also looking back to the very origins of the quarrel between the competing hypotheses that will structure this Janus-faced inquiry—beginning, middle, and end.

On one side of the agon, the chief of police in *Vice* voices a diagnostic perspective that is unpopular within the film but is still quite popular in the collective imagination, perhaps because it has a venerable tradition to support it. For him, in fact, violence directed against androids—or, as they are called, "artificial" girls played by real actresses and metaphorical of fictional representations or simulations at play in film, pornography, and video games—is unproblematic. This kind of violence not only remains safely confined within the VICE resort and the autonomous sphere of online entertainment this resort alludes to; it can also serve as an outlet with beneficial societal effects. If the taxes paid by this exclusive resort "keep the city going," as the chief of police puts it, pointing to the economic interests behind the entertainment industry, his antagonist, Detective Roy Tedeschi (Thomas Jane) initially adds a more subtle, psychological supplement to this seemingly therapeutic but actually profit-oriented hypothesis. As he starts investigating a murder that spilled from the VICE resort into what he calls "this world," for it involves the killing of a real, rather than "artificial" girl, the detective enters the VICE resort for a criminal investigation that leads directly to the theoretical riddle we are concerned with. In an illuminating agonistic scene, he walks up to Julian Michaels (Bruce Willis), who already introduced us to this utopian resort with "no laws and no consequences," and confronts the CEO with the following diagnostic hypothesis, as he says: "You'd think that if people could commit any crime they could think of, they'd get it out of their system," repeatedly punching into his hand, for dramatic, embodied, and rhetorical emphasis.

An affective participation in a fictional crime and the violence it entails, according to this hypothesis, could get violence out of people's system. How? Via a purifying/purgative process that, to this day, despite the obscurity still surrounding this concept, is still often grouped under the ancient rubric of "*catharsis*." This is, indeed, what a long-standing tradition in philosophy, aesthetics, morality, but also religion, medicine, psychoanalysis, critical theory, literary studies, and media studies, has tended to think for a long time—at least up to the past century. For instance, in *The Encyclopedia of*

Media Violence (2013) the entry on "Catharsis Theory" initially suggests that the detective's hypothesis is not deprived of theoretical foundations, for it defines "catharsis" in the exact same popular terms: "'I just needed to blow off steam' or 'I just had to get that out of my system.'"[2] From this diagnostic perspective, then, (new) media violence and the entertainment it provides is not only harmless and profitable; it could even be therapeutic, in the sense that seeing a violent fictional action in a film, or participating in a violent simulation in a video game, might purge spectators of violent affective drives internal to their system—stretching perhaps to purify the social system as well.

Intuitive in theory, and widely integrated in common-sense understandings of this problem, the scientific evidence to support the catharsis hypothesis is actually not as solid as the popularity of this perspective may initially indicate. The same entry on "catharsis" continues as follows: "There has been little direct scientific evidence to support the idea that media viewing can lead to cathartic relief of negative emotions."[3] The evaluation is confirmed by a number of other studies. For instance, in *The 11 Myths of Media Violence* (2003), after giving an informed overview of the main advocates of the catharsis hypothesis in the second half of the twentieth century, media theorist James Potter states: "As of now, the research community is skeptical of such an effect, but this effect continues to have a great deal of intuitive appeal."[4] Strangely enough, then, this rather enigmatic Greek concept, which, as we shall see, has maddened philologists for centuries, "continues to receive attention," including attention from Hollywood blockbusters that not only testify to the popularity, longevity, and mass appeal of this hypothesis but also contribute to disseminating it. Nolens volens, catharsis is not only inextricably intertwined with the debate on (new) media violence; it also plays a key role in the discovery of an Oedipal unconscious that is also modeled on the "blow off steam" hypothesis. *Violence and the Oedipal Unconscious* aims to understand the multiple and long-standing sources of its "intuitive appeal" that continues to inform a good segment of the popular imagination, making it synonymous with what many would think. In fact, if accounts of (new) media violence have currently been transferred to video games, they continue to routinely include a section on catharsis. And even in game studies there continues to be "some indicators of support for the catharsis hypothesis"[5] we shall have to consider. How? By figuring out what catharsis means or entails for the philosophers and theorists who convoked the concept in the first place, for instance.

On the other side of the agon, the opposite diagnostic perspective posits (new) media violence not as a therapeutic solution but, rather, as a contagious pathology in need of a cure. Within the film, this is, indeed, Detective Tedeschi's investigative position. Immediately after convoking the catharsis hypothesis under the rubric of what people "would think," he continues the confrontation with VICE's CEO in a more critical diagnostic mood: "But these people get a taste, and they just can't get enough." Translated in more conceptual terms, the diagnostic internal to *Vice* is double and concerns both old and new media; it addresses both passive exposure to (new) media violence as in film or television *Vice* represents at the level of the cinematic *medium*, and active participations in simulations of violence in video games the film refers to at the level of its allegorical *message*. Both the message and the medium, the detective suggests, have the potential of generating violent addictions that may not remain contained within the sphere of entertainment but have effects that spill over into the social world. The underlying hypothesis is that through repeated exposure and repetition, both via representations and simulations, violence can become eventually normalized, viewers/gamers become desensitized, fictional models of violent behavior internalized, and the violence represented or simulated online turns into an addiction to violence with the potential to spill over offline as well. This, at least, is what *Vice* allegorically suggests at both the level of the medium and the message.

And yet a mirroring confrontation between these two levels of communication also adds an interesting paradoxical twist to the affective hypothesis that sets up a mirroring agon between the medium and the message. Notice, in fact, that the diagnostic critique of (new) media violence internal to the film's *message* is mediated by a cinematic *medium* that actively represents violence as a form of entertainment. As a sf action-thriller, *Vice* is indeed fully complicit with the violence it denounces. This is already an indication that even within perspectives that promote the affective hypothesis, the diagnostic on (new) media violence may not always be clear-cut; underlying continuities may exist between violent pathologies on the side of the medium and critical patho-*logies* of violence (or critical discourses on mimetic pathos) on the side of the message. We shall have to consider both patho(-)logical sides in what follows.

If we take critical distance from this cinematic fiction, at the level of critical discourses (or *logoi*) on the contagious pathos of (new) media violence, direct causation remains difficult to prove, yet a number of scholars share the detective's view that the problem of correlation is worth taking seriously. Studies that summed up the research on media violence at the end of the last century already went as far as comparing the contagious nature of media violence to a "public health epidemic,"[6] and a number of subsequent studies, not to speak of the growing number of mass shootings, have tended to confirm this view. The philosopher and social theorist Susan Hurley, for instance, puts it in diagnostic terms that resonate strikingly with our fictional hero. As she writes, echoing Tedeschi: "One frequently hears the view that media violence may have a cathartic effect, in defusing pent up violence impulses."[7] This is indeed what many have become accustomed to think. But then Hurley immediately adds, in a similar skeptical mood: "Unfortunately, this is another piece of wishful thinking; the evidence simply does not support a catharsis effect, but rather the antithesis of it."[8] These are just some preliminary examples, but they should suffice to indicate that the diagnostic message of our fictional protagonist turns out to be more informed than the popular medium that mediates it makes him initially appear to be. In due course, we will encounter other perspectives coming from research on online violence and game studies that, contra catharsis, support the affective hypothesis.[9]

For the moment, we simply indicate that despite the diversity of perspectives at play on either side of the quarrel on (new) media violence, there is a tendency to echo an agon between the catharsis and the affective hypotheses that is still in need of close investigation. If these concepts are often mentioned in contemporary debates, they are rarely discussed in any detail, nor are they inscribed in the genealogy of thought from which they stem or contextualized within the theories of violence and the unconscious they contributed to generating. *Violence and the Oedipal Unconscious* and its mirroring counterpart, *Violence and the Mimetic Unconscious*, start filling this gap. They do so by adopting a broad view that inscribes a debate often restricted to the present within the long genealogy of aesthetic, philosophical, and psychological discussions to which it originally belongs. They also give rise to rather different theories of violence and the unconscious in the modern period that provide equally competing theoretical foundations to rethink the riddle of (new) media violence for the contemporary period.

The specific genealogical focus on catharsis and affective contagion indicated in the subtitles to both volumes 1 and 2, then, urges us to expand the scope of analysis beyond media violence in order to account for the complex relation between violence and the unconscious that tends to be left in the shadows of contemporary debates and that this study aims to bring back into the foreground. I shall thus consider a number of influential thinkers of violence and the unconscious central to philosophy and the humanities more generally, but still marginal in the social and empirical sciences—from Plato to Aristotle, Bernays to Nietzsche, Freud to Bataille, Arendt to Girard, among others. I do so not only because these thinkers give philosophical substance to concepts like contagion and catharsis; they also consider that violence operates in ways that escape conscious awareness, and thus intentional control, and are in this sense *un*-conscious. But the unconscious is as much a contested subject as catharsis and contagion; it has a long and complicated history; its legendary "discovery" can no longer be taken for granted in the twenty-first century. Hence it requires a close genealogical investigation as well. To the well-known psychoanalytical unconscious that finds in the interpretation of Oedipal dreams its cathartic via regia and shall occupy us in this volume, we shall supplement a lesser known but increasingly influential mimetic unconscious that finds in affective contagion and mirroring reflexes its clearest everyday manifestations. In a mirroring inversion of perspectives, we shall also see that modernist theories of the unconscious were born out of the ancient agonistic confrontation between the catharsis and affective hypotheses. Overall, my aim is to supplement a qualitative, interpretative, and genealogically informed (double) perspective that emerges from critical dialogues that cut across disciplinary boundaries that often simply oppose the arts to philosophy, empirical studies to interpretative studies, and would benefit from being provisionally joined to account for what is ultimately a complex, transdisciplinary problem.

The Complexity of Violence

Inevitably entangled in legal issues of gun-control regulations (or lack thereof) that, especially in the United States, polarize the debate in political terms that automatically trigger ideologically inflected answers, amplified by economic interests tied to the entertainment industries (violence sells), channeled by new, more immersive, and interactive media, the heterogeneous phenomenon of (new) media violence is, indeed, complex in the specific etymological sense (from Latin *complexus*, woven together) employed by the French sociologist and transdisciplinary thinker Edgar Morin.[10]

Complex problems tend to go beyond narrow disciplinary boundaries that drive an increasingly specialized academic world; they urge nomadic and experimental researchers to weave together a multiplicity of perspectives to form a refined texture needed to capture what is ultimately an interdisciplinary or, better, transdisciplinary problem. Complex problems also tend to be located at the juncture of the both-and rather than the either-or. As Morin makes clear, they account for a protean species called *Homo sapiens* that far exceeds this flattering and somewhat narcissistic self-definition. Not only does this *homo* go beyond gender dualities, but it opens up protean dimensions that cannot be confined to the rational, autonomous, and solipsistic creature in full possession of reason, thought, or logos constitutive of *Homo sapiens*; it is also irrational, emotional, and prone to dispossessions that can be violent, maddening, and based on affect or pathos that animates *homo demens*; it is not only individualist, consumerist, and animated by a drive for profit, or *homo economicus*, but also social, relational, and animated by the drive to play with others, or *homo ludens*,[11] among other manifestations. Given that this plurality of identities ultimately rest on a plastic, impressionable, and very imitative species that is not one for it is already double in its Janus-faced conceptual/affective orientation, and protean in its metamorphic processes of transformation, I add homo mimeticus to this list to indicate that mimesis is at the heart of an original, innovative, creative, yet still fundamentally imitative species.[12] And since the complexity of mimesis includes both rational actions and affective reactions, logos and pathos, my diagnostic will also go beyond reified binaries such as good/evil, nature/nurture, mind/body, conscious/unconscious, as well as human/nonhuman, subject/object, active/passive, fictional/real, online/offline, among other binaries that dominated the structuralist generation in the past century yet are no longer tenable in the present century.

If we take some critical distance from the cathartic and/or contagious pathos internal to our cinematic case study, it is crucial to specify that social theorists add important contextual qualifications that supplement the fictional scenario with which we started. These qualifications include but are not limited to the following: an acknowledgment of the diversity of new media involved (film, TV, video games, social media, online platforms); a discrimination between violence and aggression that distributes violence across a gradation of different (psychic, emotional, social, political, physical) levels that are part of a continuous spectrum; a focus on the overwhelming importance of social, political, and structural factors (class, race, gender, education, wealth); the consideration of decisive and often competing legal factors (free speech, gun regulations); stretching to open up broader, and equally contested and agonistic theoretical questions on the status of violence in the contemporary world in general.

For instance, the increase of violence in a globalized, hyperconnected, and overpopulated world is not always unanimously accepted among researchers and has led critics to ask: is violence really on the rise—as the daily dosages represented on (new) media suggest? Or, alternatively, have we simply become more sensitive to it because we live in times of peace animated by the "better angels of ourselves"—as cognitive psychologist Steven Pinker argues?[13] Conversely, if we do not start from transcendental angles but, rather, from immanent bodies, other critics consider that violence remains a timely problem to consider since the "estimate of the twentieth century's 'megadeaths' is 187 million, the equivalent of more than one in ten of the world population in 1900,"[14] as the literary theorist Terry Eagleton recalls at the dawn of the twenty-first century. More recently, it has become difficult to ignore that we live in an increasingly precarious and fragile world vulnerable to multiple systemic threats with violent effects on populations that go well beyond the specific issue of (new) media violence: from pandemic crises to terrorist attacks, nuclear escalations to racist brutalism, exclusions of migrants to (new) fascist insurrections and invasions, not to speak of environmental catastrophes in the age of the Anthropocene, as political theorists like William Connolly, Adriana Cavarero, and Achille Mbembe, among others, convincingly indicate.[15] At the same time, within the limits of our problematic, we should also wonder: couldn't a focus on (new) media violence run the risk of turning this protean, much-discussed yet still sociologically restricted subject of analysis into a single unifying cause of violence that masks perhaps less visible but certainly more ramified, systemic, and catastrophic forms of social violence, as Edgar Morin cautions?[16]

Indeed, the homogeneous category of media violence can all too easily serve as what mimetic theorist René Girard would call an identifiable scapegoat that stands in for a plurality of less spectacular and visible but more fundamental and systemic causes that contribute to violence in social life.[17] For these and other reasons, we shall be careful *not* to posit a singular, unilateral, and above all *direct* billiard-ball causal connection between (new) media violence and real violence in what follows; nor shall we argue that representations or simulations of violence are the main factors to consider in order to account for violence in general—for they are clearly not. And yet, at the same time, if it is possible to turn the problem of (new) media violence into a scapegoat, this does not mean that it is an "innocent" problem chosen in an arbitrary fashion. French philosopher Michel Serres, for instance, while far from inimical to new technologies, confirms that the "frenzy" with which today's new media "repeatedly represent and multiply human sacrifice" entails an "immense regression in terms of hominization."[18] In its protean manifestations, the concern with violence Girard and Serres have in common casts a long shadow on the mythic image of humanization that since the Enlightenment projected the destiny of *homo sapiens* on a grand linear narrative of progress, a metanarrative that may have worked in abstract theory, yet, as the twentieth century clearly showed, and the two first decades of the twenty-first century confirmed, generated immense regression in historical practices.

Now, if we look ahead to an increasingly precarious and uncertain future, a theoretical supplement concerning the violence that animates homo mimeticus is urgently in order. If Serres recognized that hominization oscillates, pendulum-like, between "extreme violence" and "rare wisdom,"[19] and Girard rooted this extreme violence at the origins of the "sacred,"[20] we still need a theory of violence to trace the specific oscillation, tension, or agon between the mimetic pathos of violence and the anti-mimetic distance of critical logos. This double perspective is all the more needed for it can account for the paradoxical logic that leads humans, and perhaps posthumans as well, to move from an extreme immersion in violent pathos toward the wiser critical distance of logos, and vice versa. This agonistic perspective, as we shall see, is not only reproductive but also productive; it does not simply oscillate between competing perspectives but has the power to generate paradoxical feedback loops that turn a passive infection by the pathos of violence (or pathology) into a productive diagnostic of violent pathos (or patho-*logy*). One of the goals of this study is to provide such a patho-*logical* supplement for a new theory of mimesis for the future that goes beyond universalist structural models to trace the paradoxical dynamic internal to violence and its relation to the unconscious in the twenty-first century.

Despite the number of informed quantitative studies on media violence, what is still missing is a general theory that accounts for the complex relation between representations of violence and its contradictory emotional effects on viewers or gamers, cathartic or contagious effects that might not be under the full control of consciousness and presuppose therefore a theory of the unconscious as well. Rather than approaching the riddle of the effects of representations of violence via empirical questionnaires, or taking a clear-cut position on either side of the individual freedom versus censorship fence, I shall pay significant attention to the role of catharsis and affective contagion in opening up competing theories of the unconscious in the modernist period that not only latently inform discussions on media violence in the contemporary period but also manifestly anticipate some of the most recent discoveries in the empirical sciences. This genealogical detour via the vicissitudes of the relation between violence and the unconscious will entail taking a radical step back from contemporary polarized debates on (new) media violence in order to closely interrogate the philosophical, historical, psychological, aesthetic, and epistemic foundations on which these debates rest in the first place. If the concepts of catharsis and contagion were created to account for specific genres and media, in specific historical contexts, and for specific theoretical purposes, discussions of (new) media violence tend to treat these concepts a-historically, as stable conceptual essences, without much sense of discrimination for their philosophical origins, historical transformations, and agonistic theoretical confrontations between disciplinary perspectives that carried, not without theoretical struggles, such concepts from antiquity to modernity into the contemporary period.

Suspicious of single causal and linear approaches, we shall trace complex feedback loops that go from fictions to reality and back, conscious actions to unconscious reactions, generating degrees of uncertainty that call for flexible, non-deterministic, and non-moralizing perspectives on (new) media violence. These perspectives (or logoi) on the pathos of violence favor specific contextualization over universal explanations, dynamic movements over stabilizing structures, agonistic confrontations rather than violent rivalries, all of which are vital to confronting a protean problematic in constant transformation. In fact, different people respond differently to the same representations of violence depending on their culture, economic status, age, education, and profession, not to speak of even more refined unquantifiable factors like personal history, individual character, affective disposition, and other elusive qualities. If these factors escape the large net of quantifiable questionnaires that still dominate empirical debates just as much as universalizing theories, they are nonetheless constitutive of qualitative approaches in the humanities. Hence the need to draw on disciplines like continental philosophy, critical theory, cultural studies, literary theory, film studies, feminist theory, critical race theory, media studies, digital humanities, game studies, among other emerging perspectives we shall consider in order to reevaluate both the cathartic and affective hypotheses on (new) media violence.

Since media change historically, in what follows I shall be careful not to conflate different aesthetic experiences across the ages. Instead, I will pay attention to the specific property of the medium and genre in question. If Greek tragedy provided the paradigmatic genre out of which the catharsis hypothesis was born, for instance, this does not mean that classical principles continue to structure contemporary genres like films, TV series, or video games. Conversely, if the affective hypothesis is based on dramatic impersonations of Homeric heroes staged in a still predominantly oral immersive culture, we shall have to consider the specific modes of embodiment that are at play in film and video games in a digital and no less immersive culture.

This anti-essentialist approach to the specific form of (new) media and genres applies to the content of what we shall group under the rubric of "violence" as well. Although violence can indeed be restricted to intentional forms of physical assault alone, we shall avoid a restricted, essentialist definition of what qualifies as violence. Without embracing radical forms of relativism, I think it is fair to say that what is considered violent changes historically, varies across cultures, and is entangled in power struggles that require discriminating skills in what Nietzsche called "the art of interpretation"[21] in order to be evaluated. As Judith Butler also notes more recently, "violence is always interpreted."[22] Consequently, this is a problematic that requires a training in the art of interpretation that was once central to literary cultures and now needs to be developed for post-literary, image-based cultures as well. As the genealogy of thinkers of violence we rely on—from Plato to Aristotle, Nietzsche to Freud, Bataille to Arendt, Girard to Cavarero among others—also suggests, violence is a phenomenon that includes verbal, symbolic, emotional, and physical forces that may not always be recognized or avowed as violent as such, yet have wounding effects nonetheless, and benefit from being considered as part of a continuous yet heterogeneous spectrum that calls for the discriminating art of interpretation. I argue that it is on the basis of such an art that a new theory of homo mimeticus that accounts for the entanglement of violence and the unconscious can emerge.

Given our assumptions that violence does not remain contained within mind/body dualisms that dominated philosophical discussions for a long time, I shall not strictly differentiate between (psychic) aggression and (physical) violence, if only because the former can all too easily bleed into the latter.[23] I shall thus take care to interpret manifestations of violence via specific case studies, or examples—some fictional and aesthetic, others real and historical—that will punctuate our study, especially in volume 2; due to their visibility, contagious effects are more prone to phenomenological diagnostics than inner cathartic experiences. From police murders of African Americans to (new) fascist insurrections, we shall put our genealogy to the test on contemporary examples that cast a shadow on the future as well.

Rather than attempting to address the heterogeneous phenomenon of (new) media violence in general, then, or offering a survey, categorization, or typology of the different forms of violence at play in different media, I will be both strategically selective in my theorical problematization and historically broad in my genealogical perspective. Selective because I focus on the specific relation between representations of violence and theories of the unconscious via restricted but rather influential authors and texts in the western tradition in order to account for the performative powers of mimesis that might not be conscious or intentional, yet produce psychological and physiological effects nonetheless. Coming at the problematic violence and the unconscious from the angle of contemporary developments in continental philosophy, the history of psychology, literary theory, and different schools of critical theory that have lost faith in the foundations of an autonomous, solipsistic, and rational subject or ego, I find it striking that contemporary definitions of violence that inform empirical debates on media still tend to explicitly foreground "intentionality" as one of violence's defining characteristics.[24]

Despite the important and complex implications that orient this assumption for legal theory (if violence is perpetuated unintentionally or unconsciously, can it be penalized?), it has the theoretical disadvantage of restricting the heterogeneous sphere of violence to a conscious, rational, and volitional subject qua *Homo sapiens*. As I have shown elsewhere, at least since the modernist period such a philosophical ideal turned out to be an illusory shadow or phantom that bears little resemblance with our all too human reality.[25] What I now add is that this ideal was already denounced by the very same philosophical tradition that set the stage of the debate for what we now call media violence in the first place. This also means that the subject of violence (objective genitive) might turn out to be subjected to a violent affect or pathos (subjective genitive) that dispossesses it of its proper intentionality, rationality, or logos, generating affective pathologies that operate automatically, below the register of conscious awareness, and are in this sense *un-conscious*. Time and again, we shall see that the mysterious powers of what the Greeks called, enigmatically, πάθος (pathos)—which is not restricted to *penthos*, grief, but designates the more general "experience of a force that was in [man], possessing him, rather than possessed by him."[26] The power of pathos, then, overflows the limited sphere of intentional consciousness that posits violence at a representational distance, generating unconscious pathologies that are still much in need of investigation in the digital age.[27]

Despite the specific focus on the relation between violence and the unconscious, or maybe because of it, my approach will be broad in both genealogical and theoretical scope. Tracing the theoretical developments of theories of catharsis and contagion entails taking some steps back from contemporary debates on (new) media violence in order to consider the emergence, development, and transformation of concepts that are constitutive of the birth of philosophy and aesthetics, are internal to founding texts in western thought, and, above all, pave the way for two genealogically related but theoretically distinct conceptions of the unconscious—the Oedipal and the mimetic unconscious—which organize this study in two related volumes: if the catharsis hypothesis paves the way for the Freudian discovery of the unconscious that had the interpretation of Oedipal dreams as a *via regia* (volume 1), the affective hypothesis shall lead to a Nietzschean discovery of the unconscious that had psycho-motor mirroring reflexes that are currently being *re*-discovered by the neurosciences as a privileged manifestation of what I call the mimetic unconscious (volume 2).

While rarely foregrounded, we shall see that both theories of the unconscious continue to implicitly orient fundamental assumptions in contemporary debates on (new) media violence that require a combination of critical and creative efforts to be brought to the foreground. As empirical studies of violence have also noted, what is needed is "more creativity in thinking about violence"[28]—a supplement the humanities are well-placed to provide. Consequently, this creativity should not be predicated on an artificial divide between two cultures: one hermeneutical and past-oriented, the other empirical and present-oriented. On the contrary, this book proposes a creative, experimental, and hopefully productive dialogue between approaches that still tend to be considered in isolation in an increasingly specialized academic world, yet given the complex problem under consideration, benefit from transdisciplinary collaborations.

One of the numerous advantages of broadening the historical and disciplinary focus to the riddle of the cathartic/contagious effects of (new) media violence is an impressive gain of perspectival and conceptual distance with respect to contemporary quarrels that punctuate the daily news. It reveals, in fact, how both present and futuristic evaluations of violence entail contemporary repetitions, reenactments, and representations of a rather ancient, influential, yet still little-understood philosophical riddle. Our assumption is that a lot can be learned about the much-discussed controversy concerning cathartic and contagious effects of representations of violence, if we start by reframing this ancient, long-standing yet always new problematic within the landscape of the philosophical, psychological, aesthetic, and ultimately mimetic, all too mimetic tradition that sets the stage for the debate while foregrounding its main conceptual protagonists.

Mimesis, catharsis, contagion: there is a genealogical link connecting these concepts that still needs to be traced in detail. If informed systematic accounts of the role of mimesis and catharsis in literature already exist,[29] none has so far joined these perspectives from the angle of affective contagion in order to come to terms with the problematic of (new) media violence. This book contributes to filling this gap. Given the imitative drive internal to human behavior in general, and the centrality of the problematic of imitation in the foundational agon between the catharsis and affective hypothesis that inaugurated the problematic of media violence in classical antiquity in particular, I shall repeatedly step back to what the Greeks called, enigmatically, *mimēsis*, whose origins (from *mîmos*, performance and mime) bear the traces of visual representations and affective impersonations that via new media reach into the present.[30] Located at the origins of western aesthetic predicated on the logic of visual representation considered from a theatrical distance, and central to generating an embodied pathos on the side of spectators, the Janus-faced concept of mimesis is indeed located at the palpitating heart of our genealogy of violence and the unconscious. It also sets in motion a pathos of distance that is intimately entangled with the catharsis and contagion hypotheses, generating both violent pathologies and diagnostic patho-*logies*. That is, a plurality of disciplinary discourses, or logoi, that provide new insights into the cathartic and contagious dynamic of mimetic pathos. A complex concept that includes aesthetic representation but can no longer be restricted to realism, it is becoming increasingly clear that mimesis encompasses a number of affective forms of behavioral imitation—from impersonation to identification, influence to suggestion, affective contagion to mirror neurons to brain plasticity, among other contemporary masks—that cut across disciplinary and structural binaries. Mimesis, I shall argue, is not only *the* paradigmatic concept on which western aesthetics is grounded; it is also constitutive of a thoroughly imitative species qua homo mimeticus.[31]

Furthering a mimetic turn that originates in literary and philosophical modernism whose sources of inspiration reach back to classical antiquity and ultimately concern the *re*-turn of mimesis in the present and future, I shall take a genealogical detour via some foundational texts in western thought on the question of violence and the unconscious. A genealogical awareness of the vicissitudes of concepts like catharsis and contagion in ancient philosophical quarrels between literature and philosophy, as well as of modern disciplinary formations such as psychoanalysis and mimetic theory, will help us reevaluate the value of these agonistic perspectives for contemporary debates on (new) media violence. It is my contention that only once the genealogical development of these competing hypotheses on the effects of representations of violence has been traced back to antiquity, that on the shoulders of giants from Plato and Aristotle onward, one can take a stance on such a controversial contemporary topic.[32] Reflecting diagnostically on the powers of violent spectacles to influence behavior in terms that might be therapeutic or pathological, cathartic or contagious, or perhaps an intermixture of both, is what this genealogical investigation aims to perform. In the process, *Violence and the Oedipal Unconscious* also contributes to promoting a mimetic turn, or *re*-turn of attention to mimesis on the contemporary critical and theoretical scene and will be pursued further in *Violence and the Mimetic Unconscious*. Both studies, I now add, are inscribed in a more generalized transdisciplinary theory of homo mimeticus whose conceptual foundations I briefly sketch out.

A New Theory of Mimesis or Homo Mimeticus

In what follows, I propose a new theory of mimesis that stems from the ancient realization that humans are imitative creatures, or homo mimeticus, and that is constitutive of the recent return of attention to mimesis, or mimetic turn. The conceptual and methodological foundations of this theory go back to *The Phantom of the Ego* (2013) but have continued to inform my work since and recently crystallized in a transdisciplinary five-year project titled *Homo Mimeticus: Theory and Criticism*, of which these books are constitutive part.[33] The perspectives I adopt change, but the fundamental conceptual and methodological principles remain rooted in a new transdisciplinary theory that, while not being a system, accounts for the protean transformations of homo mimeticus from the modern to the present period. Before starting our diagnostic investigation, I sketch out the main conceptual and methodological principles internal to the specific theory of mimesis that will guide us in what follows.

The distinctiveness of this method will unfold via a close investigation of the philosophical, psychological, and aesthetic texts under consideration, but it is crucial to stress at the outset that genealogy, in the Nietzschean tradition, should not be confused with history, let alone antiquarian history. While genealogies pay attention to past thinkers and traditions, dig up marginalized texts and forgotten theories, often rediscovering seemingly minor intellectual protagonists that played major roles in the development of a concept, a theory, or a discovery, the ultimate telos of genealogy is not to promote an "antiquarian" conception of history to treasure and cultivate for its own sake in what Nietzsche called the "garden of knowledge."[34] On the contrary, as the German philosopher had already indicated in the second essay of the *Untimely Meditations* (1873), the goal of what he will later call "genealogy" is to focus on the uses of history for "action and life."[35] As he specifies: "We want to serve history only to the extent that history serves life."[36] Later, in *On the Genealogy of Morals* (1887), Nietzsche will put this method to use for unmasking the transcendental origins of morality and the "ascetic ideals" it promotes. He will do so by adopting a transdisciplinary method that accounts for the disconcerting realization that "we remain unknown to ourselves,"[37] as he states in the opening sentence of the book. In a methodological address to philosophers of the future that serves as the epigraph to this book and will orient us as well, Nietzsche calls for "reshaping the original relationship of mutual aloofness and suspicion which obtains between the disciplines of philosophy, physiology, and medicine into the most amicable and fruitful exchange" (*GM* I, 17:37). Hence the vital urgency to look back to transdisciplinary—philosophical, physiological, aesthetic, medical, etc.—theories of the unconscious that emerged in the nineteenth and twentieth centuries, only to better look ahead to the problem of violence central for the affirmation of life and action in the twenty-first century.

Over a century ago, Nietzsche laid down some untimely methodological principles that are constitutive of the mimetic turn or *re*-turn to homo mimeticus and will guide our diagnostic inquiry into the ambivalent effects of representations of violence—beginning, middle, and end. These principles are untimely in the sense that genealogy, as Nietzsche practices it, is driven by an agonistic aspiration of "acting counter to our time and thereby acting on our time and, let us hope, for the benefit of a time to come."[38] The overarching goal of our genealogy of violence and the unconscious is not to look for a stable, unitary, and homogeneous "origin" (*Ursprung*) that would set the foundation for a universal, transhistorical, and thus atemporal answer to our untimely problem. Rather, genealogy looks back to past traditions of thought from which interpretations of violence descend (*genea-logy* from Greek *genea*, "descent," and *logos*, "word," "discourse") in order to cast light on present, heterogeneous, and immanent problems that can help us give birth (*gen*, "to give birth") to a new theory. The focus of a genealogy of mimesis is thus not on stabilizing origins but on destabilizing transformations. As Nietzsche puts it in *Daybreak* (1881), paving the way for a method that continues to inform genealogists of the present: "*The more insight we possess into an origin* [Ursprung] *the less significant does the origin appear*: while *what is nearest to us*, what is around us and in us, gradually begins to display colours and beauties and enigmas and riches of significance of which earlier mankind had not an inkling."[39] If our genealogy of violence and the unconscious looks back to consider "under what conditions [*Ursprung*]" (*GM* "Preface," 3; 5) a concept, a hypothesis, or a theory emerges, then, its driving telos is not an antiquarian concern for the past rooted in a single, stabilizing, and unitary origin. Rather, it is to cast light on problems that "are nearest to us" in the present in order to better see the changing "colors" of *our* world—not "*behind* the world [*Hinterwelt*]" (3; 5). This overturning of perspectives will be crucial to confront "enigmas" that are proper to our times, yet still benefit from genealogical perspectives that, to be born, must establish dialogic and agonistic continuities with logoi that descend from previous times.

The diagnostic focus internal to the genealogical method will lead me to investigate both the therapeutic or cathartic (volume 1) and pathological or contagious (volume 2) effects of unconscious forms of mimetic pathos that cross the line between representations of violence and violent behavior, vison and affect, the digital and the real world. This will entail supplementing philology, psychology, and philosophy with disciplines that further genealogy in the twenty-first century, including critical theory, literary studies, film and media studies, digital humanities, game studies, and the neurosciences, among other perspectives. Still, despite, or rather because of, this transdisciplinary approach, our diagnostic will remain anchored in a specific perspectival method that is of genealogical inspiration. It pays particular attention to the complex interplay of visual representations (or Apollonian mimesis) and bodily intoxications (or Dionysian mimesis) that provides the bedrock for our theory of homo mimeticus and will inform this study as well. Before we begin, let me briefly summarize the main conceptual elements of the new theory of mimesis that will guide our investigation throughout.

The main concepts constitutive of our theory of homo mimeticus and the re-*turn* of mimesis it promotes find in modernism rather than romanticism its starting point; yet since these concepts find in Nietzsche a major source of inspiration, they also look back to antiquity in order to propose a theory of mimesis for the future. It is well known that in *On the Genealogy of Morals* Nietzsche introduces the concept of "pathos of distance [*Pathos der Distanz*]" (I, 2;12) as part of an unmasking operation that divides the anti-mimetic master from mimetic slaves. Echoing a Platonic image, Nietzsche characterizes the slaves under the rubric of the "*herd-instinct*" (2; 13) precisely to take distance from the mimetism they not simply represent but embody. Lesser know is that this anti-mimetic philosophical stance that, since Plato, is characteristic of the philosophical subject, is balanced by Nietzsche's own avowed vulnerability to the slaves' mimetic will power, which he groups under the rubric of the "will power of the weakest" (III, 14; 102).[40] The opposition between subjects he sets up in theory is thus deconstructed in his genealogical practice. Elsewhere, generalizing this diagnostic and applying it to the strong as well, he will defined the will to power as "not a being, not a becoming, but a *pathos*."[41] In this definition of the will to power, which flies in the face of muscular caricatures of Nietzsche's thought for it renders all humans, including sovereignly affirmative humans like the *Übermensch*, vulnerable to affect, or pathos, lies if not the *Ursprung*, then at least the ground from which my theory of mimesis springs. It is, in fact, the power of this pathos that induces unpredictable processes of affective becoming that can be put to pathological and patho-*logical* use that provides, if not the solid bedrock, at least the affective flux our theory of homo mimeticus aims to channel in new directions.

I hasten to add that the *sapiens/mimeticus* binary is not stable or clear-cut but is caught in a patho-logical and dynamic interplay: the pathos of violence is, in fact, not only internal to homo mimeticus, just as a critical logos is not the prerogative of homo sapiens. On the contrary, we shall see how violent pathos equally animates homo sapiens just as critical faculties allow homo mimeticus to set up a critical distance from mimesis. In sum, both mimetic and anti-mimetic tendencies constitutive of the catharsis and affective hypotheses are internal to homo sapiens-mimeticus, and these competing tendencies generate a patho-logical contest, or agon, that informs the catharsis and affective hypotheses as well.

A specific focus on mimetic pathos, and the movement between pathos and distance it generates, has significant potential to expand, from the space

between reason and affect, the boundaries of mimetic theory beyond familiar structural configurations. Notice in fact that the enigmatic Greek concept
of *pathos* does not restrict mimesis to the stabilizing logic of representation
that freezes identity in an image, or *imago*; nor does it restrict the focus to a
master-slave dialectic caught in a violent struggle for recognition based on a
desire of the desire of the other. Instead, it generalizes the scope of mimetic
theory by including all affects, good and bad, via a relational, porous, and
impressionable conception of a phantom ego that is both open to and critical of psychic (dis)possessions of identity. Driven by a pathos of distance,
this phantom ego is both attracted to and repelled by the power of mimetic
pathos that goes beyond good and evil. Homo mimeticus is, thus, as much
vulnerable to sad passions as to joyful passions, as predisposed to a violent
pathos that can lead to sacrificial death as to a sym-*pathos* that can lead to
communal solidarity.[42]

Originally tied to a mysterious force that is linked to a type of grief or
suffering (*penthos*) that finds in Greek tragedy a paradigmatic manifestation,
pathos is an impersonal, dramatic, and affective force that requires an actor,
or *mimos*, to speak in mimetic speech in order to be fully manifested on
the stage and to generate contagious effects in the audience as well.[43] The
philosophical origins of this contagious appeal are ancient, and gave rise
to contested evaluations that are entangled in the vicissitudes of both the
catharsis and the affective hypothesis. On the one hand, pathos is central to
Aristotle's defense of tragedy in the *Poetics*, since he contrasts the *Odyssey* to
the *Iliad* on the basis that the former is a story of *ēthikē* (character), whereas
the latter of *pathē* (suffering). Aristotle enigmatically ties this catastrophic
suffering to the catharsis of related tragic emotions like pity and fear, whose
defining characteristic is that they are mimetic emotions, in the sense that
they allow spectators to partake in the pathos that a fictional "other" experiences onstage from a safe theatrical distance. On the other hand, pathos
is equally central to Plato's *critique* of the contagious powers of mimesis in
the *Republic* insofar as he ties pathos to dramatic suffering, but also to eros,
excess, and a type of frenzied and manic intoxication that blurs the boundaries between actors and spectators and that Nietzsche will later group under
the rubric of the Dionysian "imitator [*Nachahmer*]"[44]—thereby tying will to
power to a dramatic and thus mimetic pathos. Either way, across both sides
of the Platonic/Aristotelian agon that set the stage for the contest between

the catharsis and the affective hypothesis and, more generally, the quarrel between literature and philosophy, the Greek concept of pathos cannot be dissociated from the aesthetic, dramatic, and affective implications of what both Plato and Aristotle called *mimēsis*. It thus seems worth to qualify it as *mimetic* pathos to propose a new theory of mimesis that includes but also goes beyond mimetic desire. We shall do so by sitting on ancient shoulders that encourage us to look ahead to do justice to the patho(-)logies internal to both catharsis and contagion.

Pathos, distance, mimesis: a conceptual configuration is begging to take shape; but this configuration is not a stable form, or structure. On the contrary, it sets our theory of homo mimeticus in motion and can be summarized as follows. After the establishment of a human, all too human openness to others not restricted to desire but generalized to *all* mimetic affects (or *mimetic pathê*), be they good or bad—from anger to joy, violence to sympathy, ressentiment to laughter, among others—this tension, or oscillation, between mimetic and anti-mimetic conceptions of the subject (or pathos of distance) is the second main step in a general theory of mimesis that does not aspire to erect itself as a universal system, structure, or form, let alone a triangular form. Instead, it traces the dynamic movement or interplay between (anti-)mimetic tendencies constitutive of a type of porous and relational subjectivity (or phantom ego) that is constitutionally vulnerable to the experience of pathos and the dispossessions it entails (or homo mimeticus), but not unilaterally so. In fact, what was true for violent spectacles in ancient tragedies remains true with respect to the (hyper)mimetic pathos of contemporary media: for better and worse, violence continues to generate a tension, or oscillation, between an attraction to suffering (pathos) and a repulsion from it (distance).[45] Constitutive of tragic pleasure at the origins of aesthetic theory this movement of "attraction and repulsion" (Bataille's phrase) generates a pathos of distance that continues to set our contemporary theory of mimesis in motion. Interestingly, this oscillation can be linked (but not reduced) to a double movement constitutive of aggressive behavior rooted in the sympathetic and the parasympathetic system;[46] it is also integral part of the aesthetic relation of a spectator who contemplates a violent spectacle from a mediated distance, yet feels this pathos nonetheless.

Either way, both on the sides of aesthetic representations and homo mimeticus, the pathos of distance and the double movement of attraction and repulsion it generates is the core principle that sets out our theory of mimesis in motion. It is also mirrored by the problematic of the effects of (new) media violence that is not only seen outside but also felt inside.

This double movement could be phenomenologically described as follows: On one side, homo mimeticus is passively subjected to the infective type of power, or pathos, that induces affective pathologies—from emotional contagion to rivalry and the violence it entails. This bodily passivity to "Dionysian pathos" (*pathos dionysiaque*), as the French phenomenologist Michel Henry has also recognized, is constitutive of a "genealogy of psychoanalysis" that not only challenges the primacy of the logic of representation; it also reveals Freud for what he is: namely, a "belated heir" (*héritier tardif*).[47] Henry's profound pioneering study on the genealogy of psychoanalysis benefits from a supplementary genealogy of the unconscious that has the immanence of mimetic pathos in both its cathartic and contagious manifestations as a specific focal point. Henry, in fact, inscribes the Freudian unconscious as an heir of the Cartesian consciousness it seems to overcome. But in Henry's radical phenomenological reinterpretation of the Cartesian *cogito* understood as a power of auto-affection of life itself, it is actually Descartes who goes beyond mind-body, subject-object dualisms. Henry does so as he uncovers the blind unconscious feeling of life feeling-itself-feel via a blind immediacy that bypasses the visible mediation of representation. In so doing he also challenges the intentionality of the phenomenological subject to capture the invisible power of life in its immanent self-affection. It is thus no accident that Henry's genealogy of the unconscious also pays close attention to Schopenhauer's metaphysical conception of the Will as a blind, impersonal force felt immediately in sexual bodily instincts; nor is it accidental that he finds, in Nietzsche's theory of the "will to power" predicated on the immanence of Dionysian "pathos," understood in both "the suffering and joy" of Dionysus, its pre-Freudian but also post-Freudian culmination, open to "the body, action, affect [*affectivité*]" (*GP* 10, 8). This is, in a way, also our starting point. Now, if Henry's genealogy distinguishes between the "unconscious of representation," on the one hand, and "the unconscious that refers directly to the essence of life" (350), on the other, we can now go further and call the former the Oedipal unconscious based on the interpretation of dreams, and the latter the mimetic unconscious based on the inner experience of mimetic pathos. Significantly, Henry ends his genealogy by specifying that the immanent and dark "affectivity" and the Dionysian pathos it entails "undermine [*font s'écrouler*] the entire dogmatic apparatus of Freudianism" (383). Yet this pathos may be even more inimical to that dogmatic apparatus than Henry's genealogy of Freud as an "heir" of Nietzsche is ready, or willing, to acknowledge. My fundamental claim will indeed be that the living immediacy of mimetic pathos shakes the very ontological foundations of the dogma of the Oedipal unconscious and the familial representations it entails—be they cathartic or contagious.

In many ways, then, the genealogy of the unconscious that follows, while post-phenomenological in its transdisciplinary orientation and focused on a specifically Janus-faced problem of catharsis and contagion, begins where Henry's genealogy of psychoanalysis ends. The mimetic pathos of unconscious life affecting itself and, we should add, affected by others (be they human or nonhuman), as we shall see time and again, flows through the visual (Apollonian) ontology of representation and the subject of *Aufklärung* it entails—a subject whose "phantoms and myths of an afterworld [*arrière-monde*]" (*GP* 9) casts a long shadow on the Freudian unconscious, as Henry says, but also calls for a different theory of a phantom ego to emerge. Volume 1 shows how the immanence of a bodily, mimetic pathos challenges the catharsis hypothesis and the Oedipal triangular form or idea it gave birth to; volume 2 traces this Dionysian pathos back to the affective ritual foundations that flow through Nietzsche's modernist psychology of the phantom of the ego, paving the way for the rediscovering of mirroring reflexes constitutive of the mimetic unconscious.

On the other side, the balancing countermovement of our genealogy of the unconscious shows how homo mimeticus is also in a position to draw creatively and agonistically on her anti-mimetic tendencies to take critical, diagnostic, and logical distance from the powers of mimesis via what I call mimetic patho-*logies*; that is, critical accounts (logoi) on affect (pathos). In this paradoxical feedback loop that turns mimetic sickness into a critical diagnostic of sickness, passivity into activity, the immediacy of a bodily pathos into the mediation of a cognitive logos, lies perhaps the distinctive originality of our theory of mimesis. It presupposes that in order to adequately diagnose the infective powers of mimetic pathos from an anti-mimetic distance, the philosophical physician needs to be herself a subject who has experienced the powers of mimetic pathos. Or, to put it in a more clinical language, that the oscillating movement between pathos and distance turns into a spiraling diagnostic circulation characterized by the power to turn an infection from an infective sickness (or pathology) into a critical diagnostic on mimetic pathos (or patho-*logy*).[48] It is, in fact, because homo mimeticus is partially infected by affective pathologies and has a lived, experiential, interior knowledge of the affects that informs them, that she can mobilize both the immersive first-person powers of affect (pathos) and the distanced third-person powers of reason (logos) in order to all the better dissect these pathologies from both the inside and the outside.

The methodological implication of this diagnostic inversion of perspectives Nietzsche called "perspectivism," and we call "patho(-)logy" (both sickness and diagnostic), is that mimetic pathos cuts both ways for it is as much on the side of an infective sickness (or pathology) and of a therapeutic account (logos) of the good and bad effects of cathartic/contagious pathos on the unconscious (or patho-*logy*).[49] With respect to the problematic at hand, we could thus say that our diagnostic of violent pathos goes beyond good and evil: it does not simply argue that contagion is on the side of pathology and catharsis on the side of the therapy. As we shall see, there are patho-*logies* of contagion just as there are cathartic pathologies. Hence, both sick and healthy symptomatic effects will be simultaneously at play in our genealogy of both the contagious and cathartic patho(-)logies (now understood as both sickness and cure) that bring different models of the unconscious into being.

The spiraling movement of mimetic patho(-)logies brings us back to the question of the genealogical method that orients this investigation. Given the plurality of historical manifestations of mimetic pathos—from pity to fear, desire to violence, sympathy to horror, hysteria to hypnosis, suggestion to influence, contagion to mirror neurons, to many other contemporary symptoms dramatized via (new) media—an account of the powers of mimesis needs to rely on a plurality of disciplinary discourses, or logoi, in order to appropriately evaluate, diagnose, and propose elements for a cure of the multiple mimetic pathologies that affect and infect homo mimeticus in the digital age, including the cathartic/contagious patho(-)logies induced by media violence. In the process, we shall see that the genealogist qua investigative detective adopts a perspectival method that is not unitary but fragmentary, not linear but meandering, not totalizing but experimental, not discipline-oriented and territorial but problem-oriented, transdisciplinary, and nomadic—all elements constitutive of the genealogical perspectivism I call patho-*logy*.

Perspectivism should not be confused with relativism. It is rather a transdisciplinary method of rumination that calls for considerable attention to the process of emergence of theories and concepts. In *On the Genealogy of Morals* (1887), Nietzsche in fact specifies that in order to develop a "knowledge of the conditions and circumstances of their [values] growth, development and displacement" ("Preface," 6; 8), genealogists require "some schooling in history and philology, together with an innate sense of discrimination with respect to questions of psychology" (3; 4). History, philology, psychology: these are indeed some of the disciplines Nietzsche convokes in his transvaluation of moral values. I contend this pluralist methodological principle applies to reevaluate the value of theories as well. Trained in philology and informed by a classical tradition, Nietzsche took inspiration from bovine *"rumination"* to advocate the patient repetition, disentanglement, and assimilation internal to what he called the "art of reading [*das Lesen als Kunst*]," an art he considered "thoroughly unlearned" (8; 10) yet is vital to relearn in order to affirm survival in the modern age. Our diagnostic of the patho(-)logies of violence will thus vary in the logoi we rely on, yet it will consistently urge us to closely interpret case studies or examples of violence that call for considerable discrimination in the art of rumination.

Schooled in a comparative, transdisciplinary, and continental philosophical and aesthetic traditions, I have sharpened my critical and theoretical lenses by working on specific periods, authors, and texts, while at the same time foregrounding a problem-oriented, rather than discipline-oriented, approach. As this book straddles disciplinary boundaries to bring to the surface underlying theoretical continuities that lurk below the surface of disciplinary discontinuities on the subject of violence and the unconscious, it is, of course, Nietzsche's detective sense of genealogical "discrimination," more than a magic-bullet police type of investigation, that I will aspire to promote in the pages that follow. Specialized discussions on violence and the unconscious have, in fact, been articulating cathartic and contagious hypotheses for quite some time. While such hypotheses are now familiar enough to appear in Hollywood blockbusters, they still require discerning genealogical lenses in order to be properly reevaluated in their proper aesthetic, historical, and social contexts. Hence the need of a mirroring theoretical confrontation, or mimetic agon, between advocates of catharsis and advocates of contagion that both inform theories of violence and the unconscious today.

Mirroring Contents

As the contest or agon between catharsis and affective hypotheses drama-tized by the cinematic scene with which we started already suggested, these perspectives stage two antagonistic yet related philosophical traditions that articulate competing hypotheses on the relation between violence and the unconscious. Given their impressive theoretical and historical reach, which goes from antiquity to modernity, I will be discussing these hypotheses in two separate and symmetric volumes that mirror each other while also inverting the diagnostic. This form is not accidental. It is meant to reflect the content it mediates. In particular, the mirroring symmetry between the two parts of this diptych on violence and the unconscious—each divided in equal numbers of chapters that cover similar parallel historical periods from antiquity to modernity reaching into the present—is meant to signal as much the mirroring continuities between these two related yet agonistic traditions as the inversions of perspective they entail. The mirroring form, in order words, reflects (on) the mimetic content of the books.

Each volume can be read on its own for it does not presuppose the other. Ultimately, however, both parts of the diptych constitute two sides of a sin-gle, Janus-faced, and continuous genealogical argument. Hence, the reader who jumps ahead to the second volume is invited to mirror the genealogical movement of the book by subsequently jumping back to the first. Ultimately, it is the pendular, oscillating movement between the catharsis and affective hypothesis that provides the two wings whereby past theories take flight again and are carried into the present and future.

Schematically put, volume 1 stages a psychoanalytic tradition that has its modern origins in Sigmund Freud's conception of the Oedipal uncon-scious. It is aligned with a specifically therapeutic interpretation of Aristo-tle's account of catharsis as a purgation of psychic pathologies that become dominant in the late nineteenth and twentieth centuries and, in a new anthropological reformulation, finds an influential contemporary advocate in the French theorist of violence, René Girard. Internal differences between different advocates of the catharsis hypothesis will inevitably emerge as our genealogy unfolds, moving from antiquity, to modernity, into the present. Still, at the most general level, advocates of this tradition—from Aristotle to Jacob Bernays, Sigmund Freud to René Girard—tend to agree that homeopathic doses of ritually controlled violence, and their aesthetic representations thereof, keep the city, as well as individuals, going.

In an inversion of perspectives characteristic of the genealogical method, volume 2 furthers this patho-*logical* diagnostic from the other end of the theoretical spectrum. Taking Nietzsche more than Freud as a pioneering explorer of the labyrinth of the unconscious, the volume considers the recent return of interest in a marginalized pre-Freudian, "physio-psychological" tradition of the unconscious that was once dominant in the modernist period, was left in the shadow in the past, Freudian century, and is currently reemerging, phantom-like, albeit under new masks and conceptual personae such as affect theory, new materialist ontologies, and the neurosciences in the present, post-Freudian, yet no less imitative century. Once again, genealogical lenses give these recent re-turns to mimesis historical depth and philosophical perspective. They reveal that the historical origins of theories of emotional contagion harken back to Plato's diagnostic of dramatic mimesis as a trigger for irrational pathologies of the soul, which are also pathologies of the city. This perspective resurfaces in modern anti-Platonic philosophers, of which Nietzsche is the most influential representative, stretching to contribute to the birth of human sciences like crowd psychology and different schools of dynamic psychology. Ultimately, it finds its most recent advocates in transdisciplinary fields that are aware of the transformative power of that eminently plastic creature which is homo mimeticus.

Despite the diversity of traditions, methods, and areas of investigations convoked, these two perspectives share at least one fundamental diagnostic insight: namely, they give serious consideration to unconscious powers constitutive of human behavior that operate below the register of conscious awareness, tend to be dismissed as "irrational," and have been considered marginal in the past century still dominated by the myth of progress modeled on an ideal picture of *Homo sapiens*, including the myth of progress on human violence based on a rationalist faith in the "better angles of our nature." Even prior to the return of war in Europe, with the Russian of invasion of Ukraine in 2022, it was clear that we live in a historical period in which angles no longer point to ideal fables of illimited progress, let alone historical progress. If only because the wings of the "angel of history," as Walter Benjamin's interpretation of Paul Klee's *Angelus Novus* figuratively put it, are caught in a violent storm that is part of "one single catastrophe" called "progress" that "keeps piling wreckage upon wreckage."[50] What we must add is that the growth of the mimetic faculty in the digital age catches the better angels of human nature in a widening gyre of hypermimetic wreckages that threaten to go from (new) fascist insurrections to nuclear escalations, conspiracy theories to pandemic denials to climate change denial in the age that may be centered on humans in theory (or Anthropocene), yet will generate increasingly complex forms of systemic violence that escape human agentic control, decentering the *sapiens* side of the *anthropos* in practice. While I will restrict my focus to the (hyper)mimetic amplification of (new) media violence, it is crucial to realize that violent catastrophes pick up speed and intensity as they catch homo mimeticus in a widening spiral of actions and reactions that are all the more powerful for they tend to operate below the register of rational or conscious awareness and are in this sense un-conscious. I call this unconscious the "mimetic unconscious,"[51] for lack of a more original term, but also to point to the centrality of involuntary forms of imitative behavior in the amplification of anthropogenic catastrophes, including those amplified by (new) media violence.

I hasten to add that the point of this theoretical agon between the Oedipal and the mimetic unconscious, which, you will have noticed, has mimetic theory, or a new theory of homo mimeticus, sitting on both sides of the fence, is not to reenact an ancient quarrel on the virtues and vices of representations of violence—though I will eventually favor an empirical, materialist, and immanent tradition on a subject as elusive as the unconscious. Nor is it to paint a complete and exhaustive picture of the philological details that account for the underlying historical continuities and discontinuities between these two respective traditions—for a growing literature is already available on the much-discussed discovery of the unconscious.[52] As with violence, so with the unconscious: my goal is, once again, both more modest and more ambitious. More modest because it traces a genealogy of two different theoretical models for thinking about the relation between violence and the unconscious via a set of restricted, necessarily partial, yet nonetheless exemplary theoretical texts in the western tradition that continue to inform contemporary debates. And more ambitious because these books adopt a genealogical approach that looks back to the heterogeneous origins of western aesthetics in order to reflect critically, diagnostically, and from a trans-disciplinary perspective on an increasingly mediatized present and future in which fictional representations of violence have the disturbing potential to trigger mimetic or, as I shall call them, hypermimetic pathologies in the real world.

As indicated, the division between the two diagnostics is not clear-cut. While volume 2 is indeed concerned with diagnosing the affective dynamic of what I call contagious pathologies, this does not mean that it is deprived of diagnostic insights into the logic of mimetic pathos, or patho-*logies*. Quite the contrary, as we shall repeatedly see a degree of infection by the pathos of violence, if taken in homeopathic doses, has the potential to stimulate diag-nostic patho-logical reflections that serve as theoretical antidotes. Hence the divide between the catharsis and the affective hypothesis will not be as neat as the division in two volumes suggests. Both sides are genealogically entan-gled, forming a single, Janus-faced, and mirroring diagnostic of the spiraling dynamic triggered by unconscious patho(-)logies of violence constitutive of our theory of homo mimeticus.

These contexts will be strikingly heterogeneous, and our case studies will bring to the fore different—philosophical and aesthetic, ethical and politi-cal—perspectives on the catharsis and affective hypothesis. In this volume, we will go from the centrality of the case of Oedipus for the catharsis hypoth-esis—be it Girardian (chapter 1) or Freudian (chapter 2), Aristotelian (chap-ter 3), or Nietzschean (chapter 4)—to more historically specific theoretical contests like the 1966 "Structuralist Controversy" that informed a mimetic agon between deconstruction and mimetic theory (chapter 1) and provided theoretical foundations for the catharsis hypothesis. On the competing side, in the second volume, we shall consider the centrality of contagious violence that goes from Plato's concerns with the *Iliad* and the *vita mimetica* that ani-mates the Allegory of the Cave (chapter 2) to contemporary films (chapter 1) to theorize the hypermimetic potential of violence to spill from simula-tions to reality. Case studies will give specific interpretative substance to our diagnostic. For instance, we shall consider the problematic of police murders of African Americans in the United States via the case of Rayshard Brooks, a case of murder that seems modeled on TV series like *Cops*, but also reveals the

agentic power of objects like weapons (chapter 4). We shall also consider the
role of conspiracy theories that start via social media like Facebook and Twitter online yet contributed to triggering (new) fascist insurrections offline, as
the example of the storming of the U.S. Capitol on January 6, 2021, indicates,
and as the case of Waldo in the sf British TV series *Black Mirror* prefigured
(chapter 3). Last but not least we shall shift genealogical perspectives from
the untimely discovery of mirroring reflexes by philosophical physicians like
Charles Féré and Nietzsche in the 1880s—that is, over a century before the
discovery of mirror neurons in the 1990s (chapter 4)—to the role of mirror
neurons in first-person simulations of violence in action role-playing video
games like *Cyberpunk 2077* (chapter 5), among other case studies. In sum, the
perspectives on violence and the unconscious we shall adopt will be plural,
transdisciplinary, and heterogeneous, yet they will provide specific illustra-
tions on the patho(-)logies that emerge as (new) media violence operates on
the mimetic unconscious.

Clearly, my primary goal throughout will not be to offer an exhaustive
account of each perspective I will convoke. Nietzsche says "*some* schooling"
in different disciplines because a complete schooling can easily lead to the
trap of hyperspecialization that prevents the perspectival dialogues between
different schools he is advocating. In the process, we shall set up theoretical
bridges, conceptual openings, and critical conversations from a transversal
perspective that cuts across some of the major discourses that inform, at the
deepest structural level, the riddle concerning the relation between violence
and the unconscious, from its origins in classical antiquity to its various imitative models that emerge in the modern period—stretching to inform the
contemporary period as well.

Violence and the Oedipal and/or mimetic unconscious, then, is revisited from a genealogical and, ultimately, as the detective of *Vice* reminds us,
future-oriented perspective.

CHAPTER 1

The "True" Unconscious

Girard to Freud

T he threefold articulation of mimesis, violence, and the unconscious provides this study with an obvious starting point for a genealogical investigation into the vicissitudes of the catharsis and contagious hypotheses on (new) media violence. The French theorist, anthropologist, and literary critic René Girard is, in fact, one of the most important contemporary thinkers who, after a period of relative marginalization at the twilight of the twentieth century, is currently returning to the forefront of the theoretical scene at the dawn of the twenty-first century. His analyses of the relation between mimetic desire, ritual violence, and scapegoating mechanisms that look back to the sacrificial origins of culture still tend to be marginalized in critical theory.[1] And yet, in cultural practice, Girard's mimetic hypothesis provides a broad interdisciplinary framework to account for the increasing threats of violent escalations that plague contemporary societies, encouraging a growing number of theorists, philosophers, and social scientists to reflect further on the contagious powers of violence to generate irrational sameness in place of rational differences.

Despite growing recognition in the humanities, Girard's work is rarely mentioned in discussions on (new) media violence. Understandably so, since

Girard did not himself directly engage with the relation between media and violence, leaving this connection for other theorists of mimesis to pursue. At the same time, Girard's mimetic theory has not been deprived of cultural recognitions, leading Michel Serres to proclaim him as the "new Darwin of human sciences"—an emphatic designation that does not reflect a consensus on the scientific status of Girard's work but speaks to his growing acceptance within and beyond the academy.[2] This return of attention to Girard's thought is well deserved. Although I will be careful not to mechanically map his theory to the problematic that follows—if only because I have a theory of mimesis of my own—Girard's diagnostic of violence from the angle of catharsis and contagion remains relevant for the transdisciplinary genealogy that concerns us, and deserves to be taken seriously. It also allows us to further the insight that "debates over the meaning of catharsis . . . mirror the concerns of each age or school of thought,"[3] which does not mean that these mirroring effects are deprived of revealing insights into the relation between violence and the unconscious.

Over the past half century, Girard engaged with a wide range of literary, anthropological, psychological, and philosophical traditions in order to analyze how the logic of mimetic desire leads to rivalries that spread mimetically and thus contagiously, from self to others, individuals to communities, generating violent actions and cathartic reactions that are not under the full control of consciousness, yet have the power to affect us unconsciously nonetheless. This is why Girard says that "in imitation there is always a certain degree of unconsciousness involved."[4] The problematic of the unconscious is thus directly related to Girard's theory of violence, which does not mean that the Girardian concept of the unconscious can be easily identified or has been clearly defined so far. Not only Girard did not develop a theory of the unconscious, but at times he also opts for a dispensation of the hypothesis of the unconscious altogether.[5] Hence, before we set out to shed new light on Girard's account of violence and the unconscious as a step toward solving the riddle of (new) media violence, a reminder of the general scope of his theory and of the mimetic agonism that brought it into being is in order.

The Girardian Unconscious—a Genealogy

Girard is commonly identified as the thinker who founded mimetic theory, but theories of mimesis, as we shall see, have a much longer history. It would be more accurate to say that Girard's theory is based on a structural configuration grouped under three, related concepts of mimetic desire, rivalry, and violence, and the scapegoat he posits at the foundation of the world.[6] The threefold structure is not accidental. There is, in fact, a structural triangulation that finds in mimetic desire a *via regia* to the psyche that is driven by ambivalent feelings toward models or mediators. A similar dynamic was diagnosed by Sigmund Freud via an Oedipal model of the unconscious that, at first sight, does not occupy a privileged position in Girard's mimetic theory. Still, our genealogy aims to bring this structural analogy to the fore in order to rethink the foundations of both the catharsis and the affective hypothesis. In my Janus-faced titles, *Violence and the Oedipal/Mimetic Unconscious*, I thus voluntarily echo what I take to be Girard's most influential but also most Freudian book, *Violence and the Sacred*. And I do so with an aim that is double: first, I reveal the Oedipal structural foundations on which the entire edifice of Girard's theoretical foundations, including his cathartic hypothesis, rests. And second, I supplement a still missing, undervalued, yet, in our view, decisive concept—the mimetic unconscious—that lies at the foundation of our theory of *homo mimeticus*. This confrontation will not be simply rivalrous or antagonistic. On the contrary, it will develop in a respectful spirit of mimetic agonism that informs our entire genealogy of catharsis and contagion that follows.

Unlike the much-discussed concept of mimetic desire, which is manifest everywhere in Girard's work and provides the psychological foundation for his account of the ambivalences generated by mimetic rivalry and the scapegoating mechanisms it triggers, the concept of the unconscious tends to remain latent in his system and has so far been little discussed. In order to bring it to the surface, it requires an unusual combination of a bird's eye view that encompasses the overall scope of Girard's theory from a philosophical distance, while at the same time being able to zoom in on its conceptual and affective details as they emerge to confront specific problems—in short, a double sight characteristic not of a passive reader of theory but of an active theorist and creator of concepts.

One the one hand, this Janus-faced genealogical perspective should not treat specific aspects of Girard's theory in isolation but, rather, considers the complex relations between the parts and the whole by taking into account the overall synchronic structure and diachronic development of Girard's system in general—not an easy task, given that this system engages with a variety of disciplines from literary criticism to anthropology to philosophy, to name a few, and goes from the origins of hominization to its apocalyptic destinations. On the other hand, and at the same time, this perspective should consider the genealogical development of a theory of mimesis that, like all theories, builds on influential predecessors but, despite its focus on imitation, or perhaps because of it, does not always say so explicitly yet leaves traces of influences for the genealogist to uncover in order to go further. Hence the importance of taking a degree of healthy epistemological distance from Girard's hermeneutics. This will allow us to uncover that under what initially appear as rivalrous oppositions that emphasize theoretical differences, striking mirroring continuities reveal innovative inversions of rather familiar structures.

If I take the trouble to rehearse a theory that is by now well known in its general outlines and has already generated a number of informed commentaries,[7] it is with a specific genealogical perspective aimed to foregrounding the mirroring theoretical foundations of Girard's mimetic theory that are still little known. My focus in this chapter is thus less in introducing Girard's theory of violence, but in unearthing the hidden epistemic foundations on which this theory rests. This will allow us to evaluate the strengths and weaknesses of his mimetic theory, as well as of other theories of violence and the unconscious he relies on, in view of furthering a theory of homo mimeticus relevant to the contemporary problem that concerns us in this volume: namely, the problem of (new) media violence and its hypothetical cathartic unconscious effect. It is in fact only if we combine both distant and proximate perspectives that we can bring into focus how Girard's thought on desire and violence is part of a genealogical iceberg whose deep foundations have not been brought to the surface as yet. A closer genealogical look at the foundations of Girard's system will bring us very quickly to the bottom of a transdisciplinary tradition in western thought that attempted to solve the riddle of catharsis central to the Oedipal unconscious (volume 1) while also pointing to the problem of contagion central to the mimetic unconscious (volume 2).

Girard's take on violence cannot be dissociated from his conception of "mimetic desire," which he initially outlined as a literary critic in his first book, *Deceit, Desire and the Novel* (1961). In his exploration of the relation between self and others in novels by Cervantes, Stendhal, Flaubert, Proust, and Dostoevsky, Girard noticed that underneath the first layer of obvious differentiations and oppositions, the same fundamental structure led romantic protagonists to involuntarily desire what others desire. Not just any others, but admired, exemplary others, what he also calls "models," or "mediators," with whom the protagonist qua subject identifies. The structural consequences of this insight can be summarized in two foundational starting points.

First, the subject desires what the other desires, a formula that, like many other French thinkers, Girard inherited from a characteristically French Hegelian tradition mediated by Alexandre Kojève's lectures on the *Phenomenology of the Spirit*. Dominant in the 1940s and 1950s, Kojève's lectures were concerned with a master/slave dialectic of recognition predicated on what Girard himself calls "a desire for the other's desire."[8] While Girard stresses the desire for the object perhaps more than the desire for recognition, this master-slave dialectics of desires struggling for pure prestige is also at the origins of his theory of mimetic desire. As Girard belatedly acknowledged: "Many wanted to see me as the successor of Kojève, the great commentator on Hegel," which, despite the flattering genealogy, led to the accusation that "mimetic desire was only a reformulation of the desire for recognition in Hegel's theory" (*BE* 30). And Girard adds, in a confessional spirit that illustrates what I shall later call romantic agonism: "Naturally I fought back like a demon, but I cannot deny that Hegel was in the background" (30). Fighting back, we already see, is an agonistic move that betrays an anxiety of imitative proximity. For the moment suffices to say that Girard's restriction to a dialectic of desire as a starting point to establish the foundations of a theory of mimesis tout court is not accidental. It is part of the Hegelian spirit still predominant in France in the 1960s whose traces can be found in thinkers with elective affinities, from Jean-Paul Sartre to Jacques Lacan to Georges Bataille—a Hegelianism, genealogical lenses will lead us to reconsider.[9]

Second, once this master/slave dialectic of recognition is posited as the foundation of a self-other structural dynamic, the relation between the subject and the admired model becomes increasingly ambivalent. In fact, for Girard, the model not only directs the subject's desire toward an already desired object but inevitably turns into an obstacle or rival on the path of a now contested desired object. The subject, the model, and the object are thus intimately tied in a structural double bind that rests on two related yet distinct ties: namely, an identification with the model (or mimesis) and a desire for the contested object (or "appropriative desire"), which, knotted together, generate a quasi-Oedipal triangular form whose universality we shall have to reevaluate. With this structure in place, a fight to the death for the same "object," which can be a human being, often a woman, is set in motion. Thus, the "subject," the "model," and the "object" are framed within a triangular, rivalrous structure, which will inevitably trigger pathological and potentially violent feelings like jealousy, envy, and ressentiment characteristic of romantic fictions that provide both the synchronic and diachronic vectors of Girard's mimetic theory. This structuralist theory had, indeed, a strong explicative reach during the linguistic turn; it also calls for a reassessment in light of more recent theoretical turns constitutive of the *re*-turn to mimesis.

Girard infers the structure of violence from literary fictions based on familial dramas; but rather than confining his analysis within the formal boundaries of the text, he makes clear in subsequent books that this violence has a referent in the real world as well and can generate a "crisis of difference" that affects and infects the entire social body. Shifting the focus of attention from rivalries in literary fictions to rivalries in anthropological realities, from aesthetic representations to ritual referents, Girard articulates this mechanism in his second major work, *Violence and the Sacred* (1972). This is also the work where the problematic of violence and the unconscious is most manifestly articulated agonistically, with and against important, and previously unmentioned, genealogical precursors. Let us take a closer look.

Both synchronic and diachronic vectors of analysis are simultaneously at play in Girard's account of the birth of culture out of a violent sacrificial and collective murder that is not under the control of consciousness and is, in this sense, unconscious. This does not mean that human violence, for Girard, is biologically innate and part of an instinct of survival, as Konrad Lorenz argues in *On Aggression* (1963).[10] On the contrary, rather than being a cause of aggressive behavior, Girard considers violence a mimetic effect of the appropriative structure of human desires. Summing up what is presented as an anthropological narrative of lost origins in terms of the diachronic vector of his theory, while at the same time pursuing the structuralist hypothesis that mimetic desire leads to violence in line with his synchronic vector of analysis, Girard now ties both diachronic and synchronic threads in a gordian knot that centers on what he enigmatically calls the "true 'unconscious.'" As he puts it in *Violence and the Sacred*, as a consequence of the violent rivalry generated by mimetic desire, a crisis of difference occurs whereby

> the more frenzied the mimetic process becomes, caught up in the confusion [*tourbillon*] of constantly changing forms, the more unwilling men are to recognize that they have made an obstacle of the model and a model of the obstacle. Here we encounter a true "unconscious" [*le véritable* inconscient *est là*], and one that can obviously assume many forms. (*VS* 189)

This is a rather schematic account of a complex, dynamic, and wide-ranging theory that articulates the centrality of violence in the emergence of culture; and yet genealogical lenses brought us very quickly to the spiraling center of Girard's theoretical system. They also allow us to zoom in on this "confusion"—or as the French says, "vortex" (*tourbillon*)—and begin to identify the structural channels through which violent affects are made to flow. We have, in fact, not only reached the foundational mimetic principle, that, for Girard, generates rivalry, frenzy, violence, and eventually a purgative catharsis that is central to his account of the origins of culture; we are also in a position to see that the enigmatic and rather unspecified concept of an "unconscious" Girard considers "true" latently informs his structural dynamic, providing his hermeneutics with an invisible spiraling center that is nowhere and everywhere—if only because it is around this center that the *tourbillon* of frenzied affects, be they bad or good, contagious or cathartic, turns and, by extension, in-*forms* (gives a structural form to) the entirety of Girard's mimetic theory.

The French text is specific: Girard's conception of what he calls the "true 'unconscious'" is topographically located at the center of this "vortex," and is thus fluid, protean, and manifests itself in "many forms." And yet, from a genealogical distance that hovers far above Girard's theory of violence and the unconscious, we can confirm that its latent, albeit barely visible, foundations rest on a privileged form. That is, a triangular form that turns around a subject, a model, and a contested object that is not without resemblance with an alternative, perhaps not "true" but certainly dominant and influential theory of the unconscious that has become synonymous with the discovery of the unconscious tout court. This theory will play a pivotal role in developing the catharsis hypothesis, which Girard encourages us to revisit from the angle of mimesis: namely, psychoanalysis.

Of course, we should be careful in establishing our genealogical affiliation, for the continuities between mimetic theory and psychoanalysis are far from clear-cut. Consistently in his work, Girard is severely critical toward the father of psychoanalysis—so critical that he dismisses the Freudian concept of the "unconscious" as "unwieldy and dubious" (*VS* 176). Girard even hastens to add that when it comes to the unconscious, "Freud is of little use as a guide over this terrain" (189), thereby implying that he is entering uncharted psychological terrain. Thus, Girard pits a "true" unconscious contra a "dubious" unconscious, and, more generally, his mimetic hypothesis contra Freud's Oedipal hypothesis. This distancing critical move is particularly visible in a chapter devoted to "Freud and the Oedipus Complex" in *Violence and the Sacred*, from which I have just quoted. It deserves a closer consideration given the agonistic confrontation with Freud it entails, precisely on the relation between violence and the unconscious.

Girard with or contra Freud?

As the specification that this is a "true" unconscious already suggests,[11] Girard's rediscovery of the unconscious implies an intellectual confrontation with the father of psychoanalysis that is not deprived of mirroring effects. As he convincingly shows via a close reading of key texts on group psychology and metapsychology, Freud oscillates between the primacy of mimesis (identification) on the one hand, and the primacy of desire (object cathexis) on the other, a pendular movement that is revealed in what Girard calls Freud's "slip of the pen" (*VS* 172) and ultimately always leads the latter to opt for the primacy of desire and to "banish mimesis from his later work" (173). What motivates this Freudian ban? And how should we interpret this Freudian slip? Let us distinguish between the reasons of the ban, and the language Girard convokes to diagnose it.

In the philosophical tradition, mimesis was traditionally banished because of the irrational power of mimetic pathos to trouble the metaphysical ideal of the human psyche, or soul. This critique applies first and foremost to Plato's metaphysics and the rationalism and idealism that led to the ban of mimesis at the dawn of philosophy we shall consider in detail in volume 2. But why apply the Platonic allusion to this ban to Freud, given the latter's battle contra rationalist philosophers to account for humans' irrational and unconscious tendencies? Surely, the father of psychoanalysis, unlike the father of philosophy, cannot be critiqued for positing an ideal of rational consciousness at the center of what is, after all, a theory of the unconscious?

And yet this is precisely what Girard suggests. At the end of his rather detailed and penetrating analysis of Freud's Oedipal theory, Girard unmasks a rationalist exclusion of mimesis as constitutive of Freud's metapsychology. Not unlike Plato's metaphysics, Freud's metapsychology, according to Girard, rests on a traditional "philosophy of consciousness" (*VS* 176) that makes the psychoanalytical concept of the unconscious dubious in the first place. In fact, in Girard's interpretation, Freud's assumption that the Oedipal child automatically desires the maternal object without the mediation of a paternal model is predicated on an Oedipal subject that does not need to be told what to desire but, like a "traditional philosophical subject" (182)—after all, Oedipus is a solver of riddles—already has a "conscious knowledge" (177) of both his/her incestuous desire and violent parricidal intentions.[12] Thus, in an inversion of perspectives on the case of Oedipus, Girard specifies: "The incest wish, the patricide wish, do not belong to the child but spring from the mind of the adult, the model" (175). As Girard ironically concludes his diagnostic of psychoanalysis, ultimately, the theory of the Oedipus complex might actually set up a mirror to the psychoanalyst's own incestuous/parricidal desire, be it real or theoretical. For Girard, the child, not unlike the scapegoat, is "'innocent'" (174). The Oedipal/patricidal wish is unconsciously projected by the father. At one remove, both desires (for the mother and the death of the father) might be projected by the father of psychoanalysis himself who wishes to establish an Oedipal theory of the unconscious. Thus, the father of psychoanalysis is thoroughly psychoanalyzed. And in the process of the analysis, the Oedipal unconscious turns out to rest on the projection of a rationalist conception of consciousness.

Mimetic theory sets up an unflattering mirror to psychoanalytical, Oedipal desires. We can thus better understand why, in later works, Girard reiterates his "distrust" of the concept of "*the* unconscious" for the "ontological essentialism" (*EC* 86) it entails. It is, in fact, the very hypothesis of the unconscious Girard calls into question, for the primacy of mimesis over desire challenges the "repressive hypothesis" and thus "does away with the unconscious" (*VS* 183). Fair enough. It would, however, have been more accurate to say that Girard aims to do away with the Freudian unconscious. This does not mean that alternative conceptions of the unconscious do not remain central to account for the logic of mimetic violence. Girard, for one, at times prefers the pre-Freudian conception of "lack of consciousness" (*EC* 86) or nonconscious, which is collective rather than individual, based on a mimetic/hypnotic hypothesis I shall return to, rather than on the repressive hypothesis we are interrogating here.[13] For the moment, let us retain that because of Freud's quasi-Platonic ban of mimesis from his metapsychology, Girard considers that the father of psychoanalysis "failed" to apprehend the mimetic logic of desire that paves the way for a more faithful account of the relation between desire, violence, and the unconscious central to our genealogy. While Freud relies on the concept of ambivalence, which he routinely convokes to account for the double bind that ties the Oedipal subject's identificatory/rivalrous relation to the model, Girard considers this ambivalence as a symptom of a "latent conflict" dormant in Freud's theory of the unconscious, which required Girard's interpretation in order to manifest itself. This, at least, is what emerges if we limit our analysis to the manifest content of Girard's critique of the Freudian unconscious.

But genealogy is not only attentive to the content of a theory; it also considers its formal language. And it does so, not to discover a latent meaning but to highlight manifest rhetorical strategies that bring new theories of the unconscious into being. In fact, attention to Girard's rhetorical moves indicates a fundamental ambivalence in his own evaluation of Freud. That is, ambivalences, or wavering oscillations, that indicate a double movement toward/away from the father of psychoanalysis. Such ambivalences are worth attending to for they reveal important genealogical traces in Girard's own theorization of violence and the unconscious. For instance, Girard admits

Freud comes "*very close* to apprehending it [the logic of mimetic desire]" (*VS* 169; my emphasis) in his account of the male child's Oedipal triangulation of desire for the mother (or object cathexis) and mimesis (or identification) with the father, yet he also stresses that Freud ultimately "failed" to do so (169). Thus, Girard feels the need "to *continue* along the paths abandoned by him [Freud]" in order to "*discover where he* [Freud] *might have gone* had he chosen to be guided" (173; my emphasis) by the thread of mimesis in his explorations of the labyrinth of the unconscious.

A critique that explicitly sets up a distance to an opponent/model leads to a continuation implying a proximity. Or, to put it in a language both theorists share, by identifying with Freud, taking his place along the path he abandoned, he, Girard, sets out to find out where he, Freud, might have gone. If psychoanalysis paved the way for the path, then, mimetic theory is the extension that will allow Girard to discover a "'true' unconscious" Freud both failed to theorize and paved the way for. Girard even mimics psycho-analytical parlance ("latent conflicts," "suppressing mimesis," "slips of the pen," etc.) in order to reinterpret the Oedipus complex contra Freud, while at the same time furthering Freudian insights. If ambivalence may be too vague a concept to account for Girard's double reading with/contra Freud, the Nietzschean concept of "pathos of distance" provides a philosophical alternative. Its oxymoronic tension describes a double movement of attrac-tion and repulsion in which the need for distance and differentiation is actu-ally symptomatic that a mimetic pathos and similarity already connects the subject to the theoretical model.

Girard is the first to acknowledge this double movement, if not explic-itly, at least rhetorically so. Thus, from the very opening lines he recognizes "both similarities and differences" between his account of mimetic desire and Freud's Oedipus complex, acknowledging that the two theories are "at once similar and quite different" (*VS* 174). To be more precise we should rather say that they are presented as different because they are quite similar.

Difference as the effect of sameness will indeed be constitutive of agonis-tic relations we shall explore in theories of violence and the unconscious that follow. Girard's mimetic relation to Freud provides the blueprint. From his avowal that mimesis "plays an important role in Freud's work" to his speci-fication that it is "not important enough," from the recognition that Freud

came "very close" and yet he "failed," from the insight that he is "too precious
to be left to the psychoanalysis" (*VS* 178) to the decision to pursue the "path
abandoned by him" (173) to other strikingly ambivalent evaluations, such
a contradictory pathos of distance indicates to a theorist of mimesis not
blinded by the superficial primacy of difference qua originality, that a deep
genealogical connection is actually at play—the connection and pathos being
stronger in direct proportion to the need of theoretical differentiation and
distance. The "differences" Girard emphasizes between his theory and the
Oedipus complex are perhaps an indication that the "similarities" are actually
more important—a lesson that is, after all, constitutive of mimetic theory.
Precisely if we adopt Girardian lenses, when a subject is caught in a mirroring relation, rivalrous differentiation is what often ensues. Although the
claim applies to the imitative subject Girard theorizes, there is no reason to
confine the diagnostic within the boundaries of the text, for mimetic theory
also applies to subjects outside the text, perhaps stretching to include, at one
remove, Girard's own conflictual relation to his own theoretical models. If
"mimetism is a source of continual conflict" and "inevitably leads to rivalry"
(169), as Girard reminds us at the opening of his most Freudian chapter and
tirelessly repeats in all his works, perhaps this insight applies to theoretical
rivalries as well, especially when it comes to a concept as contested as the
unconscious.

   That said, we do not need to posit a latent Oedipal conflict at the heart
of Girard's theory to account for this ambivalent double bind. Although
mimesis plays a central role in relations with intellectual models, and a
form of external mediation is certainly at play in Girard's relation to the
father of psychoanalysis, strictly speaking, this is not a classical instance
of what Girard would call "mimetic rivalry." Sure, an identification exists
between subject and model (Girard's identification with Freud, the pursuit
of his path, the discovery of latent conflicts, interpretations of slips of the
pen, etc.); and yet this mimesis does not simply lead to rivalry, let alone
physical violence—though a form of rhetorical violence is certainly animating Girard's diagnostic. Nor does it lead to affective symptoms that can
be considered pathological—though Girard is the first to admit that the
great writers of mimesis can write so well about affects like jealousy, ressentiment, and vanity because they experienced them in their lives first. At one
remove, this may apply to theorists of jealousy as well.[14] Rather, and for us

more important, this mimetic relation with an intellectual model is generative of positive theoretical results that generate what I call patho-*logies*, in
the specific sense that the affect or pathos of a mimetic identification with
an exemplary precursor can be put to productive theoretical use to bring
forth a new thought or logos on mimesis.

And this is where the concept of mimetic agonism enters the theoretical
scene to cast light on the genealogy of violence and the unconscious constitutive of homo mimeticus.

Mimetic Agonism

I already alluded to the agonistic relation between advocates of the catharsis
hypothesis and those of the affective hypothesis, an agonism constitutive of
the mirroring structure of this Janus-faced study. Let me now go further by
specifying the paradoxical movement that animates what I call the mimetic
agonism generative of mirroring inversions of perspectives in the first place.
Mimetic agonism is a form of intellectual and creative contest I first identified
in Nietzsche's relation to his models, or educators, that appear at first sight
to be simply opponents, antagonists, or rivals, yet, on a closer genealogical
investigation, turn out to provide the very conceptual and theoretical tools
to establish an opposition in the first place—in a creative, productive, yet
still imitative way.[15] As we shall see, the mirroring inversions of perspectives
that entangle main advocates of the catharsis and affective hypothesis benefit
a great deal from an insight into the dynamic of mimetic agonism. As Johan
Huizinga rightly identified in *Homo Ludens* (1938), the agon is a constitutive
element of the all too human fascination for play and games.[16] We shall see
this applies to intellectual games and contests as well. If Huizinga set out
to map the agonistic element in the practices of *homo ludens*, we argue that
mimetic agonism is central to the theorization of homo mimeticus. Both are
not deprived of playful and creative elements.

This agonistic confrontation is thus not simply rivalrous, reactive, or violent. On the contrary, it is competitive, active, and productive of knowledge
for it is intended to push thought further—by pushing against the shoulders of influential predecessors. For instance, the "mysterious antagonism"
Nietzsche identifies in his agonistic relation to his former model, Richard

Wagner, early in his career, becomes particularly visible when the problematic of mimesis is at play. As Nietzsche puts it in the fourth of his *Untimely Meditations* (1873) dedicated to Wagner: "By apparently succumbing to Wagner's overflowing nature, he who reflects upon it has in fact participated in its energy and has thus as it were *through him* acquired power *against him*."[17] What follows furthers a reevaluation of the centrality of agonism by highlighting Nietzsche's debt to his colleague at Basel, the historian Jacob Burckhardt, and by emphasizing the importance of mimetic agonism for mimetic theory more generally. What applies to Nietzsche's relation to Wagner early in his career, in fact, applies to his other models qua antagonists as well, throughout his career. Be it with respect to Wagner, Schopenhauer, or Plato, in his agonistic intellectual skirmishes, Nietzsche is not simply writing against, or contra, his formers intellectual models qua educators; nor is he passively mimicking them. Rather, he writes in an agonistic identification *with and against* them by creatively appropriating the predecessors' thoughts to propose new, not fully original, yet nonetheless future-oriented thoughts affirmed in a Homeric spirit of contestation and love of honor, or *philotima*. In our language, mimetic agonism provides the affective and conceptual perspectives—the pathos and the logos—that turn romantic pathologies internal to mimetic rivalry (jealousy, ressentiment, violence, etc.) into a modernist patho-*logy*, a mimetic patho-logy that makes our theory of mimesis new by pushing with and against influential precursors. Since this method is internal to our genealogical reevaluation of both the cathartic and the affective hypotheses that posit a mirroring agonism that divides/unites this double study, let us consider the genealogy of mimetic agonism in more detail.

The mimetic dynamic of the agon is not without resemblances with other agonistic confrontations with influential predecessors that culminated in Romanticism during the first half of the nineteenth century. Yet it should not be too hastily conflated with them, for the ancient foundations of the agon and the romantic source of anxieties rest on a rather different ethos, are driven by a different power, and promote different conceptions of creation. If mimetic agonism bears a family resemblance with what Harold Bloom, on the shoulders of Freud, calls "anxiety of influence," we shall confirm time and again that the logic of mimetic agonism is not predicated on a metapsychology based on "repression," "*Nachträglichkeit*," and a romantic anxiety of originality that leads to creative but rather partial "misreadings" of influential predecessors.[18] Rather, as the concept of agon suggests, its origins are of classical rather than romantic inspiration. They go back to what Nietzsche's colleague at Basel, the cultural historian Jacob Burckhardt, in his lectures on *The Greeks and Greek Civilization* (1898–1902) called the "agonal age" constitutive of the archaic, Homeric period.[19] If the origins of the mimetic agon are ancient, modern thinkers like Nietzsche reenacted the agon, contest, or *Wettkampf* for the modern period.[20] Mimetic agonism provides an alternative to romantic rivalries and anxieties predicated on the myth of originality that did not have such a tight grip on the Greek agonal age and perhaps should not have a grip on our hypermimetic age either.

Let us recall that the Greek agon originates in the physical agonism of the Olympic games. An exemplary dramatization of this agonistic spirit in games was already at play in Homer's *Odyssey* in his journey home (*nostos*). Specifically, in the famous section in Book 8 on "The Phaeacian Games," as Ulysses is provoked to a challenge by Laodamas in "any forms of sport," Odysseus replies: "Why are you trying to provoke me with your challenges, you and your friends. I am too sick at heart to think of games. I have been through many bitter and exhausting experiences, and all I seek now is my passage home."[21] But he is insulted by another (Euryalus) who claims: "One can see you are no athlete" (*O* 8.163–64, 111). Odysseus, usually calm, is provoked to anger and accepts the agon: "I'll try my hand at the sports. For your words have stung me and put me on my mettle" (8.184–85, 111). He picks up "the biggest discus of all, a huge weight, more massive by far than the Phaeacians normally used. With one swing he launched it from his mighty hand, and the stone hummed on its course" (8.187–90, 111–12). Athena, pretending to be one of the crowd, readily announces: "None of the Phaecians will make as good a throw, let alone a better" (8.197–98, 112). It is interesting that an accusation that could have led to a violent escalation finds in the alternative space of the games a set of rules, techniques, and skills that allow the agonist to channel an aggressive pathos into a crafted physical gesture driven by the desire to overcome the offender. A base, even rivalrous, challenge can thus, in a specifically delineated space that contains the agon, give rise to the power to excel—at least if the agonistic nature is a noble, trained, and heroic one.

Beyond sports but driven by the same spirit, the agon also plays a crucial role in the development of an ambitious, noble, and creative culture that affirms a type of individualism characteristic of Greek culture that,

Burckhardt specifies, does not rely on "personal manifestations of 'genius'" and made a "lasting imprint on Greek attitudes" (*GGC* 161). As Burckhardt puts it: "The aim [of the agon] was now to develop the body to the highest perfection of beauty, a purpose for which each individual had to submit to a methodical discipline just as severe as training in the arts, denying himself any personal manifestation of 'genius'" (161). The mimetic agonist should thus not be conflated with the romantic genius based on the myth of divine inspiration; it is rather based on a rigorous training that is immanent in nature instead. Stretching from gymnastic to in-*form* (give form to) aesthetic/intellectual contests or competitions internal to drama, but also law, politics, and philosophy, the agon played a decisive role in developing a "competitive spirit" that was restricted to males but could nonetheless be partially shared in the Greek polis. As Burckhardt continues: "the agon was a motive power known to no other people—the general leavening element that, given the essential conditions of freedom, proved capable of working upon the will and the potentialities of every individual" (162)—including, of course, creative individuals cultivating artistic crafts, which, as Henry Staten recently stressed, the Greeks understood under the general rubric of "techne."[22] From music to painting, sculpture to drama (in its comic and tragic manifestations), and poetry more generally, Burckhardt claims, with passion and philological insight, that "the art of poetry develops under the determining influence of the agon" (182). This agonistic spirit, as we shall see, concerns the development of our theory of homo mimeticus as well, which we further under the influence of an ancient but still operative agon.

Important for our argument, this agon is constitutive of the quarrel between philosophy and literature as well, on which the debate on catharsis and contagion—and, more generally, media violence—has its roots. Already Pseudo-Longinus in *On the Sublime* (ca. first century A.D.) located an agonistic dynamic at the heart of the ancient quarrel between Plato and Homer. He pointed out, for instance, that the father of philosophy "from the great Homeric source drew to himself innumerable tributary streams," which Pseudo-Longinus describes according to the paradoxical structure of the mimetic agon.[23] Pseudo-Longinus is specific in his account that agonism entails a double movement with/against the opponent; it is worth quoting for it informs the movement of our genealogy as well. He continues:

> And it seems to me that there would not have been so fine a bloom of per-
> fection on Plato's philosophical doctrines, and that he would not in many
> cases have found his way to poetical subject matter and modes of expression,
> unless he had with all his heart and mind struggled with Homer for the
> primacy, entering the list like a young champion matched against the man
> whom all admire, and showing perhaps too much love of contention and
> breaking a lance with him as it were, but deriving some profit from the
> contest none the less.[24]

Since the birth of mimetic theory in Plato's thought, then, there is value in
breaking a lance or two with worthy predecessors, be they on the side of art
or thought, pathos or logos—or, as often, an interplay of both. To put it
in Nietzschean parlance, Plato developed philosophy through and against
Homer. The stakes of the agon are thus high. It is the very identity of philosophy itself that emerges from a mimetic agonism with literature in general and
the dramatizations of violence it entails in particular.

Now, if Burckhardt located the agon at the heart of ancient Greek
culture, Nietzsche reloaded it for modernist European culture, planting the
seeds for modernist theories of mimesis to come.[25] He did so in an unpub-
lished, youthful text titled "Homer's Contest [*Wettkampf*]" (1872), where,
on the shoulders of Burckhardt, but via a philological investigation of his
own already underway, Nietzsche stepped back to the Greek sources of the
agon, which, he agreed with his Basel colleague and friend, eventually go all
the way back to Hesiod and especially Homer.[26] Drawing on a distinction
first made in Hesiod's *Theogony* (eighth to seventh century B.C.) between
two manifestations of the goddess Eris, or strife, with "completely separate
dispositions," Nietzsche introduced a philological distinction that is at least
double and reaches into the present. In fact, it looks back to two conceptions
of contest central to classical antiquity; but for genealogists this move maps
two alternative paths for modern (romantic/modernist) contests that pave
the way for two competing mimetic theories for the present and future.

A genealogy of the agon confronts us with a crossroads that is ancient
in mythic origins yet still contemporary in its theoretical value. On the one
hand, Nietzsche identifies a divine Eris that "encourages bad war and strife—
cruelty!" on the basis of a life-negating ethos that is located among the gods

and generates "'resentment'" as well as "'envy'" (HC 3). This is a path central
to romantic anxieties of originality that rest on the myth of the individual
genius and is constitutive of what Girard calls "mimetic rivalry."[27] On the
other side, Burckhardt had already noticed that the good Eris "was the first
to be born," is planted in "the very roots of the earth," and "awakens even the
indolent and unskilled to industry."[28] Echoing these very same lines, Nietzsche
confirms that Zeus placed the other Eris in the "root of the earth," considers
it "good for humankind," and "drives even the unskilled man to work" in
view of "provok[ing] human beings to action" (HC 3). The crucial point,
both Burckhardt and Nietzsche agree, is that this agonistic contest leads "not
to the action of fights of annihilation but rather to the action of *contests*"
(3)—that is, affirmative confrontations driven by a "noble victory without
enmity" (*GGC* 166). Nietzsche was quick to sense that there is significant
genealogical potential in recuperating this Greek agon for the modern(ist)
creative sensibility his untimely work projected into future sensibilities as
well. It is this second, more immanent, affirmative, and aspirationally noble
path that informs the agon our theory aims to pursue in the present period.[29]
I group this contest under the rubric of *mimetic agonism*, out of which a new
theory of homo mimeticus is born.

Mimetic agonism is thus of modernist inspiration and looks ahead to a
theory of mimesis for the future; yet its foundations rest on an ancient quarrel between philosophy and poetry that is constitutive of our genealogy of
violence and the unconscious. As Nietzsche continues, confirming the agonistic view already internal to Pseudo-Longinus: "We do not understand the
strength of Xenophanes' and later Plato's attack on the national hero of poetry
[Homer] if we do not also think of the monstrous desire at the roots of these
attacks to assume the place of the overthrown and inherit his fame" (HC 4).
This ancient desire may be monstrous, but it does not lead to violence contra
a mimetic double, as Girard postulates. On the contrary, Nietzsche makes
clear the productive nature of this agonistic contest as he concludes with a
telling Olympic but ultimately human image: "Every great Hellene passes on
the torch of the contest; every great virtue sets afire new greatness" (4). There
is thus a heroic chain of virtuous figures that set up contagious continuities
between Olympic heroes of the past in a Promethean spirit of generosity that
not only is simply vertical and transcendental but also, following the example

of the Titan, brings new greatness into this world to be passed on horizon-
tally and temporally, across the ages. And making clear that the Greek agon is
itself in an agonistic confrontation against the romantic "exclusivity of genius,"
Nietzsche specifies what he considers the "crux" of the "play of powers" constitutive of the Homeric *Wettkampf*: namely that mimetic agonism "is hostile
to the 'exclusivity' of genius in the modern sense, but ... presupposes that in
a natural order of things, there are always *several* geniuses, who incite each
other to reciprocal action as they keep each other within the limits of measure" (5). Romanticism contra modernism, exclusive genius versus inclusive
creators, mimetic rivalry contra mimetic agonism: this is, in a nutshell, the
genuine antagonism constitutive of the contemporary theory of mimesis we
advocate.

Given the Greek, Olympic origins of this agon, the goal is not to escalate
intellectual confrontations to the point of rivalry that would unconsciously
reproduce in practice the type of contagious violence we aim to understand
in our theory of mimesis. On the contrary, as our genealogy makes clear,
there is indeed a reciprocal dynamic internal to the contest that keeps the
violence of pathos from escalating, endowing the powers of mimetic agonism
with a distanced measure, or limit, necessary to affirming new thoughts in a
nonviolent spirit of creative affirmation with and against worthy competitors qua precursors.[30] If we take hold of the paradoxical double movement of
opposition and continuity, pathos and distance, imitation and contestation
internal to a mimetic agonism with a plurality of figures scattered across different territories, periods, and traditions, we shall see that this torch reaches,
via influential intellectual champions that traverse the history of western
thought, into the present. In fact, this mimetic agon cannot be peeled off
from the ancient quarrel between philosophy and poetry (or mimesis); we
shall see that it is also located at the heart of the quarrel over the cathartic
and contagious (or affective) hypothesis and the competing theories of the
(Oedipal or mimetic) unconscious they gave birth to as well. Hence the need
to step all the way back to an ancient quarrel over mimesis to take the necessary run up, so to speak, to leap ahead to modern and contemporary contests
internal to the mimetic turn, or re-turn.

In sum, the logic of mimetic agonism is not predicated on a repressive
hypothesis anxiously concerned with romantic claims of originality that

continue to animate the simple logic of rivalry. Nor is it strategically selective in its misreadings that continue to rely on Oedipal father figures generative of anxieties of influence. Rather, it entails an agonistic writing with and against an influential predecessor that, in the fair spirit of an intellectual duel that ties contenders to the same rules of the game, confronts, head-on, the models' theories. It does so by going to these theories' conceptual heart, in a spirit of competitive but also generous and affirmative creation geared toward deepening understanding via the double perspectives of critical logos and mimetic pathos. Contradictory evaluations, or ambivalent intellectual tensions with predecessors, as Karl Jaspers also noted, are indeed constitutive of what he calls "understanding," which for him also entails both cognitive and emotional evaluations internal to patho-*logies*. As Jaspers puts it, also with Nietzsche as a case study: "Understanding can be linked equally with contrary value-judgments (thus Nietzsche continued to understand Socrates [and Plato as well] but sometimes he evaluated him positively, sometimes negatively)."[31] The same could be said with respect to Plato's evaluation of Homer, Aristotle's evaluation of Plato, and so on, in a long intellectual chain of intellectual heroes who pass on the torch of knowledge, reaching into the present. Our genealogy of the agon, then, both confirms Jaspers's point and goes further in the diagnostic of this agonistic understanding with and against the other. What is at play in mimetic agonism is in fact a positive assimilation of an influential predecessor's thought, or logos, which relies on the productive interplay of both affect and reason, pathos and logos. If the pathos is essential for the initial assimilation, it also provides the power necessary to turn a negative affective evaluation (bad Eris) into a productive conceptual affirmation (good Eris). Thus, the pathology of mimetic rivalry turns in the patho-*logy* of mimetic agonism.

From this genealogical detour that will inform my reevaluation of quarrels over the catharsis and affective hypothesis involving key figures in the history of western aesthetics from antiquity to the present, it should be clear that I call this paradoxical dynamic "mimetic agonism" for at least three reasons: first, to indicate that no matter how violently opposed thoughts may appear in antagonistic theories considered by passive readers from the outside, there lurks always, below the surface, a degree of productive imitation at play from the inside of agonistic confrontations—a point Nietzsche will confirm in his understanding of contest via the reciprocal dynamic of agonism as a duel; second, the emphasis on mimesis indicates that the agon originates in exemplary models worthy of imitation first encountered in the Olympic games and subsequently at play in aesthetic contests that had a theatrical agon as a privileged stage in the ancient period—a stage on which both contagion and catharsis will continue to play a key role as well; and third, the "mimetic" before the "agonism" stresses that this dynamic is intimately tied but not limited to ancient aesthetic evaluations but, rather, continues to inform the moderns as well, stretching to animate theoretical and creative conflicts between romantic and modernist theories in the contemporary period—including theoretical conflicts on the cathartic and contagious effects of violent aesthetic spectacles that operate on competing models of the unconscious. Mimetic agonism, in other words, will guide the fundamental reevaluation of all the theories of catharsis and contagion that will follow.

As this genealogy intends to make clear, theories do not come down from the sky of transcendental ideas, already formed, like Athena out of Zeus's head. On the contrary, they originate from the bottom up, from highly competitive intellectual figures who carry the torch of thought into the present by running on their own legs to pass it down to subsequent generations of thinkers. If we consider a theory, concept, or aesthetic form not as a self-contained, autonomous, and unitary entity modeled on an original idea, or transcendental form, but, rather, trace the genealogical process of conceptual emergence and genealogical transmission whereby this form comes into being via immanent, often agonistic, and sometimes dramatic confrontations with previous models, then we reach an understanding of a theory, concept, or work of art from the inside.

This type of understanding is characteristic of the active theorist and creator rather than the passive reader or faithful disciple. In this book, then, concepts shall not simply be inherited from the past idealist tradition concerned with an adequation (*homoiosis*) or identity between being and thought. Rather, they need to be created from the bottom up with an eye to solving new problems that emerge from a world caught up in a process of becoming. As Nietzsche also puts it in a fragment of *The Will to Power* that paves the ways for a definition of philosophy that has gained traction in recent years: philosophers "must no longer accept concepts as a gift, nor merely purify and polish them, but first *make* and *create* them" (409; 220). The task of philosophy, for Nietzsche, consists thus in creating concepts, as Gilles Deleuze will later echo, rendering this untimely Nietzschean insight popular for young generations of philosophers via the practice of mimetic agonism we have just outlined.

What we must add is that this agonistic principle applies to mimetic theorists as well—unsurprisingly so, given the avowed focus on mimesis. Such an agonistic stance is indeed the unavowed perspective Girard adopts toward Freud's theory of the unconscious; it shall also be the avowed perspective we adopt on both Girard's and Freud's theories of the unconscious. Attention to the patho-*logies* that emerge from agonistic confrontations allows us to see that despite the differentiating moves, or rather because of them, at the fundamental structural level the theoretical analogies between Girard and Freud in-*form* the general economy of his mimetic theory. And yet, traces of a romantic anxiety of influence responsible for Girard's disavowal of Freudian influences leads me to qualify this agon via the concept of romantic agonism.

Romantic Agonism

The similar strategies at play in the dynamic of theoretical agonism should not erase the different critical practices it leads to and the different spirits that animate them. Girard allows us to bring some of these differences into focus. Once we take hold of the paradoxical dynamic of the agon, it is clear that Girard's theory of the "true unconscious" is at least partially implicated in the unconscious principles he critiques in Freud as implicitly false. I call this strategy of differentiation "romantic agonism" for it is still haunted by romantic anxieties of influence that lead Girard, if not to repress, at least to repeatedly disavow the proximity to psychoanalysis, despite the obvious continuities with his mimetic theory.

For instance, given the focus on triangular relations based on desire, rivalry, and ambivalent psychic relations with models, it is striking but also revealing of romantic agonism, that Freud is not mentioned once in Girard's first book, *Deceit, Desire and the Novel* (1961).[32] This agonism is thus romantic (*romantique*) rather than novelistic (*romanesque*) in Girard's specific sense for it is based on a desire of originality Girard unmasks in his mimetic theory, yet still haunts, phantom-like, his thought in practice. I use the term "romantic" in this specific sense to account, in a mirroring genealogical move, for what I take to be Girard's romantic anxiety of influence. In addition to the rhetorical moves I already noted, if we zoom out from this modernist quarrel over the primacy of mimesis over desire, it is difficult not to see that Girard's emphasis on desire as the essence of subjectivity, his reliance on a triangular form that distinguishes between two distinct emotional ties (desire and identification), his emphasis on the "rivalry" and "double bind" that emerge from this familial triangulation that in turn inaugurates what he calls, mimicking Freud, a "royal road to violence [*voie royale de la violence*]" (*VS* 8) and opens the door to the "true 'unconscious'"—to list but the most manifest Freudian principles internal to Girard's mimetic theory—can be read as an agonistic extension, mirroring inversion, and romantic rearticulation of a triangular (Oedipal) unconscious initially promoted by the father of psychoanalysis.

"Be like me and don't be like me," the father figure implicitly suggests to the Oedipal child, says Freud in *The Ego and the Id* (1923).[33] And out of this "double bind," as Girard calls it, echoing Gregory Bateson, emerges a romantic agonism that may be too anxious to affirm its originality, yet has patho-*logical* value nonetheless in the sense that it generates a theory of unconscious desires, rivalries, and violence with a notable theoretical reach and explicative power. Among other things, this theory accounts for the logic of mimetic rivalries that generate affects like jealousy, ressentiment, vanity, and snobbery, in the modern period, pathological affects that find their original representations in Romantic novels, but cast a shadow on the contemporary world as well; it offers a daring anthropological hypothesis of the origins of culture, religion, and civilization based on a sacrificial murder that Girard hypothetically posits at the heart of the sacred and is subsequently reproduced in rituals across the world and, at one additional remove, in fictional re-presentations—not simply presenting again but rendering present—of sacrificial violence from antiquity to modernity; and, last but not least, it outlines an account of myth in terms of "an unconscious process [*processus non conscient*]" (*VS* 136) that, despite attempts to elude the concept of the unconscious, is not as inimical to Freud's metapsychology as Girard sometimes would like readers to believe. After all, at other times, Girard is ready to concede this proximity to the father of psychoanalysis, as he claims, for instance, that "Freud saw infinitely more in Oedipus than all Rationalist combined, beginning with Aristotle."[34] Notice, however, that a modern model (Freud) is agonistically set against the ancient model (Aristotle) in order to set up a distance from the figure who, as we shall see, set the very foundations for the so-called cathartic method. Notice also that this statement appears in an essay titled "Tiresias and the Critic" that places Oedipus as what Girard calls "the first western hero of Knowledge."[35] The unconscious, catharsis, Oedipus; Girard, Freud, Aristotle—are these alignments simple genealogical coincidences? Perhaps. Still, we shall have to reevaluate the paradigmatic choice of the case of Oedipus central to western poetics (Aristotle) in a modernist theory of the unconscious rooted in a cathartic method (Freud) that serves as a step for the development of the "true 'unconscious'" (Girard).

For the moment, one point should be clear: as Girard looks back to past ritual, violent, and tragic cultures that find in Oedipus the paradigmatic hero of "Western knowledge," he does so not only on the shoulders of Freud and other, more ancient precursors, but also in order to look ahead to the present unconscious pathologies of our modern, individualistic, capitalist cultures. That is, cultures in which rivalries, as Girard's late work suggests, threaten to "escalate to extremes" (*BE* 18) in an increasingly precarious world plagued by natural catastrophes, terroristic wars, volatile markets, and pandemic crises. Girard's mimetic theory, while rarely discussed in empirical studies on media violence, should be an integral part of it for it helps account for the contagious dynamic of violence more broadly, including nuclear escalations that, since the Russian invasion of Ukraine in 2022, cast a visible shadow on the present and future as well.

Now, if we step back genealogically to reflect critically on the genesis of theories of mimesis that cast light on the catharsis/affective hypotheses connecting violence to the unconscious, we notice that historical vicissitudes that may appear contingent play a crucial role in the development of transhistorical theories. For instance, highly volatile markets based on the logic of social differentiation provide a historical context in which Girard's theory of violence originated and eventually—not without struggles and marginalizations—culminated. Girard is, in fact, the first to admit that in the so-called sciences of man (a gender biased translation of *sciences humaines* or humanities, which now includes nonhumans as well), the "subject" of inquiry is fully implicated in the "object" of investigation along genealogical lines that introduce what he calls "a 'subjective element'"[36] in the theory.

Let me thus offer two contextual stories, or examples, taken from the alpha and omega of Girard's career, as a subjective intermezzo in our genealogical investigation of violence and the unconscious.

Two Mimetic Stories

Alpha Story: Johns Hopkins University, Baltimore, 1966 (dawn of Girard's theoretical career). A few years after the publication of his first book, *Deceit, Desire and the Novel* (1961), whose reliance on "structural models" to account for the "structural geometry"[37] of triangular desire was rather explicit, Girard played a key role in promoting a groundbreaking event that shook the foundations not only of his career but of the humanities in general, in the United States first, and, at one remove, in Europe and around the world as well. Working as a French expatriate in Baltimore, Maryland, Girard, along with Richard Macksey and Eugenio Donato, organized an academic conference, or symposium, whose explicit goal was to introduce an emerging theoretical method in the United States that was already informing the humanities and social sciences in Europe. This method was known as "structuralism."[38] Famously titled "The Languages of Criticism and the Sciences of Man," the symposium was held at Johns Hopkins University in 1966, where Girard was teaching at the time; it was hosted by "The Humanities Center," newly founded, and thus still unknown. Both Macksey and Donato were attentive to recent developments in France in philosophy and the social sciences more broadly. Their theoretical knowledge was supplemented by Girard's French connections in practice—which might have made a difference. The conference attracted major representatives of structuralism from the Parisian intellectual scene, including fields as diverse as semiology (Roland Barthes), classics (Jean-Pierre Vernant), philosophy (Jean Hyppolite), literary theory (Tzvetan Todorov), and psychoanalysis (Jacques Lacan), among other distinguished representatives of related fields. Still, despite the presence of these luminary figures, the real star turned out to be different than expected. A young, relatively marginal, and at the time still largely unknown philosopher of Algerian origins was belatedly added to the program. He ended up stealing the show. His name, you will have guessed, was Jacques Derrida.

Mainly due to the controversy Derrida's paper generated during the symposium, later redubbed "The Structuralist Controversy," the conference turned out to be an immense success. Depicted as the "French Invasion of America,"[39] Girard drew again on an Oedipal image of Freudian inspiration to convey his mimetic/agonistic stance toward it: if Freud in 1919 compared his psychoanalytical conquest of America to the plague, Girard equally depicted the 1966 conference as "the plague [*la peste*]," as he said: "When Freud came to the USA, he said, as he approached New York: 'I'm bringing the plague to them'; but he was wrong. Americans digested and American-ized psychoanalysis easily and quickly. But in 1966 we really brought the plague with Lacan and deconstructionism, at least to the universities!"[40] Belatedly we can see that the diagnostic might not be as clear-cut. In fact, the deconstructive "virus" had stopped reproducing within the U.S. academic host by the end of the twentieth century and was quickly assimilated into antithetical academic turns.

However, a glance at popular culture continues to reveal the centrality of Oedipal phantasies—from *Psycho* to *Back to the Future*, *Blue Velvet* to *Freud's Last Session*, among many other films—indicating that the psychoanalytical "plague" continues to be disseminated within U.S. culture, shaping, by exten-sion, the world imagination at large—a point I shall return to. Either way, the symposium reached, indeed, the status of a mythic, perhaps founding "event," whose influence spread contagiously, from the Humanities Center to the Comparative Literature Departments of some of the most influential North American campuses (Yale, Stanford, Berkeley, to name a few); it infil-trated the humanities in the United States more generally; and eventually, with a spatial/temporal *différance*, it boomeranged back to Europe as well.

And yet the symposium did not promote structuralism, as initially planned. Quite the contrary; it cast such a shadow on the structuralist method that it never fully reached the North American shores. Derrida, in fact, launched a seminal critique of Lévi-Strauss's structural anthropology that set the stage for a new critical method of reading philosophical and liter-ary texts against the grain (later called "deconstruction"), which went viral in the United States and across the world during the so-called linguistic turn.

Hence, this event propelled new generations of North American scholars not necessarily familiar with structuralism, let alone the long tradition in continental philosophy and the social sciences it draws from, into the age of what was grouped under the rubric of "poststructuralism." In the field of literary studies (Girard's home field), the conference inaugurated a period of intense involvement with literary theory, also known as "French theory" or, more simply, "theory." Despite its heterogeneous nature, theory in the decades following the symposium still tended to share structuralist concerns with the linguistic sign, while at the same time stressing the play of signifiers rather than signifieds (let alone referents), linguistic texts more than material contexts, writerly differences over mimetic sameness—all signatures of the so-called linguistic turn that during the 1970s and 1980s changed not only the field in theory but also academic markets in practice.[41]

Girard's position with respect to this turn was paradoxical. And this paradox arguably set in motion a romantic agonism that will orient his subsequent theoretical developments. As the senior scholar of the trio and a Frenchman at that, Girard not only contributed to the organization of the conference; he was, in many ways, at the center of this seismic event that shook the foundations of literary and cultural theory, establishing linguistic differences at the forefront of a primarily French theoretical scene. And yet Girard also soon realized that this scene was not *his* scene, after all. Thus, he remained somewhat at the margins of the symposium, his name ultimately not appearing on the cover of the conference's proceedings, titled *The Structuralist Controversy: The Languages of Criticism and the Sciences of Man* (1970). Girard was, in fact, out of sync with the main linguistic orientation of deconstruction and the "linguistic turn" more generally. In fact, he never fully let go of structuralism and of the synchronic claims about desire, violence, and sacrifice at play not only in linguistic texts and signs but also in psychic, social, and anthropological referents. Girard went as far as developing a diachronic theory of sameness rooted in a referential crisis that erases differences. He called it "crisis of difference" or "mimetic crisis," perhaps to indicate that mimesis can put not only individual differences but also theories of difference in crisis. In any case, his "economy of violence" (*VS* 7) will remain set in a silent, often neglected but nonetheless deeply engaged agonistic confrontation with a theory of linguistic difference he opposes via the paradoxical moves characteristic of romantic agonism.[42] While not explicitly manifest, this mimetic *différend* oriented Girard's subsequent career, which mostly unfolded in the shadow of poststructuralism, before receiving the due recognition of prestigious institutions, both in the United States (Stanford University) and France (the Académie Française).

This trajectory leads us to our second, more anecdotal, but intimately related, perhaps even mirroring, contextual story. This time it is not set at the alpha but at the omega of Girard's academic trajectory.

Omega Story: San Francisco, 2007 (coronation of Girard's U.S. career). Nearly half a century after the Structuralist Controversy, and many books later, I had the privilege of meeting Girard at a major international conference in San Francisco. The linguistic turn was already well in its twilight by then, and after a series of important books that had remained at the margins of theory, Girard was finally granted the "Award for Lifetime Scholarly Achievement," which gave him the academic recognition he deserved. Lost in the labyrinth of panels at what was one of my first international conferences, and one of Girard's last, I managed to miss the evening ceremony. Still, I spotted Girard's name in a panel devoted to his work the following day, which I made a point to highlight and attend. With the benefit of hindsight, it provided the most valuable insight of that conference.

Girard's talk led him to look back, genealogically, to one of his early literary sources of inspiration: namely, Stendhal's *The Red and the Black*, which had provided a key starting point for his theory of mimetic desire at the dawn of his career. After he finished his talk, I walked up to the front desk, mimicking the confident attitude of more senior scholars I had noted while lost in corridors. This time, I was driven by a goal, or telos: I wanted to ask Girard a question I did not get to ask during the Q&A and that had been on my mind for quite some time. After thanking him for both his talk and the pioneering work in mimetic theory and establishing a few genealogical connections via (French) theorists we both knew personally, I took advantage of a basic anthropological phenomenon familiar to all foreigners abroad: that a shared language and background quickens connections and justifies going quickly to the heart of the matter. And so I asked Girard, off the bat: "Vous avez parlé de Stendhal, mais si vous devriez recommencer maintenant . . . ?" Translated, it would go along these lines: "You spoke of Stendhal, but would you start mimetic theory all over again now, what would be your main focus of analysis?" This rather direct personal question caught his attention. So, I pressed on: "*Je veux dire* . . . which contemporary medium, or milieu, do you think best reveals the logic of mimetic desire and rivalry these days?"

Let me back up. As for Girard, the starting point of my interest in mimesis had been psychological; I was interested in the power of literary, but also cinematic and philosophical texts to help us reflect critically on the present. Hence, I had opted for a PhD in comparative literature with a double focus on modernism and philosophy, read via the transdisciplinary lens of mimesis. Writers like Nietzsche, but also Joseph Conrad, D. H. Lawrence, and Georges Bataille, read in the context of anthropology, crowd psychology, and different schools of dynamic psychology were providing me with distinctly modernist mimetic insights that went beyond Romanticism. I was genuinely impressed by how accurate and far-reaching modernist antennae continued to be, revealing phantoms that cast a shadow on the present as well.

And yet, at the same time, my sense was that the genre of the novel, and traditional print literature more generally, no matter how illuminating, influential, and still widely taught—one of my paradigmatic case studies was Conrad's *Heart of Darkness*—had long ceased to serve as a commonly shared societal medium that could reveal new manifestations of mimesis in the twenty-first century. Working in a Comparative Literature Department, soon to be renamed Department of Comparative Literature, Cinema and Media (now, significantly, only Cinema and Media Studies), emerging new media—cinema and television, but also TV series, computer games, and the first manifestations of social media on the World Wide Web—were already providing alternative starting points for theoretical reflections on the vicissitudes of homo mimeticus in the twenty-first century.

So, the question had been in my mind for a while. Girard's facial expression confirmed that this intuition might not have been too off the mark. He said, "It's a good question." Then he paused for a moment, looked around suspiciously, lowered his tone of voice to indicate, this is *entre nous*, and then, with a sense of French complicity and an anti-institutional spirit we also shared, he whispered with a characteristic cunning smile—half jokingly, but also half seriously—"MLA!"

Academics in literary studies will know what Girard was referring to. Perhaps they will even laugh at the joke and recognize its underlying truth. For those living outside of academia, let me clarify. MLA is the acronym for the Modern Language Association, the most important association for literary studies in the United States and, arguably, the whole world. Among other things, it organizes an annual conference that serves as an obligatory rite of passage for all international literary critics and theorists. It assembles thousands of academics over a period of three days, traditionally between Christmas and New Year, now rescheduled to early January. MLA had, indeed, organized the very conference in San Francisco that granted Girard the MLA Lifetime Award for Scholarly Achievements I referred to. Given this context, the ironies of his reply are, of course, multiple. For our purpose let us say they are at least double, since the distinguishing feature of the MLA is twofold.

First, this conference serves as the most important annual gathering in literary studies in which thousands of scholars, representative of different and often antagonistic approaches to literature, theory, and now new media, come together and are made to peacefully coexist, ignore, or, most often, challenge their respective positions during three intense and exhausting days that are considered sacred outside the sterile walls of the homogeneous Conventions Centers that host the conference, making every one MLA experience hardly distinguishable from another. If "regular" people are still enjoying the Christmas holiday, for the scholars working inside, the MLA has the characteristic of a ritual, with all the intellectual effervescence such modern rituals entail. Unsurprisingly, then, in an echo of the theoretical controversies I alluded to above, these confrontations never fail to generate intellectual rivalries triggered by a human, all too human, desire for visibility, connections, publications, all of which are driven by an all too mimetic desire for recognition and prestige that culminates in the kind of award Girard obtained. Given that all desires tend to reach for similar objects in a small, selective, and fiercely competitive context, MLA provides indeed the ideal milieu to study the emergence of mimetic desire, jealousy, and rivalry constitutive of the academic world. Girard's was being ironic, but like all good ironists, he was making a serious point nonetheless.

The second irony is even more revealing. MLA, in fact, organizes at the same time as the conference, the main annual job market for literary scholars who desire to pursue a profession in a field driven by high competition for increasingly scarce, precarious, underpaid, but symbolically coveted jobs. In a strange redoubling, the job interviews take place in hotel rooms located right above the conference venue. An intimate space usually used for private pleasure during a holyday (often a bed) is thus turned into a space for a public employment or, more often, unemployment. Finalists are thus made to compete twice: for presentations geared toward publication as well as for academic positions. Few desired jobs, hundreds of applicants. Again, one does not need to be a mimetic theorist to predict that rivalries will necessarily ensue.

Now since both the job market and the conference are part of the same event, MLA becomes a melting pot in which PhD students timidly presenting their papers (I belonged to that category), job candidates being interviewed, professors playing the role of employers, critics and theorists of all stripes and persuasion presenting their work, not to speak of exemplary theorists who are awarded prestigious prizes (Girard belonged to that category), find themselves caught in a vortex (*tourbillon*) that should generate critical discourses (logoi) that are different in theory yet often generate a pathos internal to scholarly pathologies that induces a crisis of difference in practice. Participants to this annual event qua rite of passage are driven by a desire for differentiation that leads them to nervously present ten- to twenty-minute papers, frantically attend talks, fake interest in others while highlighting individual originality, on one side; yet, on the other side, also find their individual difference in crisis as they are channeled through crowded corridors, squeezed in packed elevators, invited to sit on beds in hotel rooms, and encouraged to ritualistically clap hands in sync to celebrate papers that either support or challenge their position, not to speak of winners of prizes they were perhaps themselves striving to obtain. In such a milieu, given the structures that underlie it, desire is indeed already mimetic and always threatens to lead to rivalry, jealousy, envy, and ressentiment, among other romantic passions that, to this day, continue to plague the academia—a cradle for bad Eris. No wonder Girard had to whisper.

Let us now step back from the personal mimetic pathos of these scenes and ask, from a genealogical distance. What lessons can we draw from these two mirroring contextual stories taken from the alpha and omega of Girard's career to cast light on the joint problematic of violence and the unconscious that concerns us? The subjective nature of the sketches does not diminish their relevance to mimetic theory; just as mimetic theory is not irrelevant to account for these stories' structure or plot. The mirroring effects are again double. On the one hand, mimetic theory is particularly apt to account for an intellectual context that is characterized by the presence of eminent models (academic stars) who, in an extremely competitive field (academia), trigger a desire for an eminently contested object (a job), and the honor or recognition it might lead to (an award), inevitably leading to rivalries for pure intellectual prestige that manifest themselves at symposia like the Structuralist Controversy or at conferences like MLA, precisely along the romantic (individualistic) and rivalrous lines Girard describes. In this sense, his theory sets up an unflattering but revealing mirror to the academic context in which this theory originated in the first place. In our language a mimetic patho-*logy* offers a diagnostic on the unconscious pathos internal to academic pathologies.

But the mirroring reflection cuts both ways and is not deprived of inversions of perspectives. In fact, we could also say that the academic context is not simply external to the theory; it also offers a possibility for a genealogical reflection on what Nietzsche would call the "conditions of emergence" of Girard's mimetic theory. In this second sense, typically academic mimetic pathologies might reveal formative principles that contributed to the emergence of the patho-*logy* qua mimetic theory itself. This suspicion is internal to the genealogical method as Nietzsche understands it. In fact, what he famously says of philosophy in general is worth bearing in mind in a genealogy of theories of violence and the unconscious in particular. For Nietzsche, in fact, "every great philosophy so far" has been nothing less and nothing more than "a confession on the part of its author and a kind of involuntary and unconscious memoir [*unvermerkter mémoir*]."[43] There are no reasons to believe this unconscious principle should not apply to a self-reflective field like mimetic theory, especially since this field is avowedly autobiographical in origins and rooted in philosophies of the unconscious that rest precisely on the interpretation of confessional memoirs. As Benoît Chantre recognizes, "all his [Girard's] work was founded on a certain idea of autobiography, of which Augustine's *Confessions* as well as Dante's *Divine Comedy* served for him as models."[44] In addition to dead classical models, I suggest that living contemporary models might also have played a less visible but not less fundamental role in the development of mimetic theory. In fact, this idea of autobiography is also a confessional practice. There is thus a silent autobiographical thread running through the labyrinth of the "true" unconscious, which genealogical lenses allow us to evaluate. From this confessional perspective, in fact, general theories of the unconscious that aspire to be universal, transhistorical, and fundamentally true might also mirror personal, restricted, and context-dependent unconscious principles that apply first and foremost to the author or, in the wake of the death of the author, to the social structures in which this author develops a theory. A universal theory of the unconscious, in other words, may attempt to reveal the cathartic properties of violent subjects under investigation (objective genitive) that go from sacrificial rituals to aesthetic representations in theory; and yet it may also cast an opaque, oblique, but nonetheless mirroring self-reflective light on the specific unconscious of the investigative subject (subjective genitive) that goes from mimetic desire to violent intellectual rivalry in specialized academic practices.

In light of the two stories taken from the alpha and omega of Girard's career, a genealogical suspicion leads to the following question: could it be that Girard's mimetic theory reflects so well the imitative desires, unconscious rivalries, and intellectual jealousies, resentments, and latent aggressions that plague the academia precisely because this theory was from the very beginning in-*formed* (given form) by those same academic desires, rivalries, and romantic agonistic confrontations with exemplary models? Perhaps those very models that were already at play at the alpha of Girard's career during the Structuralist Controversy conference might have led to a romantic desire for an agonistic differentiation—by developing a theory of sameness predicated on a crisis of difference, for instance. According to this second mirroring hypothesis, mimetic theory brilliantly accounts for academic desires, jealousies, and rivalries that can lead to romantic agonism within the academia but also to contagious violence outside of it. It also mirrors a rather specific, contextual, and thus restricted (rather than universal) dynamic that is typical of academic structures in particular out of which the theory was born. Girard's mimetic theory, in other words, not only sets up a mirror to the rivalrous logic of desire and violence; it also sets up a confessional mirror to its specific intellectual context whose competitive structure promotes mimetic desire in the first place, providing the affective, subjective, but also structural foundations for Girard's theory.[45]

Let us be clear. Such an inversion of perspective is not simply critical or deconstructive; it has a constructive genealogical power as well. True, the specific focus of Girard's account of appropriative desires, ambivalent rivalries with doubles, potentially violent exclusions or marginalizations, might have led to a romantic desire for originality that erases exemplary influences structuring his theory. The romantic agonism is thus at least partially explained by the context out of which the mimetic theory emerged rather than the other way round. Yet this genealogical observation does not necessarily invalidate the theory. Quite the contrary, due to its extreme competitive nature, academic contexts like the MLA—as Girard himself suggested—serve as microcosms that put up a magnifying mirror to the mimetic and unconscious logic present at the macrosocial level. It is particularly relevant for similar contemporary structural contexts within increasingly competitive and precarious neoliberal societies, which, as Girard recognized, can lead to an "escalation to extremes" in an increasingly precarious world driven by scarcity, overpopulation, territorial wars, and appropriative greed.[46] The seeds for violent escalations are indeed internal to a number of competitive environments: from the education system (intellectual rivalries) to the profession (career rivalries), from the economy (fragile markets) to mimetic politics (elections), from the threat of nuclear war (escalation) to mass migrations driven by rapid climate change and (new) fascist exclusions (scapegoating), from online vitriol (bullying, shaming) to the proliferation of representations of violence via (new) media that, at several removes from "reality," deform information, spread conspiracy theories, and represent violent spectacles for an audience to watch and gamers to play.

And yet the point of this contextualization is also to avoid unilateral theoretical diagnostics. While certainly dominant and endemic to twentieth and twenty-first centuries' neoliberal societies, these all too human appropriative desires are far from exhausting the heterogeneous spectrum of imitative behavior. The latter includes desire and violence, but equally informs positive forms of mimesis like learning, sympathy, cooperation, and social cohesion. If the focus of Girard's theory has consistently been on the pathologies of mimetic violence, it might be at least in part because mimetic theory is the unconscious product of what Nietzsche would call the author's "personal confessions." That is, confessions that are personal but also reflect a wider academic context that privileges unconscious forms of violence that may not be physical and thus can be defined in terms of aggression, yet effectively generate mimetic desires, rivalries, and scapegoating mechanisms nonetheless. The powers of mimesis, as we shall continue to confirm, are plural: they tend to go beyond good and evil evaluations; they are not always framed within triangular, Oedipal structures and their inversions thereof; they transgress ontological distinctions that simply oppose fiction and reality, but also images and bodies, self and others, conscious action and unconscious reaction; and they tend to proliferate in heterogeneous ways that do not easily allow for grand universal and transhistorical explanations, but call for more situated, contextual, genealogical diagnostics attentive to the historicity of theories of violence and the unconscious as well as to their attunement to the intrinsic characteristics of specific genres and (new) media. Now, we have seen that psychoanalysis provides a triangular structure that, despite the romantic agonism, or rather because of it, continues to give form to Girard's account of unconscious pathos split in two emotional ties (desire and identification). We have equally seen that an agonistic academic context provided the right combination of both affective and critical insights, pathos and logos, out of which the mimetic patho(-)logies on violence and the unconscious emerge. After this genealogical detour via the logical and affective sources of Girard's theory of desire and violence that emerged from two contextual stories in the background, we have the necessary distance to return to evaluate the mirroring relation between violence and the unconscious in the foreground.

Restaging the Unconscious

That mimetic desire can lead to rivalries, irrational jealousies, and violent affects is well known, and its main symptoms are visible for all who wish to see them well beyond the walls of academic conferences or psychoanalytical couches. From the family to the nursery, the schoolyard to the office, personal quarrels to academic quarrels, films to video games, reality shows to presidential debates to territorial invasions and beyond, the occasions to be unconsciously caught up in structures of rivalry and violence generated by the appropriative nature of desire in a materialist, consumer-oriented, and increasingly digitized culture driven by greed, radical individualism, and pathological narcissism are, indeed, manifold. Such tendencies are now exponentially amplified by new social media whose pathological effects are multiple and are directly linked to our Janus-faced topic. On the side of violence, the anonymous and impersonal distance of social media like Twitter and Facebook allows for a type of abuse, psychic violence (mobbing, bullying, shaming), and dissemination of pathos that would have been unthinkable a few decades ago and is currently affecting new media users, especially (but not only) younger generations.[47] On the side of the unconscious, these new media rely on algorithms that increase human mimetic tendencies dramatically, for they exploit big data to tap into the sedimented history of users' desires that sidestep the romantic logic of the singular model, for users' data history becomes the model to induce new mimetic desires in subjects that are already posthuman.[48] Thus, algorithms reload the powers of mimesis by increasing exponentially not only the logic of appropriative desire but also the dissemination of models, values, ideologies, and beliefs (true and, more often, false), all of which induce quasi-hypnotic effects for they reinforce preexisting beliefs. Such a hypermimetic circulation of (mis)information taps into the very soul of homo mimeticus. In the process, it inflects the problematic of violence via unconscious mechanisms that require new investigations of the powers of mimesis. If we may not always be inclined to observe such imitative tendencies in ourselves, now that Girard diagnosed the unconscious logic of mimetic desire and these insights are put to use via new media, we can easily spot the violent rivalries they generate in others.

And yet the theoretical origins of this connection between mimesis and desire are less visible and require genealogical lenses that look deeper into the history of philosophy to be brought to the fore. Worthy of mention is Baruch Spinoza's diagnostic of "sad affects" in *Ethics* (1677). Spinoza is an untimely philosopher who is currently informing returns of attention to the contagious power of bodily affects constitutive of the affective turn, which are directly relevant for the re-turn of attention to mimesis as well. For instance, in Book 3 of *Ethics*, titled "On the Origin and Nature of the Emotions," Spinoza offers the following diagnostic that should not go unnoticed by theorists of imitation: "From the mere fact of our conceiving that another person takes delight in a thing we shall ourselves love that thing and desire to take delight therein"; and rooting this mimetic tendency in childhood, but with adults in mind, he adds: "they desire forthwith to imitate whatever they see others doing, and to possess themselves whatever they conceive as delighting others."[49] Left unidentified, it would be difficult, even for an experienced reader of mimetic theory, not to confuse Spinoza for Girard here. Such a confusion is accentuated by Girard's claim that the "great novelists" he discusses in *Deceit, Desire and the Novel* (1961) have originally (romantically?) unveiled the appropriative nature of mimetic desire. Stable and unitary origins are indeed precisely what a genealogical method, whose ambition is to unearth the different discourses responsible for the emergence of mimetic theory, questions. Time and again, what are presented as original insights into the laws of imitation often turn out to be voluntary or, as it is probably the case here, involuntary—that is, not conscious, and in this sense *un*-conscious—reformulations of previous theories, mimetic theories that now deserve to be inscribed in our genealogy of precursors of homo mimeticus in order to continue building on them. Again, acknowledging a precursor does not mean that Girard's theory of mimetic desire is any less true. Quite the contrary; it simply confirms the Girardian insight that the lie (*mensonge*) of originality should not be the main concern of a theory devoted to the truth (*verité*) of mimesis.

What applies to desire equally applies to the unconscious that triggers desires and rivalries in the first place. The so-called true unconscious is based on a less visible, more ancient, yet, as we shall confirm, still modern and contemporary theoretical assumption on the therapeutic value of violence, including media violence. Girard, in fact, not only explains the origins of the problem of violence via the triangular structure of mimetic and unconscious desire; he also offers a possible theoretical solution to violence by emphasizing its cathartic and equally unconscious social function. We are thus getting closer to the palpitating heart of our double genealogy of violence and the unconscious. To echo the cinematic study with which we started, for Girard, the problem of contagious violence that since the origins of socialization plagued the city, finds a therapeutic solution in a type of sacrificial violence that keeps the city going.

How does this cure for violence by violence work, if it does work? Girard supplements a catharsis hypothesis that runs deep in western culture, for it goes from tragic plays in classical antiquity to popular films in contemporary media culture. His thesis on catharsis is thus of ancient inspiration. While it is rarely, if ever, discussed in any detail in the growing literature on Girard, it plays a key role in his mimetic theory. His catharsis hypothesis can be summarized as follows: rather than confining the problematic of violence to the interiority of an individual ego caught up in artificial and quite profane fictions, which, for instance, point to future-oriented vices characteristic of digital entertainment, Girard inverts perspectives. Thus, he roots violence

back in the exteriority of collective rituals that serve as a referential, anthropological, and quite sacred function in archaic societies, stretching to inform
classical, modern, and contemporary civilizations. And he does so in order to
provide nothing less than a hypothesis on the origins of culture tout court.
Catharsis is thus the invisible hinge on which Girard's theory of violence
turns.

Starting in *Violence and the Sacred* (1972), Girard goes beyond the
analysis of the ego that had preoccupied him in his first book to develop
an anthropological theory whereby the group violence generated by the
unconscious dynamic of mimetic desire is both channeled and discharged
against an innocent victim, or "scapegoat" (*pharmakos*). For Girard, the
sacrificial killing of the scapegoat is predicated on a collective "misrecog-
nition" (*méconnaissance*) of the injustice, fundamental arbitrariness, and
self-reflective unconscious logic this kind of sacrificial violence entails. Purgation, in this sense, rests on an archaic *méconnáisssance* of the innocence of
the scapegoat that channels the collective violence. The sacrificial victim, in
fact, tends to be arbitrarily chosen in the sense that it is often an innocent,
marginal, and thus sacrificial figure, whose "bare life" is characteristic of what
Giorgio Agamben calls *homo sacer*.[50] And yet this *méconnaissance* also has
a therapeutic effect on the frenzied community caught up in the vortex of
unconscious and reciprocal violence.

Why is the French genealogically de rigueur here? Because the concept
is genealogically revealing. Girard, in fact, relies on the (Lacanian) concept
of *méconnaissance* central to the pre-Oedipal child's identification with his
imago in the "mirror stage." Psychonalytically oriented readers will recall that
Lacan had already spoken of "the *méconnaissances* that constitute the ego, the
illusion of autonomy to which it entrusts itself";[51] and he had done so by calling attention to the "mediatization through the desire of the other," which is
also "a cultural mediation as exemplified, in the case of sexual objects, by the
Oedipus complex."[52] To be sure, Girard transfers the dynamic of misrecogni-
tion from the psychology of the ego to group psychology, from an imaginary
imago to a real scapegoat, yet the illusions, misrecognitions, and fundamental
Oedipal structures are rather familiar. What is perhaps different in the effort
to tilt the (Freudian/Lacanian) conception of a private unconscious toward
the collective, sacrificial, and cathartic social sphere is that the latter also rests

on an intersubjective predilection for what Girard often calls "interindividuality" that is linked to "hypnosis" and "suggestion."[53] That is, a pre-Freudian tradition of the unconscious that Freud and Lacan disavowed yet finds a common genealogy in what I call the mimetic unconscious. In fact, mimesis—Girard and I at times provisionally agree—is an inter-individual suggestive or hypnotic process that transgresses the boundaries of the ego and finds in figures like Nietzsche major precursors. Such mirroring processes will have to wait for recent discoveries in the neurosciences in order to be confirmed.

And yet, while Girard, at times, prefers the language of *méconnaissance* over the one of the "unconscious" (see *EC* 86), the structural grammar of this language remains in our view too overdetermined by a psychoanalytical interpretation of an Oedipal, triangular, and presumably cathartic fable. Psychoanalysis, as we shall see in the next chapter, is in fact born out of a cathartic method. It is thus no genealogical accident that as violence is channeled in a single direction and discharged against the sacrificial victim, it generates what Girard repeatedly calls "catharsis." As Girard puts it: "In societies where sacrifice is still a living institution it displays [a] cathartic function" (*VS* 99). He adds: "if the sacrificial catharsis actually succeeds in preventing the unlimited propagation of violence, a sort of *infection* is in fact being checked" (30). And he further specifies: "there is every reason to believe that the minor catharsis of the sacrificial act is derived from that major catharsis circumscribed by collective murder" (102). Minor or major, catharsis, while rarely discussed in any detail in the major commentaries on Girard,[54] plays a central role in the very foundational anthropological dynamic on which his theory of violence and the sacred rest—beginning, middle, and end.

Let us take a closer look at the end, where the influences on Girard's catharsis hypothesis begin to surface, as a huge genealogical iceberg beneath the point of mimetic theory. Girard concludes *Violence and the Sacred* by summing up his view of catharsis in a passage that is worth quoting in full. In fact, it reveals multiple layers of theoretical mediation that have so far remain hidden due to the practice of romantic agonism we are now familiar with, and yet genealogical lenses can help us bring the iceberg of the catharsis hypothesis to the surface. Here is how Girard sums up his hypothesis:

The word *katharsis* refers primarily to the mysterious benefits that accrue
to the community [*cité*] upon the death of a human *katharma* or *pharmakos*. The process [*opération*] is generally seen as a religious purification
and takes the form of cleansing [*drainage*] or draining away [*évacuation*]
impurities. . . . In addition to its religious sense and its particular meaning
in the context of shamanism, the word *katharsis* has a specific use in the
medical language. A cathartic medicine is a powerful drug that induces the
evacuation of humors or other substances judged to be noxious. The illness
and its cure are often seen as one; or at least, the medicine is considered
capable of aggravating the symptoms, bringing about a salutary crisis that
will lead to recovery. In other words, the crisis is provoked by a supplementary dosage of the affliction [*supplément de mal*] resulting in the expulsion
of the pathogenetic agents along with itself. The operation is the same as
that of the human *katharma*, although in medicine the act of purgation
[*principe de la purge*] is not mythic but real.

The mutations of meaning from the human meaning of *katharma* to
the medical katharsis are paralleled by those of the human pharmakos to
the medical *pharmakon*, which signifies at once "poison" and "remedy."
(*VS* 287–88)

The vortex of unconscious violence, for Girard, is thus not only pathological.
If it is collectively channeled against a "scapegoat" (or *pharmakos*), it can also
turn into a "remedy" (or *pharmakon*), a *pharmakos/pharmakon* that serves as
a "supplement" (*supplément*) and purges, via a religious but above all medical
interpretation of catharsis understood as a "draining" or "evacuation," the community of a mimetic violence that would otherwise spread contagiously among
the crowd. The thesis is daring but it is not fully original. As the references
to the Greek (*katharsis*), the medical language (*drainage, évacuation*), and
the supplementary nature of the scapegoat as poison and cure (*pharmakon*),
Girard's catharsis hypothesis is deeply informed by multiple layers of genealogical mediation that go from antiquity to modernity, modernism to (post)
structuralism, stretching to inform Girard's exemplary contemporaries as well.

The key point, for the moment, is that ritualized violence, for Girard,
not only keeps the city going; it gets the city started. Or, better, it keeps the
city going because it reenacts a founding murder that got the city, communal
living, and, by extension, civilization started in the first place. Traces of this

founding murder, according to Girard, are still visible in aesthetic spectacles, most notably in Greek tragedies, which, as we shall see, play a key role in the genesis of the catharsis hypothesis. For Girard, in fact, humans subsequently represent (present again) this founding murder in tragic spectacles that the moderns tend to consider aesthetic classics to be contemplated from a distance yet, for Girard, are still in touch with the ritual pathos of sacrificial violence and originally occupy a cathartic social function within the ancient city, or polis. This, for Girard, is how religion, law, and aesthetics are actually born: namely, out of a ritual repetition or reproduction of the original sacrificial crisis, or collective murder, which brings about cathartic effects with unifying social functions. Catharsis of contagious violence by mimetic violence: this is, in a nutshell, what Girard's diagnostic of the *pharmakos* qua *pharmakon* suggests.

Girard is talking about the cathartic effects of sacrificial rituals that reproduce the original founding murder he hypothetically posits as a real event at the origins of hominization, in *illo tempore*. Yet, since he sees a mirroring continuity between sacrificial acts in the real world and tragic spectacles in fictional representations—or, rather, infers, via a hermeneutical effort, the (physical) violence of the sacred from the (aesthetic) violence of tragedy—his catharsis hypothesis, in a classical hermeneutical circle, also informs his specific interpretation of the cathartic effects of Greek tragedies, and by extension of aesthetic representations of violence more generally. Influential classicists like Jean-Pierre Vernant who arguably inspired Girard's reading of Greek tragedies in the first place have called attention to this circle and the philological paradox it entails. As Vernant and Pierre Vidal-Naquet put it, addressing what they call Girard's theory of "redemption and salvation": "If tragedy was a direct expression of the 'sacrificial crisis,' how is it that it is historically confined not simply to the Greek city but specifically to fifth-century Athens?"[55] They explain this paradox via the following philological observation: "As René Girard has made quite plain, it is Greek tragedy that provided him with the model of what he calls the 'sacrificial crisis.' Yet in the fifth-century Greek city, tragic sacrifice was by no means a theoretically acceptable social practice. Such representations were, on the contrary, condemned."[56] If we extend this philological critique to the catharsis hypothesis, we wonder: what comes first? The cathartic reality of Greek tragedy that informs the hypothesis, or the catharsis hypothesis that informs the medical interpretation of catharsis in Greek tragedies and, by extension, violence against a scapegoat tout court? Lest we trust authorial intentions the dynamic of romantic agonism taught us to be suspicious of, there is no easy way out from this hermeneutical circle—precisely because it is a circle.

What we can confidently say is that the genealogical detour via Girard's account of the cathartic effects of ritual violence brings us back to the question of the effects of aesthetic violence whereby we started. In the process, it allows us to see what has not been sufficiently stressed so far: namely that Girard is one of the most recent advocates of a medical interpretation of the catharsis hypothesis. This hypothesis has a long and complicated genealogy that entangles medical, ritual, religious, and psychological traditions we shall return to, which, as movies like *Vice* indicate, and continues to inform the contemporary imagination on the effects of (new) media violence, albeit at many removes from Greek tragedy. As Girard puts it, speaking of the "original" medium out of which the catharsis hypothesis is born: "If tragedy was to function as a sort of ritual, something similar to a sacrificial killing had to be concealed in the dramatic and literary use of *katharsis*" (*VS* 291). For Girard, then, catharsis operates on at least three different but related levels: First, it entails a discharge, "purification" or, as he prefers to say—reminding us that "*katharsis* has a specific use in medical language"—an "evacuation of humors [*évaquation d'humeurs*]" or "purgation" (287, 288). Second, this "purgation principle [*principe de la* purge]" (287; trans. modified) is also at play in sacrificial rituals that entail a purgation or purification of intoxicating, Dionysian affects bordering on madness. Third, this mysterious purification qua purgation continues to be "concealed", at one remove, in Greek tragedies in need of original interpretations. For Girard, in fact, tragedy re-presents (presents again, for the second time) in tragic fictions scenes of sacrificial violence from an aesthetic distance for the audience to see, feel, and perhaps cathartically enjoy.

This is the moment to note that, among contemporary thinkers, Girard is not alone in grounding the origins of tragedy in sacrificial rituals. The French transdisciplinary theorist Georges Bataille, for instance, also recognized that Greek tragedy, and western aesthetics more generally, turns the sacred experience of sacrifice into a "spectacle" that allows spectators to stare at the horror of death via the safe screen of "representation"—a tragic experience that generates a shared pathos at a distance that does not entail any risks for spectators, and that Bataille provocatively qualifies as "a comedy."[57] Before Bataille, Nietzsche had already given an account of the birth of tragedy out of an Apollonian representation of a type of ritual/ontological violence that originates in a horrifying experience of "dismemberment;" as we shall see in more detail in volume 2, it finds its ritual source in the body of Dionysus torn to pieces, or "*sparagmos*."[58] Either way, a modernist tradition in mimetic theory tends to agree that once represented on theatrical scenes via an aesthetic/Apollonian distance, such violent, contagious, and intoxicating sacrificial spectacles serve as classical precursors of modern, perhaps cathartic, and certainly entertaining fictions that, to these days, have not lost their visceral appeal as they are reloaded via new media and games. Far removed from the sacredness of ritual sacrificial practices, our mediatized culture, in fact, continues to re-present, at yet an additional remove, Dionysian spectacles that may not point to a referential violence, yet, once reloaded in the digital age, are likely to produce effects on audiences and users alike, be they therapeutic or pathological. But let us not get ahead of ourselves.

Instead, let us continue to look further back, to ancient thinkers who set the philosophical foundations for the catharsis hypothesis, which theorists of violence like Girard urge us to reconsider from a contemporary perspective. In fact, he reveals important and so far largely unexplored genealogical traces of the most influential proponent of a catharsis hypothesis that gives birth to poetics, traverses key modern representatives of western aesthetics, and, via contemporary media, continues to reach into the present. Toward the end of *Violence and the Sacred*, Girard completes his picture on the meanings of catharsis. Somewhat surprisingly, it is only at the end of this book that Girard acknowledges the precursor that had been informing his catharsis hypothesis from the beginning, as he writes:

> If we wish to complete our picture of the various meanings of katharsis we must return, once more, to Greek tragedy. As yet I have made no specific reference to Aristotle's use of the term in his *Poetics*. It scarcely seems necessary to do so at this point, for I have already established that tragedy springs from mythic and ritual forms. As for the function of tragedy, Aristotle has already defined it for us. In describing the tragic effect in terms of katharsis

he asserts that tragedy can and should assume at least some of the functions
assigned to ritual in a world where ritual has almost disappeared. (*VS* 290)

So far, Aristotle was not mentioned in Girard's account of catharsis. And
at this stage, it seems no longer necessary to do so for it is already clear that
tragedy was born out of mythic and ritual forms. Romantic agonism not-
withstanding, violent sacrificial rituals may have almost disappeared from
social life, yet an ancient poetics carries over their cathartic effects into fictional tragedies, and perhaps theories as well, from antiquity to the present.
Aristotle's account of catharsis in *Poetics* is thus the missing piece necessary
to "complete the picture [*tableau*]" on the relation between violence and
the unconscious Girard begins to sketch in *Violence and the Sacred*. And yet
this does not mean that the picture is transparently clear. If only because the
Aristotelian notion of katharsis Girard considers "scarcely . . . necessary" to
mention at the end of his study on violence, and deftly sidesteps by claiming
that "Aristotle failed to penetrate the secret of sacrificial rites" (291), is one
of the most controversial, notoriously undefined, and maddeningly elusive
concepts in western aesthetics.[59]
Genealogical lenses are now revealing how deep Girard's theory of
catharsis and the "true" unconscious it presupposes actually goes. The
death of ritual, in his view, brings about the birth of tragedy, in the sense
that tragedy re-presents in artistic fictions what rituals previously enacted in
real life. The manifestations of violence changed from reality to fiction, and
the media that mediates them continue to change as well; still, the effect of
violence remains fundamentally the same. We move from an anthropology
of violence to an aesthetics of tragedy, from reality to fiction, from rituals to
plays, or, as Nietzsche would put it, from Dionysian intoxications to Apollonian representations. In the process, violence finds itself far removed from
its bloody ritual referents, indeed; it is rendered less tangible, paler, perhaps
even ideal. And yet the cathartic effect remains, in principle if not in degree,
fundamentally the same insofar as tragedy, for Girard, "springs" from ritual
sacrifice. According to this hypothesis, there is thus a genealogical continuity between aesthetic violence and ritual violence that cuts both ways: on
the one hand, anthropological studies on ritual violence, for Girard, offer a
key to account for the effects of aesthetic violence; on the other hand, tragic

violence offers an insight into our violent ritual origins. Considered from this Janus-faced perspective, Greek tragedy does not simply represent violence from an aesthetic distance. Rather, tragedy, as an offshoot of sacrifice, retains the originary pathos of violent rituals necessary to bring about what Aristotle had enigmatically called *katharsis*.

Aristotle's *Poetics*, then, while mentioned only in passing at the end of *Violence and the Sacred*, has been informing Girard's catharsis hypothesis from the very beginning. The importance of Aristotle is rarely stressed in Girard studies, perhaps due to a romantic agonism that led the latter to downplay the importance of the father of catharsis theory. Still, Aristotle's exemplary status in western aesthetics in general and of his enigmatic theory of catharsis in particular cannot be underestimated. And this exemplarity is redoubled when it comes to the specific relation between mimesis and catharsis. The *Poetics* is, indeed, the key text or, rather, "manual," Girard follows to build a bridge between real violence in archaic religious rituals on one side, and aesthetic representations of violence in Greek tragedy on the other side. As he acknowledges: "Aristotle's text is something of a manual of sacrificial practices [*manuel des sacrifices*], for the qualities that make a 'good' tragic hero are precisely those required of the sacrificial victim" (*VS* 291). The characteristic of a manual is that it sets an example. It tends to be studied so thoroughly that one might forget to mention it; still, it provides the blueprint to paint and repaint exemplary heroes that, from the ancients to the moderns to the contemporaries, continue to generate conflicting emotions.

What, then, are the characteristics of this tragic hero? Aristotle and Girard tend to agree that "he"—for the patriarchal tradition attributes this role to a man—must be both similar and different from the community, both an insider and an outsider, noble and flawed, insightful and blind, conscious and unconscious, endowed with both good intentions and bad desires, perhaps even mimetic desires that eventually lead to a reversal of fortune, a tragic downfall, and ultimately a sacrificial expulsion of a *pharmakos* (scapegoat) with cathartic effects that work as a *pharmakon* (poison/remedy) for the plagued city. The detective we are impersonating might be scratching his or her head and wondering: who could the paradigmatic example of such a tragic hero possibly be?

The Oedipal Unconscious

Let's be honest. This is not a riddle worthy of the figure under consideration. Given his obvious distinguishing characteristic, you will have immediately guessed his identity; if only because it is impossible not to have encountered his name in the context of theories of the unconscious before. Uncovering *the* paradigmatic tragic figure whose influence goes from Aristotle's theory of catharsis to Girard's theory of the "true 'unconscious'" and beyond, the latter specifies:

> As we have seen, the tragic figure of Oedipus becomes the original *katharma*. Once upon a time a temple and an altar on which the victim was sacrificed were substituted for the original act of collective violence; now there is an amphitheater and a stage [*un théâtre et une scène*] on which the fate of the *katharma*, played out [*mimé*] by an actor, *will purge* [purgera] *the spectators of their passions and provoke a new katharsis, both individual and collective.* This katharsis will restore the health and well-being of the community. (*VS* 290; my emphasis)

We have moved from an "original" act of violence among an archaic crowd to its "sacrificial" reenactment on an altar to a "tragic" representation in a Greek theater. We are thus at three removes from the origins of violence and the "true 'unconscious'" that generates it. And yet what Girard's mirroring reflections make us see via the medium of an actor, or *mimos*, which is also the medium of *mimēsis* (*mimeisthai*, to imitate, from *mimos*, "actor" but also "performance"),[60] is the following point: fictional tragedies modeled on sacrificial rituals, which are themselves modeled on an original and unverifiable murder, may not be deprived of cathartic effects in real life, after all. What emerges from this chain of *re*-presentations, then, is not only a theory of catharsis as a ritual purification generated by a collective participation in sacrificial violence; it is also, and not less fundamentally, a theory of catharsis as a medical purgation of passions generated by tragic representations of violence whose paradigmatic model is based on "the tragic figure of Oedipus." Inscribed in a long genealogical tradition of thinkers that goes from Aristotle to Freud, when it comes to the unconscious, Girard also privileges Oedipus as the paradigmatic hero of western knowledge, in the end. It is thus no wonder that, as he sets out to solve the riddle of the "true 'unconscious'" on the basis of such a tragic figure, he inevitably found out that, despite its different dramatic manifestations, the singular truth about this unconscious has been founded, if not manifestly at least latently, on an Oedipal hypothesis.

The hypothesis that Oedipal tragedies are endowed with cathartic, unconscious effects is indeed familiar. It provides, among other things, yet another confirmation that the analogies between Girard and Freud are profound, structural, and predicated on a shared Aristotelian concern with Greek tragedy in general and Sophocles's *Oedipus Rex* (429 B.C.) in particular. During our genealogical investigation, the structural similarities have, in fact, been accumulating: Girard not only relies on *Oedipus Rex* as the paradigmatic play to frame the "true" unconscious mechanisms of triangular desire and the ambivalent/rivalrous relation to the model it entails—a psychological move reminiscent of Freud's second topography in *The Ego and the Id* (psychological hypothesis); nor does he solely develop the hypothesis of a founding sacrificial murder at the origins of culture, religion, and civilization—an anthropological move that reenacts Freud's highly speculative and much-disputed claim in *Totem and Taboo* (anthropological hypothesis); though he does both of these things.[61] Above all, and for us more important, Girard borrows the concept of catharsis from Aristotle's *Poetics* not to propose an aesthetic theory of the purifying effects of tragedy itself but, more generally, to articulate a psycho-anthropological theory of the therapeutic, purgative relation between violence and the unconscious in real life—a diagnostic move reminiscent of what Freud, at the dawn of psychoanalysis, in a book coauthored with Joseph Breuer titled *Studies on Hysteria*, called the "cathartic method" (cathartic hypothesis).

There is an interesting theoretical loop at play in this triangulation between Girard, Freud, and Aristotle that is in the maelstrom of our genealogy of violence and the unconscious. To my knowledge, it has never been addressed before and its implications still need to be unraveled. Much is indeed at stake. In fact, the validity of the catharsis hypothesis and the theory of the unconscious that promotes it, reaching into present discussions on (new) media violence, ultimately rests on such genealogical foundations. It is thus crucial to see more clearly in this theoretical triangulation that turns around the riddle of catharsis.

At the most general level, this loop traces the following movement: if Aristotle's theory of catharsis has its origins in archaic rituals and culminates in tragic plays, Girard—in a romantic agonism with Freud—inverts the process, overturns the telos of the theory, and maps the aesthetic concept of catharsis from Greek plays back to real life. The mirroring inversion, in turn, generates striking symmetries between the cathartic effects of violence in Greek tragedy (Aristotle), in the Oedipal unconscious (Freud), and in sacrificial rituals (Girard), mirroring symmetries that, despite differential and innovative moves characteristic of agonistic confrontations, all rest on a tendentious and highly disputed *medical* account of catharsis as purgative therapy for violent, contagious, and pathological affects. That is, a cathartic theory that, to this day, continues to inform discussions on the possible therapeutic effects of media violence in the digital age. These, at least, are the general theoretical outlines, stakes, and implications that emerge from this tableau seen from a genealogical distance.

If we now zoom in on the picture to see more clearly in the hypothesis of catharsis, we notice that the numerous layers of mediation by disciplines as diverse as ancient philosophy, classical philology, aesthetics, psychoanalysis, and mimetic theory generate complex, spiraling loops. These loops call for further genealogical disentanglement if we want to see more clearly into the strengths and limitations of both the catharsis and the affective hypothesis. In fact, over two millennia after the terms of the debate were set, when it comes to the question of the good and bad effects of fictional representations of violence on real behavior, we might still be going around in circles: some say that artificial violence keeps the city going; others insist that it makes the city sick. The agon dramatized in *Vice* with which we started is but a contemporary symptom of one of the most hotly disputed theoretical quarrels in western aesthetics. Hence the need to trace further back the genealogy of the catharsis hypothesis that contemporary thinkers like Girard convoke in theory, before even attempting a diagnostic of the good or bad effects of representations of violence in contemporary practices.

Exits Oedipus. Enter the Philosophical Physicians: birth of psychoanalysis.

CHAPTER 2

Birth of Psychoanalysis

Out of the Cathartic Method

The hypothesis that catharsis, for Aristotle, entails not so much a moral or aesthetic "purification" but, rather, a medical or therapeutic "purgation" of pathological affects is not new. Its modern origins date back to seventeenth-century French neoclassical theories of tragedy that, in the wake of the rediscovery of Aristotle's *Poetics* in the Renaissance, recuperated a medical understanding of catharsis as "purgation," or "evacuation of humors," to account for the affective power of the theater over the audience. For neoclassical authors such as Pierre Corneille and Jean Racine, the emphasis was more on purifying moral passions than on medical purgation—not only violent or excessive passions but passions tout court were considered morally objectionable from this Christian perspective.

And yet their understanding of "purgation" was clearly medical in diagnostic orientation and paved the way for influential psychological interpretations of catharsis that, via genealogical vicissitudes we shall trace in this chapter, will reach into the present.[1] For instance, we have seen that in his account of catharsis Girard uses precisely such a medical terminology predicated on what he calls the "purgation principle" (*principe de la purge*). He can thus be considered a contemporary heir to, and innovator of, this

French neoclassical/Christian tradition—at least in matters of purgation qua cathartic "evacuation" (*VS* 287). Girard himself is quite explicit about this genealogical connection. Thus, he specifies: "The obsessive concern during the seventeenth century with clysters and bleedings, with assuring the efficient *evacuation* [évaquer] of peccant humors, shows plainly the obsessive presence of expulsion and purification as an essential medical theme of the age" (289; trans. modified). And elsewhere he confirms this diagnostic as he claims that "*kathartic* medicine purges the body of its bad 'humors.'"[2] In a direct genealogical sense, then, Girard furthers a French-neoclassical-medical interpretation of catharsis. He does so in order to account not for the evacuation of humors or passions in general at the physiological level but, rather, for the evacuation of violent affects, or pathos, in particular a mimetic pathos that, in his view, finds in the triangular logic of mimetic desire the main road to the unconscious at the psychological level. This, at least, is the theory.

And yet, given our attention to the silent but not less formative logic of romantic agonism, a series of questions emerge in genealogical practice: is Girard erasing the traces of an important mediator when it comes to a medical interpretation of catharsis based on a triangular structure that paves the way for the unconscious? And if we have seen that the shadow of Sigmund Freud looms large over Girard's triangulation of desire and rivalry, we could go further and wonder: did the cathartic method work in practice? Or is the medical translation itself that is supposed to magically generate therapeutic effects? These questions are not as rhetorical as they initially sound. They rest on a long genealogy of skeptics concerning the medical efficacy of catharsis that actually triggered them in the first place.

Interestingly, even within this neoclassical tradition, some doubts about the efficacy of cathartic purgation in dramatic practice were already in place. Pierre Corneille, for instance, one of the most influential advocates and theatrical practitioners of this neo-Aristotelian tradition, admitted in his *Discours de la tragédie* (1660): "I do not know whether pity gives it [sorrow] to us or if it purges it"; and in a more skeptical mood, he continues: "and I fear that Aristotle's reasoning on this point is just a fine idea that has never actually produced its effect."[3] Such skepticism continued well up into the Romantic period, which is characterized not only by an agon between mimetic and expressive view of poetry that pit the Platonic "mirror" versus the romantic "lamp," as M. H. Abrams influentially argued;[4] Romanticism equally staged competing views on catharsis. On one side, it is true as Abrams states that "in the latter part of the eighteenth century, poets began to testify that, in their experience, diverse kinds of literary composition served them as a personal therapy."[5] This is a characteristically romantic shift of emphasis from the audience to the poet qua genius constitutive of a modern form of "author's catharsis."[6]

On the other side, it is equally true that figures like Jean-Jacques Rousseau, whose influence looms large on Romanticism, is even more critical in his diagnostic of catharsis. Supplementing a psychological insight into theatrical pity that cast a shadow on the value of this pathos, with Aristotle clearly in mind, Rousseau writes in his *Letter to d'Alambert on Spectacles* (1758): "I have heard that tragedy leads to pity by way of terror. Granted, but what kind of pity? A volatile and vain emotion that never lasts longer than the illusion that produced it . . . a sterile pity that feeds on a few tears and never produced the least act of humanness."[7] At play in theatrical pity there might thus be a paradoxical movement that sets up a distance from a truly shared sym-pathos with the suffering hero. Pity might, in fact, be a sentiment narcissistically tied to the ego more than to the suffering of the other. According to our theory of homo mimeticus, however, this does not exclude the possibility that a catharsis might be at play in the oscillating double movement generated by the interplay between a bodily pathos, on the one hand, and an aesthetic or perhaps even rational distance, on the other. Since we have not encountered Aristotle's reasoning on this subject, we are not in a position to judge for ourselves as yet. What we can say is that Corneille begins by translating Aristotelian catharsis as "purge," thereby endowing this concept with medical properties. Rousseau equally speaks of catharsis as a means to "purge [*purger*] passions by exciting them."[8] As they both proceed to dispute a presupposed medical efficacy of catharsis, they might actually be disputing an interpretation the translator himself attributed to Aristotle's reasoning in the first place.

We begin to wonder: who is the object of critique here? The author translated or the translator himself? The *Poetics* was rediscovered in Renaissance Italy via the mediation of Ibn Rushd's (known in the West as Averroes) Arabic translation in the twelfth century, subsequently translated into Latin by Bernardo Segni in 1549. Modern Italian, let alone French, is thus at three or more removes from the original. And yet this dynamic of reproductions renders fairly well, if not the truth of the original, at least the principle at play in such translations. *Traduttore, traditore*: rational Aristotle could not have been more irrationally betrayed.

But a perspectival, transdisciplinary genealogy also points to more modern translations endowed with ambitious therapeutic and theoretical aspirations that are even closer to Girard's account of the "true" unconscious and the romantic agonism that informs it. This theory will indeed disseminate a medical translation that will pave the way for a different, more popular, yet not necessarily effective cathartic method that bridges the gap between aesthetic theory and psychic therapy and plays an important role in our genealogy of violence and the unconscious. A medical interpretation of catharsis was indeed once again in the air during the second half of the nineteenth century, a century in which it was not uncommon for philologists to turn into apprentice physicians, physicians into apprentice philologists.[9] It is thus necessary to supplement our genealogy with a more explicitly medical and thus therapeutic perspective. As Michel Foucault—echoing Nietzsche—also recognized, genealogy is based on "an approach similar to that of a doctor who looks closely, who plunges to make a diagnosis and to state its difference."[10] As we sharpen our diagnostic lenses to see deeper into the turbulence of unconscious pathologies, then, we cannot help but wonder: how did the catharsis hypothesis turn into a therapeutic method?

As we turn to see, the birth of psychoanalysis as a science of the unconscious is born out of a philological (mis)interpretation.

A Philological Interpretation

A German philologist who is now mostly unknown outside of specialized circles played a major role in the modern transformation of catharsis from an aesthetic principle into a medical principle. His name was Jacob Bernays, a classicist specialized in Aristotle who, in the second half of the nineteenth century, relaunched interest in the neoclassical, medical interpretation of catharsis. He did so not in France this time but in the German-speaking world in general and for the Viennese intellectual scene in particular, triggering such an interest in the obscure philological concept of catharsis that it assumed "for a time the proportion of a craze."[11]

Crazes, as we know, tend to be contagious and to spread mimetically in practice. But Bernays introduced his medical account of catharsis in the sphere of theory, where it generated equally contagious effects. Bernays's philological interpretations will, in fact, infiltrate modern accounts of catharsis, stretching well beyond specialized philological circles in Vienna to inform contemporary culture at large, and casting a shadow on popular culture as well. As we have seen, his medical interpretation was so successful that it is now unwittingly echoed by cinematic police officers represented in contemporary Hollywood blockbusters. Such popular success is unusual in the sphere of classical philology and academia more generally. It is certainly not the traditional aim or telos of philological scholarship and should give us pause for thought. Given the ongoing popularity of medical accounts of catharsis, it is thus surprising that Bernays's diagnostic has not received closer scrutiny in the humanities and social sciences so far, including those studies on (new) media violence that routinely evoke the notion of catharsis yet hardly mention the name of the scholar who popularized its medical origins to start with. We have all heard that catharsis is supposed to be therapeutic, but unless we are trained in classics, we may never have heard of this German philologist who introduced this view in the first place. Genealogy, with its attention to marginalized figures, values, and theories, and its sensitivity to what Nietzsche calls the "knowledge of the conditions or circumstances of their growth" (*GM* 6; 8),[12] is well positioned to reevaluate the value of this philological hypothesis.

The first version of Jacob Bernays's widely influential but now scarcely read study was initially titled *Grundzüge der verlorenen Abhandlung des Aristoteles über Wirkung der Tragödie* (1857)—translated and abridged more simply as "Aristotle and the Effect of Tragedy."[13] It was subsequently reissued in the 1880s, and it is in this fin de siècle period in one of Europe's main cultural capitals that it achieved prominence outside specialized circles, generating what historians retrospectively described as a "craze." As Frank Sulloway puts it, "by 1880 Bernays's ideas had inspired some seventy German-language publications on catharsis, a number that more than doubled by 1890."[14] The modernists were already fascinated by an age projected into the future, and yet they knew that this future should rest on ancient foundations. It is in this Janus-faced configuration that an ancient and rather technical concept became fashionable at the dawn of modernism, paving the way for the so-called discovery of the unconscious.

What, then, was Bernays's new philological interpretation of catharsis? What is its value, and wherein lied its popularity? Theoretically, his major innovation consisted in countering previous accounts of catharsis as a moral or aesthetic purification—most notably Lessing's and Goethe's interpretations respectively—which, in his view, were too general and "explain nothing precisely because of [this] generality" ("AET" 165). He did so by adopting a different, more specific, and, above all, medically oriented perspective. Bernays's philological engagement with Aristotle implicitly shares the Nietzschean insight that every great philosophy is not deprived of a confessional element tied to the biography of the author. Although he does not make this principle explicit, for Bernays as well, personal experiences rooted in practical professions in real life can potentially inform philosophical thoughts and theories. Thus, he begins his medical reevaluation of catharsis with a biographical reminder as he writes that Aristotle was "the son of a royal doctor and himself a practical physician in his youth" (167). Aristotle was thus schooled, as the original German says, in "ärtzliche Kunst" (medical art)—a phrase the English translation slurs over but already encapsulates Bernays's fundamental thesis: namely, when it comes to the problematic of catharsis, medicine and art cannot be dissociated for they are two sides of the same Janus-faced coin.

Building on this medical genealogy, Bernays proposes a therapeutic reading of the cathartic effects of music in rituals that generate enthusiastic states of mimetic frenzy. Aristotle, as we shall see in more detail in the next chapter, discusses this ritual/musical conception of catharsis in *Politics* rather than in *Poetics*. But for Bernays this shift of perspective from the aesthetic context of *Poetics* to the ritual context of *Politics* is of strategic importance. In fact, it allows him to emphasize what he calls a "*pathological* standpoint [*pathologischer Gesichtpunkt*]" ("AET" 164) that redefines catharsis in medical terms. In fact, Aristotle, in *Politics*, uses the notion of katharsis in its common meaning of "purgation," which he links to "healing [θεραπεία]."[15] What is crucial to stress, and is rarely emphasized outside of specialized circles, is that it is on the basis of *Politics* alone that Bernays can offer the now popular view of catharsis as a medical therapy. Hence, he defines catharsis as "a removing or alleviation of an illness by means of some medical therapy—a purgation [*Linderung der Krankheit*]" (165). In this medical interpretation, then, catharsis excites states of physical frenzy linked to affects (*pathēmata*) such as pity and fear, and, by doing so, purges what Bernays calls the "unbalanced man" of these affective pathologies. A philological blurring of texts and a new interpretation of catharsis is indeed underway: with this move Bernays posits the hypothesis that catharsis, for Aristotle, has a balancing effect that is not merely aesthetic or moral, as Goethe and Lessing had stated, but instead therapeutic and medical.

Philological interpretations, we are beginning to sense, can have far-reaching consequences. Bernays was a philologist, not a physician. Hence, his focus was on a philological interpretation of a philosophical text dealing with the effects of ancient tragedies rather than on a medical interpretation of mental pathologies among modern "unbalanced" subjects. Yet, without consciously knowing it, he was contributing to turning a philological interpretation into a therapeutic practice.

Does Bernays's philological theory generate an uncanny feeling of déjà vu? Sometimes, interpretations that look back to ancient texts can cast shadows so long that they not only form modern theories but also inform and transform contemporary practices. Bernays's interpretation is now disputed by the overwhelming majority of philologists, but it had an impact that went way beyond specialized intellectual circles in fin de siècle Vienna, and spread to inform twentieth-century physicians, patients, and popular views across the world. How? Thanks to a stroke of genealogical luck even a popular philologist like Bernays could not have possibly foreseen in his wildest dreams. Bernays was, in fact, not only interested in Aristotle qua ancient physician. He also happened to become the maternal uncle (by marriage) of another soon-to-be-modern physician qua apprentice philologist concerned with the articulation of physical and affective pathologies of unbalanced men and women in real life. His name, you will have guessed, was Sigmund Freud.

How an Interpretation Became a "Method"

Genealogy traces filiations that are not simply personal and familial but conceptual and theoretical; yet, in the case of psychoanalysis, the distinction between the two is blurry at best. Even self-proclaimed masters of psychoanalysis would not disagree. Jacques Lacan, introducing Bernays in his seminar to account for the success of the concept of catharsis in its "medical connotation," regrets that "little attention has been paid to him," and says, "It is nevertheless difficult to imagine that Freud, who was by no means indifferent to the reputation of the Bernays family, wasn't aware of him."[16] And he adds that had disciples and editors of Freud like Ernst Jones referred to Bernays, "it would have been a way of referring Freud's original use of the word catharsis to its best source."[17]

Lacan makes a good philological point that still needs a supplement. Inspired by his uncle-in-law's definition of "catharsis," the young Sigmund Freud, in collaboration with the physician and experimental psychologist Joseph Breuer, not only took Bernays's medical interpretation of catharsis seriously in theory; they also transposed it into their medical practice.[18] The physicians were, in fact, in need of a theory, or at least a working hypothesis, to cure a destabilizing mental pathology that rendered both men and especially women unbalanced, generating theatrical symptoms that were already manifest in some patients. It is thanks to this fortuitous and familial genealogical conjunction that Bernays's catharsis hypothesis turned into a therapeutic method with far-reaching cultural implications.

Uncovering personal tragedies internal to an oppressed and conflicted psyche, the method suggested, could provide a door for a cathartic discharge with balancing therapeutic effects. Before turning to Freud's and Breuer's method, it is important to stress that Bernays had already laid the theoretical foundations. Lacan rightly mentions Freud's general debt to his uncle-in-law's medical interpretation, but the so-called original source had an influence on the vicissitudes of catharsis that even Lacan does not seem to have fully realized. The philologist (Bernays) had, in fact, offered the following medical definition of "catharsis" along with an embryonic theory of affective drives that must have made a strong impression on the physicians (Freud and Breuer). Here is a philological passage that physicians in search of a method are unlikely to have overlooked; we need to consider it carefully, that is, philologically, by paying attention to both the theory and language that mediates it. As Bernays diagnoses,

> *katharsis* is a term transferred from the physical to the emotional sphere, and used of the sort of treatment of an oppressed person which seeks not to alter or re-press [*zurückzudrängen*] the oppressive element [*beklemmende Element*] but to excite it, to draw it out [*hervortreiben*], and thereby to effect a relief" ("AET" 167; trans. modified).[19]

Both the language and the dynamic proposed here are genealogically interesting. They are particularly interesting to account for the birth of a psychological theory, if only because the passage articulates, in the same breath, a diagnostic and a possible cure. A psychic pathology generated by oppressive affects, on the one hand; a medical therapy based on the excitation and the injunction not to repress such affects, on the other. Picture Freud and Breuer reading this passage. "This sounds like an interesting method," the philological physicians must have thought. Let us call it the "cathartic method."

Our genealogical investigation is now uncovering intriguing and previously unexplored connections on the genesis of the catharsis hypothesis that allow us to ask more specific theoretical questions. Here is a hypothesis on the birth of psychoanalysis: could it be that on the basis of this philological interpretation of Aristotle's *Poetics*, Breuer and Freud felt justified in transferring the enigmatic Aristotelian concept of catharsis from aesthetics to medicine in order to attempt to cure a destabilizing mental pathology that was much *en vogue* in fin de siècle Europe, had attracted the attention of other exemplary physicians who had made an impression on Freud—most notably Jean-Martin Charcot—and still remained largely unexplained in fin de siècle Europe: namely, hysteria? The analogies, as we shall soon confirm, are uncanny enough.[20] Should this hypothesis prove correct, would then the cathartic method developed at the dawn of psychoanalysis be nothing more than the offshoot of a philological speculation? Either way, since this speculation not only is constitutive of the birth of psychoanalysis but continues to inform popular culture more generally, going as far as being reproduced in contemporary cinematic fictions, it is legitimate to ask: is this medical speculation qua interpretation true? Or is it rather the product of a philological error? Given the stakes for psychoanalysis, mimetic theory, and cathartic theory, these are delicate questions. Let us thus not rush to conclusions and consider them one by one, instead.

The mirroring effects between the philologist and the physicians are actually striking and support the hypothesis of the birth of the psychoanalytic method—out of a philological interpretation. Bernays, in fact, spoke of medical katharsis in relation to the dangers of *zurückdrängen*; Freud and Breuer develop a "cathartic method" to cure pathologies Freud will consider generated by repression—that is, *Verdrängung*.[21] The words are not exactly the same, but the semantic difference between *Zurückdrängung* and *Verdrängung* is minimal, and both can be rendered as "repression." Further, both terms appear in the context of a diagnostic of a medical therapy linked to the catharsis of pathological affects: Bernays speaks of "oppressive" (*beklemmende*) affects; Freud and Breuer, as we shall see shortly, speak of "strangulated affects" (*eingeklemmten Affekte*). Again, one term is psychic, the other physical, but in matters of physio-psychology the distinction between *beklemmen* and *einklemmen* is blurry at best. This is especially true if we consider that what is at stake is a psychic dynamic concerning the pathological danger of repression and the therapeutic virtues of discharge. Last but not least, the concept of *Verdrängung*, which, we should not forget, is the fundamental concept of psychoanalysis and provides the hypothesis on which the Freudian unconscious stands or falls, appears for the first time in 1893, that is, at the same time the cathartic method is being developed. Are these simple coincidences along the way of the so-called discovery of the unconscious? The philological analysis I am tracing suggests not only that reading Bernays helped Breuer and, later, Freud formulate the cathartic method; at an additional remove, it also helped Freud catalyze the concept of *Verdrängung*—that is, nothing less than the concept on which hinges the Freudian door to the unconscious. A hypothesis for future historians of psychoanalysis to confirm.[22]

Genealogical lenses attentive to the conditions of emergence of theories by thinkers haunted by romantic anxieties of influence teach us to be suspicious of striking mimetic symmetries, especially when direct filiations are at play in a theory particularly concerned with the psychic problem of filiation. Given all of the above, it seems we have sufficient indications to postulate the following hypothesis: Bernays's medical interpretation of catharsis and the embryonic cautionary theory against repression it entails could be the missing genealogical link in the account of the birth of the repressive hypothesis that paved the way for a theory of the (Oedipal) unconscious and the contemporary variants that ensued, which cast a long shadow on the twentieth century. True or not, this unconscious and the interpretations it gave rise to are still manifestly with us today. In its protean manifestations, it continues to latently inform contemporary accounts of the therapeutic relation between catharsis and violence that go beyond the walls of medical cabinets, are still part of academic programs in the humanities, and continue to (mis)inform popular culture as well.

Given the stakes of this theory of violence and the unconscious, it is thus important to take a close genealogical look at the birth of psychoanalysis—out of a catharsis hypothesis.

The Philological Physicians—Bernays, Freud & Co.

At the time of *Studies on Hysteria* (1895), psychoanalysis, as Freud would later develop it, was not fully born but was already in an embryonic stage. Freud and Breuer were, in fact, relying on hypnosis, not dreams, as a main door to access the unconscious. They were not alone in doing so. Freud in particular was under the spell of influential physicians he had met during his stay in Paris in the winter of 1885/86. I mentioned Jean-Martin Charcot, whose legendary *leçons du mardi* at the Salpêtrière Freud religiously attended. Freud fell, indeed, under the spell of what Michel Foucault calls an "apparatus for observation [*appareil d'observation*]" qua "incitement machinery [*machinerie d'incitation*]" generated by a carefully staged "theater of ritual crises" meant not simply to represent but to produce the "truth" about presumed sexual pathologies.[23] This productive "will to know" (*volonté de savoir* in French is not far from *volonté de pouvoir*), as many historians of psychiatry have recognized, was not deprived of performative effects that generated the symptoms they were meant to cure.[24]

We shall return to this performative power, or will to power, as it pertains to the problematic of (new) media violence as well. At the same time, we should not forget French philosophical physicians like Alfred Binet and Charles Féré, who worked under Charcot and will play a central role in the affective hypothesis, as well as critical visitors such as the Belgian philosopher

Joseph Delboeuf. Especially worthy of mention are two towering figures whose influence in the genesis of psychoanalysis is more important than Freud will later be willing to acknowledge: first, the French philosopher and psychologist Pierre Janet, founder of a method he called "psychological analysis" (*l'analyse psychologique*), whose "story of Marie and her cathartic cure" in *Psychological Automatism* (1889), as the medical historian Henri Ellenberger points out, in his monumental *The Discovery of the Unconscious* (1970), Freud "could not have failed to become acquainted with" and subsequently emulated;[25] and second, Charcot's main rival, the psychologist Hippolyte Bernheim, from the competing School of Nancy, whose method of "hypnotic suggestion" Freud directly borrowed to develop his own cathartic method.

As Mikkel Borch-Jacobsen, one of the most informed historians to reopen the Freud dossier in recent years, has shown in "Sigmund Freud, Hypnotiseur" (2015), the impact of hypnosis qua "*voie royale* of neurosciences" on the birth of psychoanalysis has been profound; it made lasting impressions on its practitioners, practices, and theories. Under the spell of the "Napoleon of neuroses," Borch-Jacobsen argues, the young Freud will follow the mesmerizing example step by step: "He too will conquer the neuroses; he too will lead a School, journals collections; he too will publish his lessons; he too will attract to his cabinet the worldly, millionaires and princesses."[26] Borch-Jacobsen's diagnostic is as concise as it is historically precise. The young Freud, he writes, echoing Delboeuf, returned from his stay in Paris under the spell of such a theory—that is, "*salpêtrisé*."[27] Although Freud will later manifestly reject hypnosis via a romantic agonism we shall confirm as central to his method as well, the shadow of hypnotic suggestion, Borch-Jacobsen demonstrates in seminal works that establish a genealogical bridge between psychoanalysis and mimetic theory, will continue to latently haunt major concepts such as catharsis, transference, and identification.[28]

This genealogical hypothesis should be taken seriously by anyone seriously interested in the development of psychoanalysis from the point of view of the active theorist rather than the passive disciple. Such concepts are, in fact, central not only to the Freudian unconscious but to mimetic theory as well. It is thus essential to look back to the birth of psychoanalysis out of a catharsis hypothesis that held sway in the twentieth century to better evaluate how mimetic theory paves the way for an affective hypothesis crucial to account for the dynamic of unconscious violence in the twenty-first century. It is on the shoulders of these modern doctors of the soul, and with Bernays's philological work to remind them of a more ancient philosophical physician as well, that Freud and Breuer turned into apprentice philological physicians ready to test the cathartic theory in their medical cabinets. Hence, they converted Aristotle's philosophically obscure notion of catharsis into a therapeutic "method" to cast light on a once widely diffused, yet now no longer actual, psychic pathology, or *maladie de l'âme*. While the method did not yield successful results in practice and Freud would go on to eventually abandon it, it was not deprived of theoretical success: it paved the way for the discovery of an unconscious based on an interpretation of a tragic play that was erected as a universal model for psychic traumas and is still very much with us.

With respect to catharsis, Breuer was the true pioneer. As Frank Sulloway reminds us, Breuer not only "had a special interest in Greek drama" and "had long been concerned with the dramatic concept of catharsis";[29] Breuer also convoked this concept to attempt to cure a young woman who suffered from hysterical symptoms: the case of Bertha Pappenheim, better known as Anna O. Famous for being the first patient of psychoanalysis and for coining the celebrated phrase "talking cure," Anna O. provided the clinical foundations for Breuer's and Freud's general hypothesis in *Studies on Hysteria*: namely that "hysterics suffer mainly from reminiscences" and that a recollection of—or, better, an affective reaction to—these reminiscences is necessary for a cathartic therapy to ensue.[30] As the philological physicians put it: "The injured person's reaction to the trauma only exercises a completely 'cathartic' effect [*eine völlig "kathartische" Wirkung*] if it is an adequate reaction—as, for instance, revenge" (*SH* 7). Catharsis, in this medical sense, then, rests on an "adequate reaction" to the violent action that caused it in the first place. This also means that catharsis rests on a mimetic reaction in a sense that is at least double for it concerns as much the affective content of the reaction and the formal medium through which it is expressed. At the level of content, a violent, traumatic action (sexual abuse) is cured by a mimetic reaction to a violent affect (revenge)—an indication that an affective response to an event suffered in the past can make a therapeutic difference in the present. At the level of form, the patient does not simply represent or narrate the trauma from a diegetic distance but dramatically reenacts it via mimetic speech—an indication that dramatic narrative categories that go back to antiquity continue to structure the content of these modern representations.[31] A dramatic conception of mimesis we shall discuss in relation to contagion is thus central to the cathartic method as well; and it is from these mimetic foundations that a method is born—out of a classical theory of mimesis.

Given these explicit classical allusions, it should not come as a surprise that the echoes of the philologist's catharsis hypothesis are still audible in the diagnostic of the physicians, working as apprentice philological physicians. Breuer and Freud now specify the therapeutic properties of the cathartic method as they articulate the following hypothesis:

> [catharsis] brings to an end the operative force of the idea which was not abreacted in the first instance, by allowing its strangulated affect [*eingeklemmten Affekte*] to find a way out through speech [*Rede*]; and it subjects it to associative correction by introducing it into normal consciousness (under light hypnosis) or by removing it through the physician's suggestion, as is done in somnambulism accompanied by amnesia. (*SH* 16)

Abreacted ideas, strangulated or, rather, stuck affects, therapeutic words— the language of this method is still somewhat contorted, but a structural dynamic is beginning to take form. If the violence of a past trauma prevented the abreaction of an idea, accompanied by the blockage of an affect, and the pathological dissociation of the personality in a conscious and unconscious part, the cathartic method allows the affect, and the idea with it, to come to the fore with therapeutic effects. How? Through a type of linguistic ritual that resembles a confession. Or, better, through a first-person dramatic and thus mimetic re-presentation and reenactment that makes present the very affects that had not been allowed outlet in the first place, were strangulated and stuck, and are now introduced into "normal consciousness." Alternatively, these affects could also be removed, as previous hypnotists (Bernheim, Janet, Delboeuf) did for somnambulists, by unconscious means. In sum, the cathartic method relied on a hypnotic-mimetic technique ("suggestion") in order to put the patient in an altered state of consciousness ("light hypnosis") and, through the medium of speech—it is still Anna O.'s "talking cure"—attempt to cure hysterical symptoms via a catharsis of "strangulated" (*eingeklemmt*), later called "repressed" (*verdrängt*), affects. This can be done in two ways: either by bringing these affects into consciousness or, if that does not work, by operating directly on the unconscious via hypnotic suggestion and dissolving them from consciousness altogether. "Upon awakening, thou shalt remember the trauma—or thou shalt forget it!"[32]

Does this sound confusing? Yes, these theoretical oscillations generated some confusion, contemporary philosophical physicians would agree. Even influential psychoanalysts who advocated a return to Freud were never convinced. Lacan is, once again, a case in point. As he puts it: Freud's and Breuer's account of "abreaction" and "discharge of something that is not so simple to define . . . remains a problem for us, the discharge of an emotion that remains unresolved."[33] If we are also confused, there is thus no reason to worry or, worse, suspect a traumatic pathology. It is a normal response to a confusing hypothesis.

On his side, later in his career, Freud will conveniently reminisce a simpler, clearer, and clean version for posterity to remember and, if not to "work through," at least to compulsively repeat: "Under the treatment, therefore, 'catharsis' came about when the path to consciousness was opened and there was a normal discharge of affect [*Entladung des Affekts*]"; and, pointing to the importance of the catharsis hypothesis, he adds: "an essential part of this theory was the assumption of the existence of unconscious mental processes [*unbewußter seelischer Vorgänge*]."[34] From philology to psychology back to philology. The theory of catharsis might have gone through a circular logic in theory, but it was certainly off to a successful and quite contagious start in practice. In a spiraling move that brought the cathartic method back to the theatrical practices from which it originated, contemporary philologists even invoked Freud's and Breuer's theory to account for the cathartic effects of tragedy on the audience.[35] This is, in fact, the version that still tends to be remembered today, is routinely repeated in textbooks, and continues to be passed down to future generations of students in the humanities, most notably literature departments—arguably one of the few remaining fields, along with philosophy, that is still under the spell of psychoanalysis—as the essential insight that made the Freudian discovery of the unconscious possible.

In sum, my genealogical point is that the cathartic method, mimetic violence, and Freud's account of the unconscious cannot easily be dissociated—if only because it is thanks to this method that Freud reopens the long dossier on the unconscious from an Oedipal, cathartic, and thus Aristotelian perspective.[36] This is how an obscure philological riddle, thanks to Freud's heroic efforts, will achieve the status of a legend.

The Freudian Legend

We know the histories and vicissitudes of what followed. Freud would abandon the cathartic treatment via hypnosis as well as the so-called seduction theory it presupposed in favor of the method of "free associations," and turn from the idea of real familial traumas to phantasmal Oedipal traumas on the basis of a repressive hypothesis that, in his own account, opened up the door to the true unconscious that has dreams as its legendary *via regia*. Freud himself will indeed retrospectively give an autobiographical account of the birth of psychoanalysis emerging from the cathartic method. As he puts in his "Autobiographical Study" (1925), once "repression" became the "cornerstone" of his understanding of neuroses, the goal was "no longer to 'abreact' an affect which had got on to the wrong lines but to uncover repressions and replace them by acts of judgment."[37] That is, judgments constitutive of a colonizing rationalist perspective resumed in the famous expansionist formula: "Where id was there ego shall be." As Freud also puts it, this principle led to the "recognition of the new situation by no longer calling [his] method of investigation the treatment of *catharsis* but *psycho-analysis*."[38] Somewhat ironically, then, psychoanalysis was born out of the abreaction of the cathartic method: where catharsis was, there psychoanalysis shall be. Given the status of psychoanalysis as what Karl Jaspers calls a "popular psychology," which he qualified as a "mass-phenomenon"[39]—that is, a mimetic phenomenon—this dominant metanarrative of how Freud single-handedly discovered the unconscious spread contagiously, imposing itself on the popular side of the cultural scene.

Over the past decades, historians of psychoanalysis have provided ample evidence to seriously doubt the validity of this metanarrative, revealing it as the product of what Henri Ellenberger influentially called the "Freudian legend" (*DU* 547). The main characteristics of the Freudian legend, Ellenberger specifies, include the theme of the "solitary hero struggling against a host of enemies," and the stress on the "absolute originality of the achievements in which the hero is credited with the achievements of his predecessors, associates, disciples, rivals, and contemporaries" (*DU* 547).[40] The hero might erect himself as a model to be imitated but that does not mean that the achievements are original, or even true. They might be the product of a romantic agonism we need to continue unmasking. Yet the defining characteristic of legends is that they do not need to be true to affect the popular imagination.

This applies not only to the legendary Oedipal unconscious but also to the catharsis hypothesis that paved the way for it. The success of the legend can in fact still be gauged by the following symptom: it is primarily thanks to Freud that when the notion of catharsis is invoked outside of specialized philological circles, it is still generally understood in Bernays's medical sense—that is, as a purgation of psychic pathologies that allows for an unconscious discharge of violent affects with therapeutic effects. This is, of course, not without deep theoretical, historical, and therapeutic ironies. To be sure, psychoanalysis was always quick to counter alternative philosophies of the unconscious on the basis of the sacrosanct principle of what Michel Henry calls "incontestable, pathological material" that endows the Freudian theory with its distinctive "originality"; yet Henry also adds that "all theoretical legitimation on the basis of a practice is always suspect, and Freud apparently never thought that only a believer was legitimated to talk of religion."[41] Despite the belief that the psychoanalytical unconscious and the legendary discovery it entails tend to elicit, or rather because of this belief, the legend should indeed remain open to alternative and potentially dissident interpretations.

What we must add is that even, or once again, especially on therapeutic grounds, the so-called pathological material proved rather resistant to the theory—ultimately driving a nail in the coffin of the cathartic theory itself. Contrary to what Freud claimed, the first patient of psychoanalysis was far from cured by the cathartic method. As Ellenberger was quick to point out: "It is ironic that Anna O.'s unsuccessful treatment should have become, for posterity, the prototype of a cathartic cure" (DU 484). In fact, he adds: "the supposed 'prototype of a cathartic cure' was not a cure at all" (483; see also 480–89). Sulloway confirms the diagnostic thus: "The patient apparently had many relapses and was eventually institutionalized. Breuer even expressed the hope, a year after he discontinued personal treatment of the case that his patient might die and so be released from her suffering."[42] And as Borch-Jacobsen summed it up in the last decades of the twentieth century, this theoretically disastrous diagnostic finally came to an end after a "century of mystification."[43]

Still, here is a disconcerting fact: the failure of the cathartic method in practice did not prevent the further development of the catharsis hypothesis in theory. Even in scholarly discussions, as we have seen in the preceding chapter, this medical interpretation is still in circulation. Girard, for one, in his account of catharsis as a "purgation" predicated on a discharge of violent affects remains in line with the genealogy of psychoanalysis we have just mapped, though the logic of romantic agonism led him to studiously never mention Freud's cathartic method in the context of his own discussion of catharsis. The specific context is, of course, different. Girard is concerned with the catharsis of ritual violence at the heart of the social, whereas Freud is concerned with the catharsis of violent psychic pathologies at the heart of the ego. But the general theoretical move of transposing a medical interpretation of catharsis from an aesthetic context to a psychic context remains uncannily similar, especially if we remember that overarching triangular structure predicated on the paradigmatic case of Oedipus on which Girard's interpretation also rests, despite his overturning move. If we sum up the latent theoretical steps that silently structure Girard's account of violence, catharsis, and the "'true' unconscious" we have been progressively unearthing, we discover an impressive, multilayered, but no less derivative tour de force: it consists of recuperating the classical aesthetic theory of catharsis (Aristotle) as a paradigmatic example of a medical rather than moral treatment (Bernays) predicated on an Oedipal model of the unconscious (Freud) presumably originated in a primordial sacrificial killing of the father (Freud again) in order to propose a therapeutic solution to the contagious pathologies generated by human, all too human, violence (Girard).

Girard, then, on the medical shoulders of Freud, who, in turn, sits on the philological shoulders of Bernays, manifestly derives the notion of catharsis from Aristotle's *Poetics* "itself." Before drawing any conclusions on the eventual therapeutic value of the catharsis hypothesis, then, it is legitimate to ask: What is the meaning of catharsis in *Poetics*? Why is a Greek tragedy such as Sophocles's *Oedipus Rex* the paradigmatic text of modern theories of the unconscious? And, closer to our initial questions: what shall we make of contemporary appropriations of a classical aesthetic theory that attempts to deal with the therapeutic effects of representations of violence on spectators populating a "real" yet increasingly mediatized world? Now that we have reopened this can of worms, there is no turning back. Confronting these modern riddles that continue to shape contemporary attitudes on the relation between violence and the unconscious entails plunging deeper into our genealogical past so as to take a closer diagnostic look at the ancient riddle of catharsis in Aristotle's *Poetics* itself.

CHAPTER 3

The Riddle of Catharsis

Aristotle's *Poetics*

f our genealogy has taken the form of a detective investigation, we should recognize that we reach here one of the oldest, most influential, and, above all, most enigmatic fragments of evidence concerning the riddle we are trying to solve. And what the evidence tells us is not encouraging. I am sorry to say that there are no easy scholarly answers to the question concerning the original meaning of catharsis in the *Poetics* (ca. 335 B.C.). Aristotle's passing and much-quoted remark on catharsis is, in fact, notoriously obscure. Its "incurable vagueness" has puzzled classicists since the rediscovery of the *Poetics* in the Renaissance, and ultimately—*pace* Bernays—it continues to elude unilateral definitions.[1]

To frame this riddle in light of our genealogy, let us begin by recalling that in the *Poetics*, Aristotle accepted Plato's challenge as he set out to develop a philosophical defense of poetry from the exclusion advocated by his teacher and influential predecessor. In the *Republic* (ca. 375 B.C.), in fact, after a lengthy dialogue that started with the pedagogical dangers of dramatic spectacles and concluded with a metaphysical critique of mimesis, "Plato," under the mimetic mask of his own teacher, Socrates, (in)famously concluded Book 10 by excluding poetry on the grounds that "if you grant admission to the honeyed Muse in lyric or epic, pleasure and pain will be lords of your city instead of law."[2] For "Plato," then, pleasure and pain have dangerously contagious effects on the irrational side of the soul for reasons based on an affective rather than cathartic hypothesis. And in a passage that must have made a major impression on the young Aristotle, Plato/Socrates opens up the following possibility: "But nevertheless let it be declared that, if the mimetic and dulcet poetry can show any reason for her existence in a well-governed state, we would gladly admit her, since we ourselves are very conscious of her spell" (*Rep.* 832; 607c). Plato ends the *Republic* with an open invitation to an intellectual challenge, contest, or agon, for an ambitious student or agonistic contender it to pick up and run with it.

Aristotle's *Poetics* in general, and the theory of catharsis of emotions like pity and fear in particular, picks up the challenge, enters the mimetic agon, and sets out to provide a rational reply to Plato's agonistic invitation that will have lasting effects in theories of art through the ages, reaching into the present. In fact, Aristotle argued, contra Plato or, better, as an agonistic reply to Plato, that Greek tragedy does not generate irrational forms of contagious pathos that threaten to violently disrupt the stability of both the soul and the body politic; nor should it be opposed to philosophy because it generates illusory phantoms that are at two removes from the truth. On the contrary, the mirroring dynamic of the mimetic agon leads to the inversed reflection: namely that tragedy, and by extension literature and theatrical spectacles more generally, turns out to have philosophical potential. In fact, for Aristotle, tragedy is based on a representation (*mimesis*) of an action whose formal properties of causality and necessity not only mirror the rational properties of the intellect; they also have the affective power to generate the catharsis of contagious and painful emotions, such as pity and fear. If Plato restricted mimesis to a poetic genre (namely, tragedy and comedy) that triggers a contagious pathos, Aristotle, while focusing on tragedy, generalizes mimesis as the principle constitutive of *poetics*, that is, the making (from *poiein*, to make) of poetry tout court, which he endowed with enigmatic cathartic properties. Before we even being to unpack this concept it is crucial to realize that Aristotle's catharsis hypothesis is born out of a mimetic agon with an influential model (Plato) who is not simply opposed to mimesis. He might also provide young agonistic contenders with the very invitation—and perhaps the very concepts—to readmit this accursed concept in the lawful city, or polis.

Catharsis is *the* concept Aristotle picks up to respond to Plato's contest. As he famously puts it in chapter six of *Poetics*, which I quote in Stephen Halliwell's translation:

> Tragedy, then, is a representation of an action which is serious, complete, and of a certain magnitude—in a language which is garnished in various forms in its different parts—in the mode of dramatic enactment, not narrative—and through the arousal of pity [*eleos*] and fear [*phobos*] effect the *katharsis* of such emotions [*pathēmata*].[3]

These lines have received numerous illuminating commentaries, but to this day the specific meaning of the Greek action noun κάθαρσις, rendered in English as "catharsis," continues to remain obscure—hence it is usually left untranslated. And aptly so, for it is a concept that belongs to what Barbara Cassin groups under the category of "untranslatables."[4] It is generally understood that by watching a tragic play, spectators identify with the suffering hero; feel pity and fear mimetically or vicariously by identifying with the protagonist's tragic destiny; and, through this affective, dramatic, and identificatory participation in fictional events, experience the catharsis (purgation, purification, clarification?) of these painful and violent emotions in real life, which can have "medical, religious, moral, psychological, or aesthetic connotations" reflecting the concerns of the age.[5]

That much is known. But it still does not tell us what catharsis means, let alone how it actually works. In order to better understand why tragedy in particular and, by extension, representations of violent actions—originally in the theater, then in the movie theater, and now on any digital screens—catharsis, and the unconscious psychic reactions it triggers in viewers, should be linked in the first place, contemporary scholars have stressed the importance of adopting at least two related perspectives. The first consists in reinscribing this enigmatic concept in its original ritual context in ancient Greece (let us call it anthropological); the second, in situating catharsis in the philosophical context of Aristotle's thought in general and of the *Poetics* in particular (let us call it formalist). Let us thus schematically recapitulate these two related genealogical perspectives and the mimetic agonism that gives birth to the *pharmakon* of catharsis.

The *Pharmakon* of Catharsis

On the anthropological side, it is possible to frame the Aristotelian concept of catharsis in its original ritual context from which Aristotle presumably derives it. In their entry in *Dictionary of Untranslatables* (2014), Barbara Cassin and her collaborators usefully remind us that catharsis has ritual origins that can be traced back to the ritual of Thargelia, in which a scapegoat (*pharmakos*) was sacrificed for purification purposes. As they put it: "*Katharsis* is an action noun corresponding to the verb *kathairô* (clean, purify, purge). Initially it had the religious sense of 'purification,' and referred particularly to the ritual of expulsion practiced in Athens on the eve of the Thargelia," a spring festival linked to good omens for activities like harvesting. As Harpocration noted: "'The Athenians, during the Thargelia, drove two men, as purifying exorcisms, out of the city, one for the men, the other for the women,' and then scapegoats, according to the ritual of the *pharmakos*."[6] And summing up the diagnostic of the original ritual function of catharsis, Cassin and collaborators specify:

> as a remedy—Greek, *to pharmakon*, the same word, in the neuter gender, as the one designating the scapegoat—*katharsis* implies more precisely the idea of a homeopathic medicine: purgation is a way of curing harm by harm, the same by the same, and it is also why every *pharmakon* is a "poison" as much as a "remedy," the dosage of the harmful thing alone producing a good result.[7]

This theory of the original, ritual meaning of catharsis as both poison and cure is thus steeped in classical antiquity. Jean-Pierre Vernant addressed the double role catharsis served in ancient Greece, specifically via the duplicity of the Oedipus case who embodies both the role of "*divine king* and *pharmakos*," or scapegoat—an association that must not have been lost on Girard.[8]

This is the moment to pull some genealogical strings and recall that Vernant was one of the invited speakers at the 1966 Johns Hopkins symposium co-organized by Girard, which sparked the structural controversy discussed in chapter 1. Let me now add that in his intervention on Greek tragedy, Vernant had been very critical of modern interpretations of *Oedipus Rex*. He had in fact argued that "what the Freudians have to say about the Oedipus myth constitutes a new myth,"[9] which, as we have seen, stretches to inform the cathartic myth. At the same time, a genealogical perspective equally reveals that the connection between *pharmakos* (scapegoat) and *pharmakon* (poison and remedy) is not original either. It bears the traces of contemporary influences, mimetic influences, which again were present during the same symposium, an exemplary symposium that, we are now in a position to confirm, played a seminal and so far largely unacknowledged role in the development of Girard's theory of violence.[10] In particular, Girard's concluding remarks on the cathartic properties of the scapegoat resonate directly with Jacques Derrida's influential account of the pharmakon in "Plato's Pharmacy" (1968)[11]—a seminal text for mimetic theory as well. In fact, Derrida's deconstructive reading of Plato's evaluation of writing in *Phaedrus* as a pharmakon that serves simultaneously as both poison and remedy, directly informs Girard's claim that "Plato's *pharmakon* is like Aristotle's *katharsis*" (*VS* 296) in the double sense that the cathartic effect of sacrificing a scapegoat (*pharmakos*) functions both a poison and a cure (*pharmakon*).[12] Hence Girard, echoing Derrida and Vernant on this specific genealogical point, writes: "The mutations of meaning from the human *katharma* to the medical katharsis are paralleled by those of the human pharmakos to the medical *pharmakon*, which signifies at once 'poison' and 'remedy'" (*VS* 288). Catharsis is thus both a poison and a remedy. As in all medical evaluation, it is a question of good dosage: what is a remedy in homeopathic doses might turn into a poison in massive doses. Something that applies to (new) media as well, as we shall see.

Now, as the reference to catharsis as a pharmakon already suggests, the dynamic of mimetic agonism does not simply oppose Aristotle to Plato, as it is often assumed. On the contrary, it generates mirroring effects characterized by both visible inversions and less visible, but not less fundamental, continuities. Despite Aristotle's antagonistic relation to Plato's theory of mimesis and the pathological contagion it generates, or rather because of it, the opposition between the two founding figures of mimetic studies on the affective and conceptual value of aesthetic representations may not be as opposed as is often repeated. Recall, in fact, that according to the paradoxical

dynamic of the agonism that was constitutive of Greek intellectual confrontations, as both Burckhardt and Nietzsche have shown, the new contender
(in this case, Aristotle) is not simply opposed to the predecessor (in this case,
Plato). Rather, the former draws on the predecessor's concepts in order to
stage an intellectual contest *with* and *against* the model in view of affirming
a new logos on pathos, or patho-*logy*. If our account of mimetic agonism is
of any worth to account for mirroring inversions and continuities between
influential thinkers, here is another test: could it be that the very notion of
katharsis that Aristotle mobilizes in order to provide an answer to Plato's
scapegoating exclusion of the poets to purge the ideal city stems precisely
from the intellectual antagonist qua predecessor Aristotle is up against?

Outside of specialized circles, it is not often mentioned that Aristotle
is not the first philosopher to propose the concept of catharsis. Plato had
already introduced it as constitutive of philosophical thought. In the *Sophist*, for instance, under the mask of the Stranger, Plato had already inscribed
catharsis at the very core of his own dialectical method, as he specifies: "Every
discernment or discrimination of that kind [that throws away the worse and
preserves the better] is called a purification [catharsis]"; and then sets out
to distinguish between the "arts of purification" of bodies inside (medicine)
and outside (bathing), making clear that the goal or telos of philosophy
is the "purification of the soul or intellect."[13] The very concept of catharsis
can thus not easily be detached from Plato's dialogues; it provides the very
method to achieve the purification of the intellect from the irrational pathos
his dialectical logos aspires to accomplish. Later, in the *Laws*, Plato, this
time under the mask of the Athenian, goes as far as contradicting his negative evaluation of wine and inebriation in the *Republic* by considering it as a
Dionysian "*pharmakon*," poison and cure. In a discussion that furthers, dia-
lectically, the negative view that a "diseased body which has been subjected
to medical purgation" should be considered healthier than a "body which
has never stood in need of such treatment,"[14] the Athenian introduces the
opposite hypothesis: namely that there might be a cathartic value in wine,
if not for the young at least for the elderly, which he is happy to allow now,
taken in homeopathic doses at symposia, for instance. For the elderly Plato,
in fact, the intoxicating effects of wine can be used to "bring your citizens in
a state of fear and test them under its influence, thus constraining a man to
become fearless."[15] In other words, by triggering fear via a pharmacological

Dionysian substance, a paradoxical effect ensues that purges citizens of fear, thereby operating its catharsis.

The analogies with Aristotle are striking enough. It even led classicists to posit the hypothesis that "the *Laws* directly influenced Aristotle's views on tragic catharsis."[16] This possibility is especially plausible if we consider that the Dionysian symposia in which wine was drunk, for Plato and Greek culture more generally, is directly connected to the theater—a mimetic art under the patronage of Dionysus. Moreover, both symposia and the theater are concerned with education, which provides the context of the discussion of catharsis in *Laws*. The fact that the Athenian sets out to define a "choric performance" in terms that are strikingly reminiscent of Aristotle's definition of tragedy further strengthens the connection. Plato defines it as follows: the "choric exhibition is a mimic presentation of manners, with all variety of action and circumstance, enacted by performers who depend on characterization and impersonation" (655d). Taken together, all these analogies strongly suggest that a mimetic agonism is indeed at play in this ancient quarrel on catharsis and contagion, a mirroring quarrel that may not be as clear-cut as dominant accounts made it appear. In fact, *with* Plato Aristotle appropriates the concept of catharsis to put it to philosophical use; yet *contra* Plato he does so not to defend wine but rather to defend tragedy and poetry more generally. Then Aristotle sets out with and contra Plato to redefine tragedy as a mimesis of an action that, through dramatic impersonation, generates the catharsis of emotions like pity and fear. The agon is thus clearly set. Still, the structure of the contest generates destabilizing mirroring effects we shall have to consider in our genealogical reevaluation of the value of the catharsis hypothesis. To give specificity to this mimetic agon, we need to consider in which specific context catharsis serves as both remedy and poison, or *pharmakon*, for Aristotle as well—which takes us to ritual catharsis in *Politics*.

Ritual Catharsis in *Politics*

If *Poetics* is the paradigmatic text in which Aristotle influentially launches the concept of catharsis on the philosophical scene as an aesthetic concept, this is the moment to consider that Aristotle discusses the ritual and medical conception of catharsis in *Politics*, not in *Poetics*. And he does so in a context devoted to the formative qualities of education in general and of music in particular, not of poetry—let alone the specific genre that he is discussing in the *Poetics* and on which both Freud's and Girard's interpretations hinge: Greek tragedy. Speaking of the pedagogical and cathartic effects of music, Aristotle writes in *Politics* 8.7, in the concluding pages of his treatise:

> For feelings such as pity and fear, or, again, enthusiasm, exist very strongly in some souls and have more or less influence over all. Some persons fall into a religious frenzy, and we see them restored as a result of the sacred melodies—when they have used the melodies which excite the soul to mystic frenzy—we see them restored as though they had found healing (*therapeia*) and purgation (*katharsis*). Those who are influenced by pity or fear, and every emotional nature, must have a like experience, and others insofar as each is susceptible to such emotions, and are all in a manner purged and their souls lighted and delighted.[17]

In a ritual context, then, music that generates emotions such as pity and fear, as well as enthusiasm, has the power to purge these affects via a form of irrational and pleasurable participation Aristotle compares to a "mystic frenzy" characteristic of religious rituals, which, as Lacan also recognized in a Nietzschean echo, generate a state of "Dionysian frenzy."[18] Although the cathartic diagnostic of ritual mimesis in *Politics* resonates directly with catharsis in theatrical mimesis in *Poetics*,[19] important differences need to be signaled. What is at play here is a musical ritual, not a tragic spectacle; it is not a question of (visual) representations but of (ritual) participation; not of Apollonian mimesis but of Dionysian mimesis, to use Nietzschean categories. Thus reframed, mimesis is a constitutive part of the diagnostic of ritual catharsis, for Aristotle is attentive to the mimetic effects of music, such as frenzy and enthusiasm. That is, affects that take possession of the participants via the dispossessing pathos of mimesis. This is why he writes in *Politics* 8.5 that "rhythm and melody supply imitations of anger and gentleness" (*Pol.* 8.5: 1340a19; 2126), making clear that this form of imitation is not primarily representational and visual but affective and embodied. Ritual catharsis can thus not easily be peeled off from mimesis understood as contagious or intoxicating ritual affects, if only because they are two sides of the same Janus-faced problem.

The specific question, then, is not whether catharsis is a mimetic or an anti-mimetic concept, but rather it is a question of which diagnostic catharsis entails. Should this diagnostic be restricted to religious rituals based on mimesis understood as a frenzied pathos? Or should it also be linked to tragic and violent spectacles based on mimesis understood as representation of an action? In a passage of *Politics* that introduces the cathartic effects of music and establishes a link with *Poetics*, Aristotle writes: "We maintain further that music should be studied, not for the sake of one, but of many benefits, that is to say, with a view to education, or purgation"; and then he adds, in parenthesis: "(the word 'purgation' [*katharsis*] we use at present without explanation, but when hereafter we speak of poetry we will treat the subject with more precision)" (*Pol.* 8.7: 1341b.36–40; 2128). If we follow carefully the vicissitudes of the catharsis hypothesis in Aristotle's thought, we are caught in a hermeneutic circle: one clue in *Politics* leads to another clue in *Poetics*, which then leads back to the same clue "without explanation," in a circular hermeneutical process that might promise therapy in religious rituals but is maddening in philological practice. No wonder that philologists had to play the role of detectives.

In this circular account of catharsis much remains, indeed, without explanation. Still, at least two related points are clear. Despite its irrational, frenzied, and contagious character, the mimetic effects of music, in a carefully ritualized context that is not restricted to the aesthetic notion of mimesis understood as an "imitation of an action" (*mimesis praxeôs*), are not only pathological for the "frenzy" they entail; they are also potentially therapeutic, for catharsis generates "benefits" that are compatible with "education" and perhaps with an aesthetic education as well. Hence, catharsis does not have a single explanation but, not unlike its conceptual counterpart, mimesis, is simultaneously tied to both intoxication and education, mimetic pathologies and patho-*logies*. In short, both mimesis and catharsis have the Janus-faced patho(-)logical characteristics of a pharmakon.

This genealogical detour via Aristotle's *Politics* puts us in a position to better evaluate Bernays's medical interpretation of catharsis. Despite the fact that catharsis is left "without explanation" in *Politics*, the passage I quoted is the very foundation on which Bernays's entire medical interpretation, and at one additional remove, its psychoanalytical, mimetic, and popular appropriations, had actually rested. The passage is well chosen for such a philological operation.

In fact, the language Aristotle mobilizes in *Politics* is clearly medical and ritualistic more than aesthetic or moral. Hence, it allows Bernays to take a stance against the aesthetic/moral interpretations that were dominant in the neoclassical period. This also means that in this ritual context, catharsis does not entail a type of observation of a theatrical representation from a rational *distance*, a distance that is doubled in case a tragedy is not seen but read, as Aristotle envisioned. Rather, this passage entails a direct ritual and thus bodily and collective participation in musical rituals that generate irrational states of enthusiastic frenzy, or pathos. True, this mimetic pathos, especially in excitable and unbalanced souls, was part of what Aristotle calls a "crowd" (*Pol.* 8.7:1342a20; 2129), triggers a pathological state of enthusiastic frenzy akin to "Bacchic frenzy" (1342b5)—hence its analogy with what Plato had already defined as a pharmakon in the sense of "poison."[20] Still, for Aristotle, the ultimate effect of this mystical participation is therapeutic in the end for it generates a *katharsis* of pity and fear that purges the frenzied soul of this affective excess—hence its evaluation as what Aristotle considers a pharmakon in the sense of "cure." The mimetic agonism, indeed, generates mirroring effects that allow us to reflect critically on the more general problematic of the effects of representations of violence.

From Aristotle to (New) Media Violence

Reaching back to the ritual origins of the catharsis hypothesis in classical antiquity brings us back to the contemporary cinematic scene with which we started, urging us to consider both the pathological and patho-*logical* effects of frenzied rituals. This is, in fact, the very same riddle at the center of *Vice*, a film that, we are now in a position to confirm, reloads an ancient riddle on catharsis and contagion in the sphere of cinematic and virtual phantasies, which are representative of contemporary manifestations of (new) media violence characteristic of the digital age. The media change and new diagnostics are called for. Still, the agonist evaluations of the effects of violent rituals and representations thereof remain eerily similar—that is, Janus-faced.

On one side, you will recall that participants in the VICE resort partake in frenzied and sexualized musical rituals with so-called artificial women (played by real actresses) in which they dance to the sound of intoxicating

Julian Michaels (Bruce Willis) and VICE Resort in *Vice* (dir. Brian Miller, 2015)

techno music that generates ecstatic states characteristic of what we call "raves"—a ritual experience supposed to get violent affects out of people's system and "keeps the city going," as the chief of police puts it.

What the movie suggests, then, is that an embodied enactment of mimetic pathos in ritualized, musical contexts can be potentially therapeutic if the necessary measures are present to prevent contagious outbreaks of violence. On the other side, *Vice* also indicates the diagnostic possibility that such experiences do not remain confined within the sphere of fictional representations but generate pathological effects, leading to contagious addictions, numbing, physical violence, and, in extreme cases, assault and

murder—a pathological experience of which people "can't get enough"—as
the detective suggests.

This Janus-faced diagnostic is, in turn, redoubled if we consider that
what is at stake in *Vice* is not simply an evaluation of the pathological and
therapeutic effects at play in bodily experiences whose aesthetic origins can
be traced back to Dionysian rituals characterized by intoxicating music,
frenzied dances, sexual orgies, and sacrificial violence. Rather, the world of
Vice with its "artificial" girls and transgressive experiences is, as we noted,
metaphorical of digital societies with reduced physical participation further
diminished by pandemic crises in which people rarely participate in potentially therapeutic qua violent ritual experiences, on one side. But on the
other side, they regularly observe such artificial and violent spectacles from a
digital, representational distance via all kinds of (new) media and immersive
experiences (film, TV, internet porn, video games, etc.) that increasingly
stand in for "reality" itself. This second level concerns spectators of films like
Vice, for instance, but also applies to the post-cinematic world of TV series,
internet pornography, video games, and the violent second lives played out
in artificial virtual platforms to which *Vice* clearly alludes. This brave new
world of media violence now stretches to include "reality-crime shows" that
are popular in the UK, United States, and Russia and go as far as "showing
corpses from car crashes, fires and murders."[21] In a distant echo of a gesture
that goes back to the origins of cathartic theory, *Vice* is interesting for our
genealogical reevaluation because it poses the key question of the transition
of violence from a ritual (embodied) context to an aesthetic (visual) context,
from something felt to something seen, from representational mimesis to
homo mimeticus; and above all, it questions the therapeutic value of catharsis
in this paradigmatic transition that is constitutive of (new) media violence in
the digital age.

If we now step back to observe the ground covered so far, we are in a position to see that, in a general sense, our genealogy generated a loop that goes
from modernity to antiquity and brought us back to the present. Overall, it
lends support to Girard's anthropological hypothesis of the pharmaceutical
properties of catharsis when it concerns ritual experiences in real life. In a
carefully ritualized, musical, collective context, an affective participation in
states of communal frenzy can potentially have cathartic effects that are beneficial for individual and communal bodies and souls alike—thereby being

beneficial for the body politic more generally. If Girard stresses the cathartic properties of violence discharged on a pharmakos that cannot strike back, Aristotle has a much broader understanding of katharsis that does not rest on sacrificial murders but on ritual music and festivity instead. Think of a carnival more than of a lynching. The ritual context of *Politics* also partially justifies renderings of the meaning of catharsis in terms of "purgation" of pathological emotions that require an affective, ritual, and thus embodied participation in order to turn the poison into the remedy. Last but not least, in the sphere of theory, it also opens the door to a model of the unconscious that, in its Freudian, Girardian, or Derridean variations, continues to hinge on the case of Oedipus as a paradigmatic example to account for tragic identifications with potentially cathartic effects.

And yet the diagnostic is not unilateral. Since these contemporary accounts of catharsis stem from a representation rather than from a ritual, from *Oedipus Rex* rather than from the ritual paeans the play alludes to, a number of complications arise. In fact, a ritualized form of affective participation in frenzied song and dance is not the same as a visual representation of an action, no matter how fearful and pitiful this action is or may be. The fundamental distinction between competing forms of mimesis (representation/impersonation, visual/embodied, Apollonian/Dionysian) central to the mimetic turn or re-turn toward homo mimeticus is thus the key to the rather masked problem internal to the riddle of catharsis. A diagnostic approach to the embodied effects of representations of violence also reframes the riddle of the discovery of the unconscious by asking a more specific genealogical question we are now ready to confront: why of all possible myths available in the western tradition, one particular myth, or rather, tragedy, continues to serve as the paradigmatic example when it comes to theories of the unconscious that advocate a cathartic method?[22] Michel Henry in his "radical critique of psychoanalysis" (*GP* 343) is right to point out that "Freudian mythology has the seriousness of all mythology" (14), which also means that other myths ought to be equally considered. Is, then, the obsessive focus on *Oedipus Rex* due to its universal ahistorical truth, or is it rather the effect of a series of philosophical, philological, and psychological choices?

The stakes of these questions are particularly high when it comes to the Oedipus myth, and the theories of catharsis and of the unconscious it triggered. In order to answer them, or at least attempt to provide the genealogical foundations for answering them, there is no real shortcut; we need to shift from the ritual context of Aristotle's discussion of catharsis in *Politics* to the aesthetic context of one of the most influential philosophical texts in western aesthetics.

Aesthetic Catharsis in the *Poetics*

Aristotle's *Poetics* (*Peri poietikês*), as the title says, is a treatise on the art or techne of poetry understood as the making of poetry in general and tragic drama in particular. It is in many ways a continuation of Aristotle's agonism with Plato's condemnation of mimesis as irrational, pathological, and far removed from the truth. What we must immediately recall now, if we approach it from the angle of modern interpretations of the unconscious, is a basic philological fact: namely that Aristotle's *Poetics* in general, and his account of catharsis of emotions generated by this incestuous, murderous, and familial drama in particular, also happens to rest—you certainly guessed it—on Sophocles's *Oedipus Rex*. Of all possible plays, *Oedipus Rex* serves as a paradigmatic aesthetic example of a complex tragic plot based on a unity of action, a recognition of a tragic fault, and a reversal of fortune, which the treatise sets up as a model for future playwrights to imitate. As Aristotle puts it, "the finest recognition occurs in direct conjunction with reversal—as with the one in the *Oedipus*" (P 43). And then, via the example of *Oedipus Rex*, Aristotle sets out to articulate the aesthetic principle of tragic plots that rest on reversals of fortune and tragic recognition, which gives birth not only to western poetics and to a number of tragedies predicated on this model, but also to theories of catharsis, mimesis, and the unconscious—all of which are primarily based on this particular fictional model.

Does the privilege given to *Oedipus Rex* of all tragic plays available in classical antiquity originate in Aristotle? The logic of mimetic agonism urges us to look for precursors. Note that the figure of Oedipus already makes a surreptitious entrance in Plato's critique of the pathos generated by desires that occur in dreams in *Republic*, as he writes: "In the matter of our desires, I do not think we sufficiently distinguish their nature and number" (*Rep.* 571a, 798). And addressing "lawless desires" that are "awakened in sleep" and speak to the "beastly and savage part [of the soul]" he—Plato, that is,

Socrates—adds: "You are aware that in such case there is nothing it will not venture to undertake as being released from all sense of shame and all reason. It does not shrink from attempting to lie with a mother in fancy or with anyone else, man, god, or brute" (*Rep.* 571 c–d). *Pace* Freud's originality, the link between the myth of Oedipus and theories of dreams is indeed as old as Plato, which does not mean that the myth must be true. On the contrary, it simply suggests that due to the cultural primacy of *Oedipus Rex*, Oedipal dreams have an influential genealogy in theory that can be mimetically reproduced in a series of footnotes to Plato and Aristotle, to be traced in modern and contemporary thinkers, from Bernays to Freud to Girard.

With this genealogical point in mind, let us ask a theoretical question by adopting the point of view of the active theorist, not of the passive disciple: is it a simple coincidence that ambitious modern theorists, such as Freud and, later, Girard, will gravitate toward the very same Greek play at the center of Aristotle's influential "manual," to develop their theoretical accounts of catharsis based on Oedipal triangles? And is their theory of the unconscious, true or false, not ultimately dependent on the interpretation of this particular play? Since the past, Freudian century mimetically conditioned us to do so, it is of course tempting to answer such question by automatically relying on the so-called universality of the Oedipal myth.

This is, indeed, a well-traveled route, even among sophisticated theorists whose refined historical and aesthetic judgment can at times succumb to the spell of a psychoanalytic myth. A literary theorist well versed in the art of tragedy like Terry Eagleton, for instance, rightly notes in his historically informed and passionate book on tragedy, *Sweet Violence* (2003), that "it is remarkable how many general theories of tragedy have been spun out of a mere two or three texts [*Oedipus Rex in primis*]."[23] And yet even a Marxist theorist intimately at ease in materialist and dialectical thinking like Eagleton does not see the historical contradiction in uncritically endorsing "Freud's teaching that the most tumultuous crisis of our early lives is scripted by an ancient tragic drama."[24] We may wonder: Is this script designating a universal truth? Or is it the historical product of a general theory of tragedy spun out of the same old myth?

In the dialectical agon confronting a universal interpretation contra a contingent genealogy, it seems that it is Eagleton the Marxist more than Eagleton the Freudian who might be closer to historical reality. To be sure, the advantage of scripting the plurality of our psychic lives within a universal monomyth has not gone unnoticed by epistemically oriented theorists, but this does not mean that the Oedipal myth provides the only key to all interpretative riddles. From the perspective of science studies, Bruno Latour puts it succinctly: "With one word in the critic's repertoire, for instance 'Oedipus complex,' you can explain four dozen novels and five hundred plays."[25] In an age dominated by the academic imperative of publishing or perishing, there is a certain advantage in mechanically reproducing the same critical formula over and over again. It might make the difference between a published and a perished academic. Yet, even if the pressures to conform are high, lest we essentialize the unconscious in an ideal tragic universal form, couldn't we take the less traveled route, inverse the diagnostic, and aim to do genealogical justice to the conditions of emergence of a theory? This entails setting up a mirror to Oedipal critics and theorists and ask again: couldn't it be that it is because theories of tragedy were spun on the model of few plays of which *Oedipus Rex* is the primary example, that Freud developed a theory of tumultuous Oedipal crises modeled on that play and subsequently generalized it to a universal complex?

Genealogical lenses suggest that the latter is the most likely hypothesis. It pays attention to the emergence of a theory from the point of view of the theorist that creates—one needs to be a theorist to unmask another theory. We are, of course, not alone. This mimetic hypothesis has a chain of genealogically connected texts to support it, rather than dreams that mimetically conform to the theory of the analyst doing the interpretation—one needs to have shared texts to develop falsifiable interpretations. Equally remarkable is how theoretical allegiances to schools of thought formed early in one's career can lead masters of dialectical thinking to miss striking historical contradictions. Rather than taking this circular logic as proof of the universality of the Oedipus complex, I propose the following genealogical principle: what may appear to be theoretical coincidences, or the product of universal truths about the unconscious, turn out on closer examination to bear the traces of genealogical influences. The problem when it comes to the evaluation of mimetic theories is that their genealogical connections with classical antiquity actually complicate, rather than support, modern medical theories of catharsis and the unconscious based on an Oedipal myth. This leads us to our second genealogical perspective necessary to come to a better understanding of the untranslatable concept of catharsis.

For some time, contemporary commentators of the *Poetics* have tended to be skeptical of medical (or pathological) standpoints on catharsis and the ahistorical psychoanalytical interpretations they gave rise to. Instead, they have offered more nuanced textual and contextual accounts of the relation between affective and rational, conscious and unconscious responses at play in this enigmatic concept in the *Poetics* itself.

On the textual front, the classicist Gerald Else, for instance, in a lengthy and authoritative study on the *Poetics*, frontally challenges Bernays's assumption that "we come to the tragic drama (unconsciously, if you will) as patients to be cured, relieved, restored to psychic health."[26] What is Freud's uncle-in-law's evidence for this now popular view, Else critically asks? For him, the evidence is one that you can textually confirm yourself: "There is not a word to support this in the *Poetics*, not a hint that the end of drama is to cure or alleviate pathological states"; Else adds: "On the contrary, it is evident in every line of the work that Aristotle is presupposing normal auditors, normal states of mind and feeling, normal emotional and aesthetic experiences."[27] A pathological state, then, is not originally presupposed, and thus neither is a therapeutic cure, which does not mean that both pathologies and cures cannot be belatedly projected onto the text by apprentice philological physicians in urgent need of a therapeutic method.

More recently, Stephen Halliwell, one of the leading commentators and translators of Aristotle's *Poetics*, while disagreeing with Else on other minor philological points—they are not in a conspiracy—is equally skeptical about the purgation hypothesis, which he calls nothing less than a "travesty" or "falsification of Aristotle's position and of the larger philosophical psychology that underpins it."[28] Instead, Halliwell stresses the aesthetic (as opposed to the therapeutic and ritual) properties of Aristotle's account of catharsis. As he puts it in his commentary of *Poetics*:

> the likelihood presents itself that *katharsis* does not stand for a notion of pure outlet or emotional release, still less for a discharge of *pathological* emotions. It is more probable that the idea of release is only part of a more complex concept built around Ar.'s belief that the emotions have a natural and proper role in the mind's experience of reality (*P* 90).

It is true that this reduction of emotions to the mind, pathos to logos, affect to reason, in a passage that after all has to do with visceral affects such as pity and fear, may sound excessively rational and analytic to ears—like the present author's—more accustomed to continental philosophy. On such a divisive academic riddle, academic quarrels between competing schools of thought, and thus of interpretation, are likely to play an important role. But it is equally true that Halliwell has a nuanced formal point in mind that is not at all inimical to continental approaches to the *Poetics*.

The French philosopher Philippe Lacoue-Labarthe, for instance, one of Girard's most acute early interlocutors and a key figure in the recent mimetic turn to homo mimeticus, makes a similar point when it comes to the role understanding plays in cathartic relief. Lacoue-Labarthe writes, in fact, that if catharsis "relives pain [*soulage*], if it renders the unbearable bearable, it is because it offers the possibility to *understand* what, for thought or reason alone, would otherwise remain strictly incomprehensible."[29] This is, after all, a point in line with Aristotle's defense of poetry and thus of mimesis. As Aristotle famously states, contra Plato, "poetry is both more philosophical and more serious that history" (*P* 41). Why? Because the laws of causality and necessity that are at play in the construction of a tragic plot, or *muthos*, generate a pleasure in understanding that is akin to philosophical pleasure. This is why Lacoue-Labarthe qualifies this affective understanding at play in catharsis in terms of "emotions of thought [*emotions de la pensée*]." Halliwell speaks of "emotional understanding." Their point is essentially the same. For both French and North American philosophers, what is at play in the contemplation of aesthetic representations of violence is not a process that takes place through reason alone or emotion alone, fully consciously or completely unconsciously. Rather, it emerges, perhaps not from the harmony but from the dynamic interplay between body and mind, affect and reason, or, to use the more ancient terms characteristic of our theory of imitation, pathos and logos, or patho-logy that is constitutive of tragedy qua mimesis of an action, which is "serious, complete" and thus endowed with a "beginning, middle and end" (*P* 37, 39).[30]

Shifting to a more general contextual level, Halliwell develops this hypothesis in *Between Ecstasy and Truth* (2011), a book that situates Aristotelian catharsis beyond the case of Oedipus by considering the broader context of Greek poetics in general. In his view, such a poetics, of which

Aristotle's is the most exemplary manifestation, oscillates between a concern with emotional states of enthusiasm, entrancement, or ecstasy (pathos) on the one hand, and more rational concerns with truth and reason (or logos) on the other, generating a form of "emotional understanding" that, in order to be properly diagnosed, requires philological physicians "to integrate psychology, ethics, and aesthetics."[31] The phrase "emotional understanding" might still sound oxymoronic to some modern (Cartesian) readers. Still, the idea that rational diagnostics stem from an involvement in the sphere of affect is not unfamiliar to self-proclaimed philosophical physicians qua gene-alogists concerned with the discovery of the unconscious who are currently informing recent returns of attention to embodiment, affect, and mimesis. The philosopher who, for us, acts as mediator between the ancients and the moderns and provides important foundations for our theory of homo mime-ticus, namely, Nietzsche, is a case in point. From *The Birth of Tragedy* (1872) onward, Nietzsche's genealogy of mimesis oscillates between Dionysian and Apollonian principles, violent unmediated pathos and rational mediating distance, generating patho-*logies* that inform an account of the mimetic unconscious that does not set up a dualism between affect and reason, the mind and the body.[32]

This does not mean that affect (pathos) in general, and painful affects triggered by violent tragic scenes in particular, are not constitutive of Aristo-tle's account (logos) of catharsis. Aristotle, for one, mentions representations of suffering, including "a destructive or painful action, such as visible deaths, torments, woundings, and other things of the same kind" (*P* 43) crucial in the generation of pity and fear and the catharsis that follows. Hence, he includes suffering as a main component of the plot-structure. Yet, and somewhat significantly, Aristotle does not make a visual representation of suffering a necessary condition for catharsis to take place. As he puts it: "even without seeing a performance, anyone who *hears the events* which occur will experience terror and pity as a result of the outcome; this is what some would feel while *hearing* the plot of the *Oedipus*" (45; my emphasis). Hearing, or simply reading, a tragedy, for Aristotle, generates tragic affects.

Given this focus on listening, Lacoue-Labarthe, in a dialogue with Jean-Luc Nancy on the Aristotelian concept of the "scene" or "spectacle" (*opsis*), notes: "Aristotle, it is clear, doesn't like what I call here—for convenience's sake but I hope without forcing—the spectacular [*le spectaculaire*]."[33] This

Aristotelian dislike, or "sobriety," as Lacoue-Labarthe also calls it, includes the spectacle of violent acts, of course, based on "gesture, mimicry, figural corporation . . . and music."[34] Thus Lacoue-Labarthe concludes: "trying to provoke katharsis by other means, that is by the use of spectacular means, does not correspond to the essence of tragedy."[35] This insight relies on the fact that Aristotle develops a poetics that, contrary to Plato's, as we shall see in volume 2, no longer relies on the primacy of oral performance but focuses on textuality and listening. Being able to agree on this basic philological point would already go a long way in excluding a number of contemporary spectacles from the scope of Aristotle's catharsis hypothesis. To put it bluntly, for Aristotle, you need a tragic plot, not a violent show, for catharsis of pity and fear to potentially ensue.

The Italian classicist Pier Luigi Donini comes to the same conclusion from a different perspective. He points out that it is "impossible" that the ritual context of musical catharsis in *Politics* "could be directly transferred to the effects of tragedy, which as Aristotle repeatedly said with absolute clarity, reaches its goal even only when read, without representation, music and signing."[36] Nor does it mean that the pathos of tragedy is subordinated to, contained, let alone repressed by a rational logos. For although poetry, in Aristotle's famous formulation I already mentioned, is "more philosophical and more serious than history," tragedy (or poetry) is not a philosophical treatise (or poetics); it is the dynamic interplay between emotion and thought, pathos and logos, generated by a complex plot that can potentially generate catharsis in theory—and perhaps in practice as well.

The essential point for us to bear in mind, then, is the following: the father of a cathartic theory so influential that it traverses western aesthetics, informs nineteenth-century theories of the unconscious, is constitutive of twentieth-century theories of violence, and even resurfaces in contemporary blockbusters and popular culture more generally at the dawn of the twenty-first century, consistently subordinates such representations of violence to the specific formal properties of Greek tragedy—most notably the "reversal" (*peripeteia*) and "recognition" (*anagnôrisis*) that, for Aristotle, define a "complex" plot-structure (*mythos*) whose paradigmatic example is, as we saw, Sophocles's *Oedipus Rex*. Thus, Aristotle writes in chapter 7 that "tragedy's greatest means of emotional power are components of the plot-structure, namely reversals and recognitions" (*P* 38). That is, it plots a reversal of fortune and recognition of a tragic fault characteristic of an exemplary hero who is neither base in character (as in comedy) nor infallible but, rather, is "like ourselves" (44), and thus occupies the position of a figure with whom balanced, sane, and sympathetic spectators can potentially identify.

Aristotle confirms this formal point repeatedly. For instance, as he writes that "for such a combination of recognition and reversal will produce pity or fear (and it is events of this kind that tragedy, on our definition, is a mimesis of)" (43). Or again, in chapter 14, as he states: "The effect of fear and pity can arise from theatrical spectacle, but it can also arise from the intrinsic structure of events, and it is this which matters more and is the task of a superior poet" (45). Time and again, Aristotle stresses that it is not representations of violence, nor even emotions, that make a tragedy superior and thus potentially cathartic, but the "intrinsic structure of events" or the making of a complex *muthos* instead. On the basis of such passages and other accounts of catharsis in Aristotle's work that had already attracted Bernays's attention (most notably those from *Politics* we have considered), Halliwell argues that what is ultimately at stake in catharsis is a "form of conversion of painful into pleasurable emotion within the contemplation (*theória*) of mimetic simulations of reality."[37]

Mimesis can indeed not be peeled off from catharsis; nor is the mimetic patho-*logy* constitutive of homo mimeticus inimical to cathartic pathos. An identification on the side of the audience that triggers a sym-pathos with the tragic hero, who is a victim of his tragic destiny rather than a mere perpetrator of violence, is thus implicitly presupposed for the representation of a complex action to generate a patho-*logical* interplay constitutive of cathartic effects. It is, in fact, once spectators' identification with the tragic pathos of the suffering hero—who, again, is not a simple murderer but an exemplary individual or king with a tragic flaw—is channeled by the reversal and recognition mechanisms internal to the mimetic action of the plot that a pleasurable cathartic conversion can potentially take place. Notice also that although pity and fear are routinely identified as manifestations of tragic pathos, there is an interesting push-pull between these rather different affects that sets in motion a pendular movement we are by now familiar with. If pity implies an affective movement that goes from the self to the tragic hero whose pathos is contemplated from a distance, fear is predicated on a mirroring inversion that starts from the recognition of a danger that may be perceived from a distance yet is intimately felt nonetheless.[38]

This double movement between pathos and distance constitutes the palpitating heart of our theory of mimesis. It traces the oscillating, vibratory, and intersubjective interplay of mimetic communication Nietzsche grouped under the concept of "pathos of distance"; Georges Bataille identified it in terms of "attraction and repulsion." In our language, it is because homo mimeticus is a relational, porous, and affective creature fundamentally open to the experience of pathos coming from the outside that the ability to set up a protective distance is vital for the preservation of individuation. Conversely, the boundaries of individuation that appear stable and close from a distance are easily blurred by the experience of sym-pathos that attracts us toward others, including tragic others impersonating violent roles via fictional spectacles or representations we can safely contemplate with pathos from a distance. The riddle of the pleasure of tragedy and its potential cathartic effect may thus well emerge from this tensional push-pull between pathos and distance characteristic of an affective identification with a tragic hero on one side and the realization that this tragedy is but a fiction to be contemplated from a safe distance on the other.[39]

There are a number of indications that support this oscillating hypothesis constitutive of our theory of mimesis. Reformulating Aristotle's tragic principles for his Romantic theory of the sublime, Edmund Burke expresses this pathos of distance as follows: "for terror is a passion which always produces delight when it does not press too close, and pity is a passion accompanied with pleasure, because it arises from love and social affection."[40] More recently, neuroscientist Vittorio Gallese suggests an analogous principle in line with our genealogy. Promoted to reflect on the Aristotelian riddle of catharsis from a neurological perspective attentive to mirroring reflexes, Gallese states: "It's too early to answer the question [of catharsis]." In a speculative move, he turns to Girard's treatment of mimetic rivalry in search of a source of inspiration. Interestingly, however, rather than engaging directly with Girard's own theory of catharsis, Gallese proposes the following hypothesis: "We enjoy watching comedy and tragedy as much as we do because we see a conflict reenacted—a conflict from which we feel safe, because we stare at it from a safe distance. . . . So it's a blend, so to speak, of identifying with the conflict while simultaneously feeling it from a safe distance."[41] I fully subscribe to this view, which, it should be noticed, focuses on aesthetic pleasure rather than cathartic therapies. My only genealogical correction is that this pathos of distance internal to the safety of a visual (Apollonian) representation and the proximity of an embodied (Dionysian) identification may not be central to Girard's theory of desire and violence, which is based on structural (or triangular) foundations we considered in some detail. It is, however, constitutive of a dynamic movement (or oscillation) between pathos and distance central to our modernist mimetic theory. In fact, a dynamic interplay between affective identification and aesthetic representation, emotion and understanding, pathos and logos is at the palpitating heart that sets a theory of homo mimeticus in motion. It might also serve as the affective-rational patho-logical movement at play in Aristotle's passing yet influential and untranslatable mention of catharsis.[42]

Now that some specific textual and contextual evidence has been presented, and an attempt at translation of an untranslatable concept has been made, we are ready to reevaluate the riddle of catharsis from a more distant and informed perspective.

The Riddle of Catharsis Reevaluated

We were wondering if violence, or, at an additional remove, a representation of violence that makes a pathos present, could have unconscious, purgative, therapeutic effects. We wanted to know if deep down, and quite universally, all boys unconsciously want to reenact in phantasy or reality the bloody deeds of Oedipus, and, for girls, of Electra, originally performed on a fictional stage. Killing the father and desiring the mother; desiring the father and killing the mother—fictional models for the audience to identify with generating a strange world of phantoms, indeed. And last but not least, we wanted to know if a dramatic reenactment would entail a recognition that could cure us from the very violence internal to such representations. While a modern conception of the Oedipal unconscious influenced a centenary generation to automatically believe in such cathartic hypotheses as they were applied to contexts as diverse as sacrificial rituals and theatrical plays, psychoanalytic couches, and now cinematic fictions, a genealogy of the mimetic theories on which the discovery of this unconscious rests teaches us otherwise.

Despite the scholarly disagreements on what catharsis means exactly, or what role it plays in aesthetic theory, the most scholarly informed accounts of the *Poetics* make at least one point clear: it is not violence as such, or a simple representation or reenactment of violence—let alone Oedipal violence—that is in itself cathartic. Rather, it the complex aesthetic structure of a carefully construed tragic plot—what Gerald Else calls "a feature of the structure"—that generates a form of "emotional understanding" with potential cathartic effects among healthy individuals.[43] Even philosophical readers sympathetic to Freud and not particularly concerned with the contagious dimension of dramatic mimesis confirm this fundamental aesthetic point. Paul Ricoeur, for instance, writes: "Whatever the term *catharsis* means it is generated by the plot itself."[44] In the absence of such complex formal features based on reversal and recognition constitutive of the art of poetry, no catharsis can possibly ensue.[45]

To put it in a Nietzschean diagnostic, catharsis is not triggered by an automatic discharge of tragic emotions such as pity and fear anytime we see representations of violence on a stage or screen—bodies shot, torn to pieces, exploded, etc.—and may vicariously experience some pathos from a distance. It is rather the product of a complex mimetic patho(-)logy understood as both mimetic pathos and critical logos, affective participation and rational understanding, which, once set in a systolic and diastolic movement by a complex narrative structure, can potentially have beneficial cathartic effects. In sum, it is not representations of violence itself but the dynamic interplay of pathos and logos, conscious actions and unconscious reactions that may, in the case of aesthetic texts with a very specific formal structure that are represented in homeopathic, not massive, doses, have the power to convert violent pathologies into pleasurable, instructive, and potentially transformative patho-*logies*.

If we join our two genealogical perspectives constitutive of our attempt to translate an untranslatable concept, we can say this to conclude this rather technical but hopefully clarifying chapter: both the ritual context on the side of life *and* the aesthetic text on the side of fiction, ritual mimesis and aesthetic mimesis, constitute the defining cultural frames that, for Aristotle, have the power to put a mimetic experience to cathartic and educational use. Yet this is a far cry from saying that violence as such, or identification with the perpetrator of violence characteristic of contemporary (new) media such as film or video games, can automatically benefit from a catharsis hypothesis. Quite the contrary.

For the moment, a consideration of catharsis in Aristotle's classical yet enigmatic diagnostic encourages us to continue to rely on modernist thinkers who dared to go beyond the cathartic principle in order to open up alternative accounts of the unconscious—which does not mean that mimetic principles stop being at play.

CHAPTER 4

Beyond the Cathartic Principle

Nietzsche on Influence

After this genealogical investigation in some of the most prominent theoretical vicissitudes of the catharsis hypothesis in the so-called Freudian century, the original meaning of catharsis continues to remain elusive in theory, not to speak of its therapeutic efficacy in practice. Yet stepping back to ancient theories has given us a fresh, more distant, and, I would hope, more informed perspective to reevaluate the value of what remains a modernist hypothesis for our post-Freudian century. This detour via the ancients allows us to re-turn to the moderns in order to lay out psychological and aesthetic principles that go beyond the catharsis hypothesis. For this genealogical operation, I will rely on an influential modernist figure who, due to his genealogical training and future-oriented diagnostic aspirations, plays a critical role in both mediating between the ancients and the moderns in general, and in articulating a theory of homo mimeticus that speaks to contemporary concerns directly relevant to the problematic of violence and the unconscious in particular: a self-proclaimed "philosophical physician" whose name is Friedrich Nietzsche.

Nietzsche's distinctive contributions to our theory of the mimetic subject are multiple. He provides the genealogical method we pursue to account for both the pathologies and patho-*logies* of homo mimeticus central to the modernist and contemporary period, and are constitutive of the mimetic turn, or re-turn of mimesis.[1] For the purpose of our genealogy of violence and the unconscious, I recall three mimetic perspectives we shall continue to pursue in his company. First, relying on his training in classics, Nietzsche recuperated the ancient realization that not only desire but all affects generate contagious continuities between self and others that disrupt the boundaries of individuation—a point constitutive of what I call mimetic pathos. Second, Nietzsche developed a physio-psychological approach to the unconscious that does not set up an opposition between mind and body, psyche and soma, but is attentive to the affective power of the body to influence the psyche and vice versa via actions and reactions that are not under the volitional control of consciousness—a point characteristic of what I call the mimetic unconscious. And third, Nietzsche foregrounds a characteristic modernist ambivalence, tension, or oscillation with respect to the power of mimesis that is not simply inimical to mimetic pathos. Instead, it exploits a partial implication or vulnerability to pathos and the pathologies it entails in order to develop a perspectival clinical distance to diagnose the body and soul of homo mimeticus via the tools of a type of reason (or logos) that is deeply entangled in bodily affects (or pathos)—what I call mimetic patho-*logies*.

Let us now join these three related patho-*logical* perspectives in order to deepen our diagnostic evaluation of the riddle of catharsis from the angle of Nietzsche's genealogy of the moral, aesthetic, and psychic influence of art on spectators. As Robert Pippin recognizes, for Nietzsche there is a "deep interconnection or inseparability between psychology and genealogy"[2] in general, and this applies to his genealogy of the catharsis hypothesis in particular as well. Nietzsche never devoted a complete study to catharsis, but given his training in classics, his specific focus on tragedy, and the centrality of this concept to aesthetics and psychic drives more generally, his take on catharsis punctuates his corpus beginning, middle, and end. While changing in perspectives and evaluations, Nietzsche's diagnostic is fully inscribed in our genealogy for it entails a critical evaluation of Aristotle's cathartic theory in the *Poetics*, and, closer to him, of Jacob Bernays's medical interpretation of catharsis in favor of a more aesthetic reevaluation we shall soon consider.

Before we do so, however, let us change perspective, invert chronology, and consider Nietzsche's psychology from the angle of his most famous contemporary and successor who, on the shoulders of the very same genealogy, relied on the cathartic method to discover, or, perhaps, rediscover the unconscious. If we saw that Freud's reliance early in his career on the cathartic method and all it entailed (the case of Oedipus, the medical interpretation of catharsis, the centrality of tragic recognitions, etc.) was crucial to his conceptualization of the unconscious, this is the moment to recognize Nietzsche's influence in this discovery as well, which has tended to be erased. There might indeed be a romantic agonism between Nietzsche's psychology of the unconscious and his most famous successor qua competing disciple. Hence the urgency to reassess the value of a theory of violence and the unconscious that was dominant in the past century and still casts a shadow on the present century.

Freud contra Nietzsche (to Read or Not to Read)

For a long time, Nietzsche has been routinely considered a precursor of psychoanalysis—and rightly so given the striking continuities between Nietzsche's and Freud's unmasking operations. Well before Freud, Marx, and Nietzsche were celebrated as the "three masters of suspicion,"[3] in a much-repeated phrase rendered popular by Paul Ricoeur in the 1960s, Nietzsche had in fact long been recognized as a master of "uncovering" or "unmasking" psychology—a less known evaluation proposed by the German philosophical psychologist Ludwig Klages already at the dawn of the century.[4] Let us thus revisit the continuities and discontinuities between Freud and Nietzsche from a genealogical perspective that does not simply reproduce the dominant view rendered popular by the "Freudian legend" (Ellenberger's term) but, rather, opens up a minor yet nonetheless innovative and agonistic perspective on the unconscious for mimetic theorists of the future.

Freud's debts to Nietzsche are more profound than the former is willing to acknowledge, and these debts touch precisely on psychic processes and mechanisms that are constitutive of the discovery of the unconscious. Nietzsche's anticipation of insights commonly attributed to Freud are many and striking. They include not only Nietzsche's diagnostic of the "interiorization" of the soul due to a self-reflective turn in psychic violence and the "bad conscience" it generates (*GM* II, 16; 65), but also his theory of "sublimation" of cruel drives into artistic pleasure, including the pleasure of "tragic sympa-thy" (II, 7; 49), which is constitutive of cathartic experiences—an indication that, well before Freud, a tragic pathos was already operative in a psycho-logy of the unconscious. But the similarities go deeper. Nietzsche, in fact, also sets up an agon at the heart of the psyche in his theory of conflicting drives as a manifestation of the will to power; he develops a sustained critique of both idealist metaphysics and Christian religion as a "fable" or illusion; he articu-lates an account of "unconscious resistances [*unbewussten Widerständen*]" that urges psychologists to look into the "depth" and go beyond good and evil (*BGE* 23; 53) for it rests on the realization that even "good actions are sublimated [*sublimierte*] evil actions" (*HH* 107; 75); he even speaks of the dynamic of "dream-thoughts [*Traumdenken*]" (13; 21) located in what he— we are still talking about Nietzsche—repeatedly located beyond the "ego" (*Ich*) in the bodily "self" (*Selbst*) or, alternatively, in the "it" (*das Es*),[5] among other psychological insights that are, nolens volens, constitutive of the dis-covery of the unconscious.

The echoes are loud, the mirroring concepts numerous. They are so loud and numerous that it is actually surprising that Nietzsche is not the first name that comes to mind when what is at stake is a depth psychology deal-ing with sublimation, interiorization, bad conscience, and other unconscious mechanisms that, among other things, take very seriously the violence consti-tutive of all too human drives. After all, Nietzsche spoke repeatedly about the centrality of unconscious processes for psychic life in his career. He claimed for instance that "the greatest part of our spirit's activity remains unconscious [*unbewusst*]";[6] or, alternatively, that "a thought comes when 'it' wants, not when 'I' want . . . *It* thinks [*Es denkt*]" (*BGE* 17; 47); or, again, when he stated that "we as conscious, purposive creatures, are only the smallest part of us. . . . By far the greater number of motions have nothing whatever to do with consciousness" (*WP* 676; 357), among many other claims that precede the Freudian "discovery."[7]

Given these analogies, it is perhaps no accident that influential thinkers from Thomas Mann to Karl Jaspers have noted striking analogies between Nietzsche and Freud, often privileging the former as the most insightful psychologist. Mann called Nietzsche "the greatest critic and psychologist of morals known to the history of human kind" (qtd. in *DU* 272). Jaspers, in his

General Psychopatholgy (1913; revised in 1946), redoubled the compliment as he aligned Nietzsche in a genealogy of thinkers of "meaningful psychological understanding" that goes from Plato to Augustine, Montaigne to Pascal, and claimed that the German thinker along with Kierkegaard "stand out unique as the greatest of all psychologists interested in meaning."[8] The absence of Freud from Jaspers's list of insightful psychologists and the marginal role of psychoanalysis in his monumental study is significant; it also confirms the diagnostic of the more recent historians of psychology I considered in chapter 2.

Jaspers is an important precursor of critiques of psychoanalysis that will have to wait for historical approaches to come to the fore. He evaluates psychoanalysis as follows: "*As a cultural, historical phenomenon*, psychoanalysis is *popular* psychology. What Kierkegaard and Nietzsche had achieved at the highest cultural level was again achieved at a lower level and crudely reversed to correspond with the lowest level of the common man and metropolitan civilization."[9] Jaspers specifies: "Psychoanalysis made use of it [the previous psychological tradition] in a misleading way and this blocked the direct influence of psychopathology of great people such as Kierkegaard and Nietzsche. Psychoanalysis therefore is partly responsible for the general lowering of the cultural level in psychopathology as a whole."[10] What we must add is that psychoanalysis also contributed to disseminating a medical interpretation of catharsis that lowered the cultural level of theories of violence and the unconscious. Hence the importance of recuperating the pre-Freudian tradition that psychoanalysis helped erase, a psychological tradition that finds in Nietzsche a major representative who, while critical of the catharsis hypothesis, serves as a main source of inspiration for the Freudian rediscovery of the unconscious.

Freud was writing at a time Nietzsche was still alive, his influence spreading rapidly beyond the German-speaking world, infiltrating artistic circles as well. Freud could thus certainly not have ignored his closest psychological precursor. This also means that Nietzsche's psychology of the unconscious casts a long shadow on Freud's originality. The analogies listed above inevitably lead genealogists to ask the following question: did Freud read, or perhaps even plagiarize, Nietzsche? Can the origins of the Freudian discovery of the unconscious, which we saw entangled with the catharsis hypothesis, also be traced back to a disavowed Nietzschean influence that will turn out to be critical of catharsis?

Perhaps. What we can say is that Freud's influences were multiple, heterogeneous, and cannot be traced back to one single origin, for they include disciplines as diverse as medicine and psychology but also literature, anthropology, religion, mythology, and, despite his claims to the contrary, philosophy as well.[11] Still, Nietzsche stands out both for the intellectual proximity to Freud and the distance the latter consistently kept from his precursor who fostered psychology as an art of suspicion. This pathos of *distance* is by now familiar to us for it is constitutive of romantic anxieties of influence we have encountered in chapter 1. Historians of psychoanalysis have in fact long recognized the importance of Nietzsche's influence on fin de siècle European culture in general and on the discovery of the unconscious in particular. As Henri Ellenberger concisely puts it: "For those acquainted with both Nietzsche and Freud, the similarity of their thought is so obvious that there can be no question about the former's influence over the latter"; hence he adds: "Nietzsche may be considered the common source of Freud, Adler, and Jung" (*DU* 276–77)."[12] Nietzsche scholars have found a number of clues that confirm this diagnostic. As Roland Lehrer puts it in one of the most comprehensive studies devoted to this genealogical connection, "it was virtually impossible for Freud not being influenced by Nietzsche."[13] What is not fully clear as yet is the mimetic paradox that animates Freud's ambivalent attitude toward Nietzsche that can be summarized as follows: on one side, Freud openly acknowledged Nietzsche's "introspective" genius and sporadically remarked on how the latter's intuitions "agreed in the most astonishing way with the laborious findings of psychoanalysis" (qtd. in *DU* 277). On the other side, Freud consistently denied having been influenced by Nietzsche whose works he claims to have acquired only in 1900 (though he mentions him in some correspondence with Eduard Silberstein as early as 1875). To increase suspicion among genealogists he claims not to have studied Nietzsche because he (Nietzsche) was too close to psychoanalysis and/or because he (Freud) was "too lazy."[14]

To read or not to read Nietzsche—that seems to have been Freud's question.

Of course, Freud was anything but lazy. Hence, genealogists like Foucault admit having been "struck by Freud's astonishing silence" on Nietzsche, finding it "enigmatic."[15] Subsequent attempts at explaining this silence exist, but the enigma is not fully solved. Lehrer at times considers it plausible that Freud forgot to have read and have been influenced by Nietzsche. Conversely, Ellenberger notes that Nietzsche's ideas permeated fin de siècle culture so profoundly that "it was not necessary to study Nietzsche to be permeated by his thought" (*DU* 277). While both possibilities remain open, a dose of suspicion remains in order when an original discovery is claimed, and the influence of a predecessor is carefully erased so as to affirm one's originality. We have seen the dynamic of romantic agonism generate paradoxical double binds in Girard's intellectual relation to Freud. What we must add is that Freud had already anticipated the same dynamic with respect to Nietzsche. As Freud puts it in *On the History of Psycho-Analytic Movement* (1914), in a passage concerned with the "originality" of psychoanalysis: "In later years, I have denied myself the very great pleasure of reading the works of Nietzsche, with the deliberate resolve not to be hampered in working out the impressions received in psychoanalysis by any sort of anticipatory ideas."[16] Commenting on these and other paradoxical claims in which Freud expresses a strong attraction to Nietzsche's psychology only to reject the notion of having read him—let alone having been influenced by him—Lorin Anderson, after a close examination of Freud's fundamental debts and ambivalences toward Nietzsche, expresses a plausible anti-mimetic hypothesis as he writes: "Freud refuses to compete with Nietzsche; nor does he care to use him, to 'stand on his shoulders.' Instead, he barricades himself against Nietzsche's stylus. Nietzsche is not to be spoken of, not to be read."[17] And he concludes: "Ignorance assures that one is the father of all one's ideas."[18]

On the shoulders of this realistic anti-mimetic hypothesis, I add a mimetic supplement that allows us to confirm the view of the self-proclaimed father of psychoanalysis as a "reader of Nietzsche, borrower from Nietzsche—Freud, Nietzsche's secret disciple."[19] Freud's double movement of attraction and disavowal toward an influential precursor finds a direct explanation via our theory of the romantic agon. In fact, it has all the characteristics of a romantic and less noble variation of the mimetic agonism we found at play in Aristotle contra Plato, Nietzsche contra Wagner, in a romantic iteration, Girard contra Freud, and now, to close the circle, Freud contra Nietzsche as well.

As in the case of mimetic agonism, the admired predecessor's thoughts are avidly assimilated with pathos in one's youth, but the subsequent movement of dissociation and erasure of traces in order to affirm one's independent originality is characteristically romantic. If in mimetic agonism we have seen that the model/opponent is confronted and countered directly, by challenging the predecessor's theory in a spirit of noble competition that puts an aggressive pathos to productive patho-*logical* use (Nietzsche's strategy), this romantic variation of the agon rests on a deft but not exactly brave, let alone honorable, move. For romantic spirits it is, in fact, more convenient to deny the influence altogether so as to kill two or, rather, three birds with one stone, and from a safe distance too (Freud's strategy). The advantages are, of course, many: first, no direct intellectual confrontation and thus risk of defeat ensues; second, the maximum possible distance from the model is also guaranteed; third, a disavowal of influence turns an all too mimetic practice into an "original" theory. It takes genius, but also a high degree of anxiety about one's originality, to come with such a romantic solution. Given Freud's Oedipal obsessions with father figures, this "anxiety of influence" (Bloom's term) would indeed be in line with Freud's own theory of the unconscious.[20] To close this vicious circular logic, the same move Freud was quick to define as plagiarism in others could subsequently be taken by disciples as a proof of the truth of his psychological theory.

And yet, precisely because of the imitative proximity that ensues between disciple and model caught in the dynamic of romantic agonism, important differences between Nietzsche's and Freud's theories of the unconscious need to be signaled as well. Just as romantic agonism is not the same as mimetic agonism, a closer genealogical look reveals that it would be a gross genealogical mistake to conflate Freud's and Nietzsche's respective theories of the unconscious.[21] For instance, Nietzsche did not consider dreams as the *via regia* to the unconscious. On the contrary, he even denounced dreams as a source of metaphysical illusions. As he puts in a section of *Human, All Too Human* aptly titled "Misunderstanding Dreams":

> In the ages of raw, primordial cultures, people believed that in dreams they
> came to know a *second real world*: here is the origin [*Ursprung*] of all meta-
> physics. Without dreams, there would have been no reason to divide the

world. The separation into soul and body is also connected to the oldest views about dreams. (5; 18)

The interpretation of dreams, for Nietzsche, is not at the origins of immanent facts but of metaphysical illusions instead. Had he lived a decade longer, he might have added that it can also lead to illusory meta-psychologies. A biblical practice par excellence, interpretations of dreams that divide the world between appearance and reality, manifest symptoms and latent meanings can indeed cast a shadow on a theory of the unconscious that looks for a transhistorical truth in the analysis of symbolic meanings and is no longer rooted in immanent physiological processes manifested in the body. Despite Nietzsche's early claim that psychologists should look into the depth, consistently in his investigations he turns to manifestations of the unconscious that are at play on bodily surfaces, via gestures, mimicry, movements, and related physiological phenomena. As Foucault also recognized: "There is in the work of Nietzsche a critique of the ideal depth, the depth of consciousness that he denounces as an invention of philosophers."[22] In this genealogical sense, then, Nietzsche's critique of idealism and its religious avatars stretches into the future to include interpreters of dreams as the door to a truer, more subtly abstract, and intelligible reality—part of the history of an error he sets out to dispel as Platonism for the people.

Now, if we have seen that Freud's reliance on the cathartic method led him to the development of the repressive hypothesis and the Oedipal unconscious it entails, we shall see that Nietzsche sets out to puncture that hypothesis in order to open up an alternative door to the unconscious.

Puncturing the Hypothesis

In *On the Genealogy of Morals* (1887), Nietzsche offers us a methodological advice for a diagnostic of the value of theories that we already mentioned at the outset and is worth recalling in the middle, for it applies to mimetic theories and concepts we will explore through the end. As he puts it, this evaluation "requires a knowledge of the conditions and circumstances of their growth, development, and displacement."[23] What Nietzsche implies, contra a long-standing idealist tradition in continental philosophy, is that theories and the concepts and values that go with them do not descend top-down and ready-made from the transcendental sky of intelligible ideas. On the contrary, they develop historically, bottom-up, from a process of theoretical development and displacement of previous theories, an agonistic process that needs to be carefully evaluated first in order to subsequently test if the construction holds to further build upon it. Romantic and mimetic agonism are the concepts I propose to trace the emerges of theories and test their strength and value for life. While it is well known that Nietzsche's genealogical suspicion of accepted concepts applies to the value of morality, philosophical truth, and ascetic ideals, it has not been sufficiently emphasized that it applies to the inherited value of the concept of catharsis as well.

Having followed Nietzsche's genealogical advice so far, we are now in a better position to understand why a rather technical, notoriously obscure, and untranslatable concept like catharsis eventually came to be identified with a pathological perspective that defined it either in terms of moral purification and cleansing, or in medical terms of "purge" and "discharge," generating a moral/medical picture of catharsis that—by a sort of mimetic contagion—spread well beyond specialized academic circles to inform the popular imagination as well. With respect to its medical inflection, Stephen Halliwell confirms what we have been suspecting all along. As he puts it: "The main reason in recent times for the irresistible but largely fanciful obsession with the term [catharsis] is undoubtedly the appeal of such speculations to a Freudian age" (P 90). Despite the philological obscurity on the meaning of catharsis, or perhaps precisely because of this obscurity, the idea that violence—be it fictional or real, imaginary or symbolic, ritualized or aestheticized—has purgative medical effects continues to (mis)in-*form* dominant roads to the unconscious (psychoanalysis), anthropological theories of the origins of culture (mimetic theory), stretching to inform new media (films, but also TV series, computer games, etc.) as well, which are now responsible for informing or, more often, disinforming future generations living in an increasingly precarious and unpredictable world. We can equally better understand why this so-called science of the true unconscious predicated on a catharsis-hypothesis-turned-repressive-hypothesis continued to obsessively zoom in on a privileged tragic play (Sophocles's

Oedipus Rex) as *the* paradigmatic model of a universal structure of the psyche that frames violence, desire, and the unconscious in a triangular (i.e., Oedipal) form.

To be sure, this form, like all ideal forms, claims to be true, intelligible, ahistorical, and, above all, universal. Yet genealogical lenses reveal that the transcendental ideas we inherit from the past are the product of an immanent history. It is, in fact, because an Oedipal play once served as the privileged formal *exemplum* at the dawn of aesthetic theory (Aristotle) that—due to a series of (un)fortunate genealogical vicissitudes—this play and the violence it entails came to cast such a spell on philological physicians in search of a cure (Freud and Breuer) in the nebulous zones where the twilight of reason opens onto the magical sphere of dreams. Contemporary theorists attentive to the processes of "development and displacement" of theories can only wonder: what interpretations of catharsis would have emerged had the *Poetics'* section on tragedy been lost, and the one on comedy preserved? Which comic plays would have served as paradigmatic cases for future theories of the psyche? We can only speculate, but what is likely is that we might have inherited a gayer science of the unconscious. To be sure, since classical antiquity, fictions have constantly provided a powerful starting point for theoretical speculations, but this does not mean that these fictions are literally true. They need to be ruminated first via a method of close reading Nietzsche considered vital for his genealogy of morality and we consider vital for a genealogy of catharsis as well.

Nietzsche's reading lenses were initially trained on classical texts, yet he hesitates when it comes to evaluate the riddle of catharsis. There are moments in his corpus in which he simply appears to echo the translation of catharsis as "purge" of "pathological" affects such as pity, thereby relying on a medical terminology that he, like Freud after him, likely inherited from Bernays and, before him, neoclassical theories of tragedies.[24] As he puts it late in his career, in *Antichrist* (1895): "Aristotle, as is well known, considered pity a pathological [*krankhaften*] and dangerous condition, which one would be well advised to attack now and then with a purge: he understood tragedy as a purge [*Tragödie als Purgativ*]."[25] We have heard this interpretation before, albeit not in Aristotle's *Poetics* itself but in neoclassical and modernist theories of the psyche. Should we then align Nietzsche with this medical tradition?

It is not so simple. As always with Nietzsche, his recuperation of classical theories must be understood in the specific context of his diagnostic
concerns with the mimetic pathologies of modernity. In this case, the focus
of his perspectival approach is clearly on critiquing a specific affective pathology (*Mitleid*), more than on promoting a medical cure (catharsis). Thus, via
a characteristic mimetic agon, he proceeds to confront his former models
and educators—Schopenhauer and Wagner, as well as the modern aesthetics
they represent—as he writes: "From the standpoint of the instinct of life, a
remedy [*Mittel*] certainly seems necessary for such a pathological and dangerous accumulation of pity as is represented by the case of Schopenhauer
(and unfortunately by our entire literary and artistic decadence from St.
Petersburg to Paris, from Tolstoi to Wagner)" (*A* 7; 574). Nietzsche's agon
is of classical rather than romantic inspiration because he does not erase
his predecessors; he confronts them to contest their theories instead. And
what emerges from this contestation is a patho-*logical* suggestion: a remedy
to the life-negating drives Nietzsche sees internal to pity is needed in order
to affirm life. Still, this does not mean that he fully advocates the cathartic
method. Thus, Nietzsche concludes his diagnostic evaluation of the Chris-
tian/Schopenhauerian/Wagnerian celebration of pity by denouncing it as a
life-negating, pathological affect he considers necessary "to puncture . . . and
make it *burst* [*damit sie* platzt]" (7; 574). To genealogical ears, this sounds
like a conceptual—more than bodily—explosion: the power of thought
(logos) bursts an unhealthy celebration of mimetic affect (sym-pathos) by
denouncing it as a pathology to be overcome.

Now that the real target of Nietzsche's patho-*logy* is identified, let us
reconsider his overall genealogical evaluation of catharsis by selectively tracing it throughout his entire corpus. Given the pathos of distance that informs
Nietzsche's diagnostic of mimetic matters, we should not be surprised to see
that his evaluation is not stable but oscillates between pathos and distance
in view of operating a characteristic overturning of perspectives. The view
of catharsis as "pathological discharge" he convokes via Bernays for specific
patho-*logical* reasons in his later period should not be confused with the
evaluation of catharsis he traces from his early, middle, and final periods.

As Nietzsche had already made clear in his first book, *The Birth of Tragedy*
(1872), which was dedicated to Wagner and written under the influence of
Schopenhauer, he takes issue with both moral and medical interpretations of

catharsis understood as a "triumph of the moral world order, or the purgation of the emotions [*Entladung von Affekten*] through tragedy, as the essence of the tragic" (*BT* 22; 132). From the outset of his career, then, Nietzsche's position on catharsis, which he ties to the spectators of Apollonian/Dionysian mimetic "excitement" (*Erregung*), is neither moral nor medical; it is neither in line with neoclassical French theories nor in line with Bernays's medical theory. Thus, he deepens his diagnostic *contra* medical/moral interpretations as follows:

> Never since Aristotle has an explanation of the tragic effect been offered from which aesthetic states or an aesthetic activity of the listener could be inferred. Now the serious events are supposed to prompt pity [*Mitleid*] and fear [*Furchtsamkeit*] to discharge themselves in a way that relieves us [*erleichternden Entladung*]; now we are supposed to feel elevated and inspired by the triumph of good and noble principles, at the sacrifice of the hero in the interest of a moral vision of the universe. I am sure that for countless men precisely this, and only this, is the effect of tragedy, but it plainly follows that all these men, together with their interpreting aestheticians, have had no experience of tragedy as a supreme *art*. (*BT* 22; 132)

Nietzsche's sharp philological lenses put him in a position to stress what twentieth-century commentors of the *Poetics* will later stress as well. While he does not a priori dispute the possibility of moral/medical effect, he is quick to see that Aristotle's focus is not on morality, let alone on medicine, but on aesthetics instead. An experience of tragedy, for Nietzsche, should be first and foremost an aesthetic experience, lest one is unfamiliar with the experience of tragedy as an art. It is thus from the angle of aesthetics that the young Nietzsche enters the fray on the much-discussed riddle of catharsis.

Critical of contemporary "interpreting aestheticians" that foreground morality and medicine, Nietzsche is not alone in his aesthetic evaluation of catharsis. He sits on the shoulders of a towering modern artist and theorist who made art the supreme telos of experience. Thus, Nietzsche continues:

> The pathological discharge [*patologische Entladung*], the catharsis of Aristotle, of which philologists are not sure whether it should be included among medical or moral phenomena, recalls a remarkable notion of

Goethe's. "Without a lively pathological interest," he says, "I, too, have
never yet succeeded in elaborating a tragic situation of any kind, and hence
I have rather avoided than sought it. Can it perhaps have been yet another
merit of the ancients that *the deepest pathos* [das höchste Pathetische] *was
with them merely aesthetic play?*" (*BT* 22; 132; my emphasis)

Aesthetics contra morality, Goethe contra Bernays, surface contra depth,
playful mimetic pathos contra serious medical pathos. Nietzsche's early
allegiances on the question of catharsis are clear. Contra moral and medical interpretations, on the shoulders of Goethe's aestheticism, and thinking
of Wagner's musical tragedy, he replies to his own question thus: "We can
now answer this profound final question in the affirmative after our glori-
ous experiences, having found that the deepest pathos can indeed be merely
aesthetic play." (*BT* 22; 132–33).[26] Put differently, aesthetic (Apollonian) play
serves as the mimetic (representational) medium for a bodily (Dionysian)
pathos whose mimetic (contagious) power goes beyond the cathartic principle reaching into the sphere of "unconscious emotions" that cannot easily
be diagnosed—let alone discharged and cured. Thus, Nietzsche trenchantly
concludes siding with aesthetics contra both moral and medical interpretations of the catharsis hypothesis: "Anyone who still persists in talking only of
those vicarious effects proceeding from extra-aesthetic spheres, and who does
not feel that he is above the pathological-moral process, should despair of his
aesthetic nature" (22; 133). Aesthetics over morality, play over pathology: this
is, for the early Nietzsche, the genuine antagonistic ground on which the
catharsis hypothesis stands, oscillates, and eventually decays and falls.

The Decay of Catharsis

Nietzsche's concern with the problematic of the cathartic/contagious effects
of art in general and tragic representations of violence in particular runs
through his entire corpus, beginning, middle, and end. His position, while
not always clear-cut, continues to be manifested early in his career, in the
book that marks his intellectual independence from his models. Thus, in his
subsequent work, *Human, All Too Human* (1878), Nietzsche picks up the
riddle of catharsis by shifting from an aesthetic to a psychological perspective

in an aphorism titled "Old doubts about the effect of art [*Wirkung der Kunst*]."²⁷ There Nietzsche wonders, with Aristotle, in a questioning, psychologically oriented, and ironically detached mood: "Can it be that pity and fear [*Mitleid und Furcht*], as Aristotle claims, really are purged [*entladen*] by tragedy, so that the audience returns home colder and calmer?" (*HH* 212; 141). And he ironically adds: "Can ghost stories really make people less fearful and superstitious?" (212; 141). The answer is not univocal, for Nietzsche is ready to make fine distinctions. Thus, he continues: "With certain physical processes, for example with sexual pleasure, it is true that the drive is eased [*Linderung*] and temporarily moderated when the need [*Triebes*] is satisfied" (212; 141). In the case of physical pleasures like erotism and love that take place at the immanent level of immediate bodily gratification, Nietzsche seems to generally agree with Aristotle and, closer to him, Bernays, thereby anticipating Freud: the catharsis hypothesis could, indeed, be invoked to account for the "purification" (*Linderung*) that ensues from the discharged (*entladen*) libidinal drive (*Trieb*). The specific focus on catharsis puts us in a position to confirm the hypothesis we already posited: the hydraulic dynamic of the drives, with the damming up and discharge it entails, and the cathartic effects that ensue, paves the way for the psychoanalytical discovery of the unconscious.

That Nietzsche's diagnostic of tragic anticipates discoveries that, to this day, are routinely attributed to Freud is confirmed repeatedly if we look closer at some mirroring psychological analogies we surveyed in the preceding sections. For instance, in *On the Genealogy of Morals* (1887), which offers a genealogy of the origins of "bad conscience" predicated on the psychic mechanism of "internalization" of aggression that prefigures the Freudian discovery, Nietzsche writes: "Every instinct which does not vent itself [*entladen*] externally *turns inwards*—this is what I call the *internalization of humans* [Verinnerlichung *des Menschen*]" (*GM* II, 16; 65; trans. modified). Considering the constraining force of civilization a source of discontent, Nietzsche makes clear that these interiorized instincts constitutive of a bad conscience Freud will later group under the rubric of the "superego" are primarily violent instincts: "Hostility, cruelty, pleasure in persecution, in assault, in change, in destruction—all that turning against the man who possesses such instincts: *such* is the origin of 'bad conscience'" (II, 16; 65). In addition to prefiguring Freud's account of the superego, Nietzsche's diagnostic of the formation of the psyche or soul cannot be dissociated from the problematic of aesthetic representation of violence. It is in fact on the basis of a quintessential tragic emotion like "tragic sympathy" that Nietzsche anticipates another major Freudian concept: namely, sublimation.

Furthering his genealogical insight that even "good" moral sentiments have their origins in aggressive drives that continue to operate subliminally, below conscious awareness, Nietzsche opens up a hypothesis that casts a long shadow on the presumed moral goodness of tragic pity. He continues in the second essay of *On Genealogy* devoted to "'Guilt,' 'Bad Conscience,' and Related Matters":

> Perhaps the possibility might even be entertained that pleasure in cruelty need not actually have died out: considering the extent to which pain hurts more nowadays, all that it had to do was sublimate [*Sublimierung*] and refine itself—that is, it had to appear translated into the imagination and the psyche, embellished only with such harmless names as were incapable of arousing suspicion of even the most delicate hypocritical conscience ("tragic sympathy" [*tragische Mileiden*] is such a name). (*GM* II, 7; 49)

Here we see Nietzsche, the self-proclaimed master of "great suspicion," using his psychological lenses to unmask the violent pathos that drives tragic sympathy. If we have seen that tragic pity, contrary to fear, which is viscerally felt inside the ego, implies a certain distance from the pathos of the other, Nietzsche now takes the diagnostic a step further by rooting tragic *sym-pathy* (*Mit-leiden*) back in violent aggressive drives constitutive of the genealogy of homo mimeticus—what psychoanalysis will group, via Sade, under "sadism." Thus reframed, tragic pleasure turns out to be a refined aesthetic manifestation of pleasure in cruelty. Or, better, it is a refined, subterranean way to extend pleasure in cruelty within the constraining bulwarks of civilization and the discontent it generates. Similarly, tragic sympathy (*Mitleid*) is not feeling *for* or even *with* (*sym, mit*) the suffering (*pathos, leiden*) of the other. On the contrary, it is a strategy to extend a pleasure in witnessing the pathos of the other from an aesthetic distance masked under a benevolent moral sentiment. How? By way of sublimation (*Sublimierung*). Nietzsche, again paving the way for Freud, introduces a concept that he, Nietzsche, understands as a process of translation of cruel unconscious drives into culturally refined aesthetic and moral categories. Sublimation is thus an unconscious dynamic he describes as follows: "the unconscious disguise of physiological needs under the cloaks of the objective, ideal, purely spiritual goes to frightening lengths" (*GS* 3; 34). It would be useless to deny it. A diagnostic of tragic emotions based on a psychology of suspicion that sees violent drives where others see moral values and cathartic effects has indeed discovered the unconscious long before Freud.

And yet, in a move contra the catharsis hypothesis and the repressive model of the unconscious it gave birth to, Nietzsche earlier in his career had also developed alternative psychological approaches to aesthetic emotions that often operate below conscious awareness. Thus, in *Human, All Too Human*, he turns to consider an affective hypothesis that opens the door to an alternative, more immanent, and physiological conception of the unconscious as he continues, in a more clinical mood:

> But fear and pity are not in this sense the needs of specific organs, which have to be relived. And in the long run, every drive is *intensified* by the practice of satisfying it, despite the periodic easing [*Linderungen*]. (*HH* 212; 141).

Nietzsche speaks as a psychologist more than as a philologist here. Better still, he speaks as a philosophical physician. Hence, he does not pay specific attention to the philological fact that fear and pity are tragic affects triggered by the mimetic plot of complex ancient tragedies in general and of *Oedipus Rex* in particular, as we stressed in the previous chapter. Instead, he distinguishes between organs and affects in order to point out that tragic pathos, be it pity or fear, is not itself in need of discharge or relief. There is thus no biological drive or medical therapy at the origins of catharsis. Nietzsche seems to correctly assume that, for Aristotle, pity and fear are artificially produced by an identification with the pathos of the tragic hero represented in an aesthetic fiction. That he immediately generalizes his diagnostic of tragic affects to apply it to modern genres such as ghost stories is revealing. It indicates that he is ready to take his critique of Aristotle's cathartic theory beyond the limits of a specific tragic myth or play into the sphere of modern aesthetics, an aesthetics that is dominated by the rise of the novel, which is traditionally considered an anti-tragic genre.

At one remove, he paves the way for future genealogists to extend the diagnostic beyond the novel or literary genres, into the post-literary sphere of visual entertainment—from film to TV to video games.[28] Even farther removed from tragedy, these new media provide new forms of entertainment whereby the catharsis and affective hypothesis confront each other. In this shift of perspective, Nietzsche also tilts the focus from philology to psychology, or, as he will later call it, physio-psychology, in order to introduce important distinctions between mimetic drives that are constitutive of his genealogical discrimination.[29]

Nietzsche is, in fact, extremely sensitive to the dynamic of specific drives that require a sense of differentiation in order to be properly evaluated. His bodily attunement to the psycho-somatic effects of tragic pathos triggered specifically by the tragic affects of pity (*Mitleid*) and fear (*Furcht*) lead to the two following diagnostic principles we shall have to take seriously in our diagnostic of the affective hypothesis in volume 2: first, mimetic drives that are stimulated are activated rather than purged; and second, a drive gratified by the pleasurable experience of tragic pathos is thus not discharged and weakened but innervated and strengthened. As Terry Eagleton also recognized, "Nietzsche espoused the mimetic theory and rejected the doctrine of *catharsis*: for him, instincts were strengthened the more they were expressed."[30] What we should add is that if the catharsis hypothesis paves the way for an Oedipal unconscious that dominated the past Freudian century (and continues to inform psychoanalytically oriented theorists), the affective hypothesis paves the way for a mimetic unconscious that is emerging in the present post-Freudian century (and informs more recent turns to affect, performativity, and embodiment constitutive of the mimetic turn). It is worth noting that Nietzsche did not have contemporary neuroscience ready at hand to confirm that "neurons that fire together wire together" in mirroring/plastic terms reinforced by habitual behavior and patterns of consumption. And yet his physio-psychological sensitivity to the dynamic of drives, his experiential knowledge of the power of bodily habits and practices, coupled with a strong genealogical distance with respect to the construction and displacement of past theories, supplemented by an alternative conception of the mimetic unconscious we shall return to, puts him in a position to anticipate insights into the immanent dynamic of imitation that will have to wait until the twentieth and twenty-first centuries in order to be confirmed.

After a career devoted to philological, psychological, and aesthetic considerations on the patho(-)logical powers of artistic influences, Nietzsche articulates a final diagnostic of the catharsis hypothesis in a fragment of *Will to Power* from 1888 titled "What is tragic?" where he states: "On repeated occasions I have laid my finger on Aristotle's great misunderstanding in believing the tragic affects to be two *depressive* affects, terror and pity" (*WP* 851; 449). For Nietzsche art is not a depressant in the service of tragic and pessimistic emotions; on the contrary, tragic aesthetics is "the great stimulant of life, an intoxication with life, a will to life" (851; 449). And with respect to the complexities internal to the catharsis hypothesis, he sums up his final diagnostic with unequivocal clarity: "that one is 'purged' of these affects [pity and fear] through their arousal, as Aristotle seems to believe, is simply not true" (*WP* 851; 449).[31] As with moral prejudices so with aesthetic prejudices: the catharsis hypothesis is eventually unmasked as part of the history of an error.

But on what foundations does Nietzsche affirm such a genealogical reevaluation? Going beyond his previous aesthetic/textual refutation of medical/moral interpretations of catharsis, at the end of his career, Nietzsche deepens and finalizes his immanent approach by turning to the empirical reality of bodily reflexes in order to refute the catharsis hypothesis. Hence, paving the way for empirical investigations yet to come, Nietzsche advises future philosophical physicians to adopt the following empirical method in order to test the validity of theories based on concepts as elusive as catharsis: "One can refute this [cathartic] theory in the most cold-blooded way: namely, by measuring the effects of a tragic emotion with a dynamometer" (*WP* 851; 449)—that is, a device for measuring physical force or power. In a mirroring inversion of perspectives, this device will play a crucial role in confirming the affective hypothesis that is now taken seriously in the neurosciences precisely on empirical foundations. Perhaps for fear of accusations of reductionism that still inform "two cultures" debates that simply oppose science to the humanities, perhaps due to the primacy of concepts over empirical realities that still dominate older generations of philosophers, or perhaps simply due to lack of careful consideration of Nietzsche's consistent interest in physio-psychology, such empirical insights are rarely stressed in Nietzsche studies and do not inform the commentaries of catharsis I know of.[32]

And yet, it did not escape philosophers who went beyond commentary by picking up Nietzsche's diagnostic arrow and throwing it further in the twentieth century. Georges Bataille, for instance, whose debt to Nietzsche is well known, and whose relevance for the affective hypothesis on violence we shall return to, is a case in point. In the context of the discussion of the effects of "tragic representation" on the "crowd [*foule*]" of spectators, Bataille notices that violent scenes of "horror, death, or mutilation . . . uncontestably produce a stimulating effect [*effet excitant*] on the spectators"; and, with Nietzsche's posthumous passage clearly in mind, Bataille immediately specifies his source of inspiration as he adds: "Nietzsche proposed to measure this stimulation with a dynamometer."[33] Nietzsche and Bataille are certainly not reductionist thinkers, yet they fundamentally agree that a dose of empiricism in the thorny matters of catharsis and contagion, violence and the unconscious, can be sobering. "You want to know the effects of tragic and violent spectacles?" they seem to be asking. "Then, do not consider the psyche in isolation, or as detached from your body. Above all, do not interpret dreams or linger on the Oedipal hypothesis," these masters of suspicion seem to whisper to philosophers of the future. "Instead, carefully observe the movements of your body first, and you'll have access to the movements of your soul." In sum, from a Nietzschean, immanent perspective, be they ancient or modern, tragic or gay, violent spectacles that convey mimetic pathos do not keep the city going. On the contrary, they cause decline, degeneration, and decadence in the city.

We have seen that genealogy looks back to ancient theories; but it does so to better look ahead to contemporary realities. In the process, it urges new generations of theorists to trace the development of influential hypotheses, reevaluate their value in light of more contemporary insights, and, if proven insufficient, replace them with alternative hypotheses. With Nietzsche, we are thus encouraged to shift from an unconscious based on a catharsis hypothesis used to solve an Oedipal riddle toward an unconscious based on an affective hypothesis that calls for the explanation of mirroring riddles. This also entails shifting perspectives from an ideal (triangular) form structured around a conflict between desire and mimesis toward an immanent (spiraling) movement that calls for the complex articulation of pathos and logos. If the past century has favored familial triangulations based on a classical (theatrical) medium that served as the model for the catharsis hypothesis, we are not rediscovering the contagious powers of modern (digitized) new media that call for the exploration of the affective hypothesis.

In *Violence and the Mimetic Unconscious*, I shall follow Nietzsche's empirical advice literally by turning my diagnostic lenses to contemporary attempts in the neurosciences, if not to empirically measure, at least to account for the contagious effects of violent representations on the brain and to the genealogies these contemporary physicians unconsciously reopen. We have seen so far that the catharsis hypothesis, which cast such a long spell on theories of the unconscious and of violence in the past, Freudian century, might have lost some of its hypnotic power in the present, post-Freudian century. Tracing a genealogy of the catharsis hypothesis in some exemplary thinkers who contributed to spreading it in the modernist period does not offer a homogeneous interpretation of what catharsis originally means in theory, let alone of how it works in practice—when it works. Instead, it allows us to uncover underlying and previously little studied continuities between intellectual figures that our current academic drive toward specialization tends to split into different areas of investigation such as philosophy (Aristotle), philology (Bernays), psychoanalysis (Freud), literary theory (Girard), and a transdisciplinary combination thereof (Nietzsche); and yet, genealogical lenses reveal that these thinkers are clearly inscribed in the same tradition of thought. From different perspectives, modern advocates of the catharsis hypothesis contributed to promoting a medical translation of catharsis that, while doing hermeneutical violence to its original aesthetic meaning, continues to inform the critical, theoretical, and popular imagination.

To be sure, genealogy does not claim to reveal a single, homogeneous truth at the origin of concepts. Already Aristotle, for one, was not fully original in his own definition. He was, in fact, recuperating the definition of catharsis from his agonistic model. In *Phaedo*, for instance, Plato already writes that catharsis "consists in separating the soul as much as possible from the body."[34] Since the separation of the soul from the body, psyche from soma, is a classical idealist move that orients Plato's metaphysics of ideal Forms, this might as well serve as a reminder of the idealist origins of a seemingly empirical hypothesis. In his *Poetics* Aristotle was thus perhaps more Platonic than he is usually thought to be, if only because he sets out to defend poetry contra Plato—with what turns out to be a Platonic concept. Is the cathartic method, then, a Platonism for contemporary theory?

Perhaps. This is, in any case, a hypothesis we shall have to consider in the sequel to this study. More immanent theories, in fact, show, on a physio-psychological basis that roots the soul back in the immanence of bodily reflexes, that representations of violence may not lead to any purification, let alone medical purges. On the contrary, they might generate contagious reactions that have the potential to trigger more violence instead. By showing that these concepts have a long, conflicted, and heterogeneous history, this genealogical operation reveals that what was thought to be a valid medical hypothesis is part of the history of a philological error—or, at least, of a spectacular theoretical simplification.

After this genealogical detour via Nietzsche's overall evaluation of catharsis, we can confirm that our ears had heard correctly. The aesthetic philosopher turned physician of the soul who relied on his sick body to test and evaluate the value of theories, punctures the catharsis hypothesis, which is quite exploded in the end.

CHAPTER 5

An Attempt at Self-Critique

Contra Hyperspecialization

To shift our genealogical perspective from catharsis to affective contagion, the answer to a question with which we started can no longer be postponed. We have seen that the catharsis hypothesis is overwhelmingly disputed by the most influential classical scholars who devoted a lifetime, if not to fully solving, at least to clearly framing, contextualizing, and reevaluating the riddle of catharsis. We have equally seen that once turned into a medical therapy, the cathartic method generated spectacular therapeutic failures that have not reached the popular imagination as yet but are becoming increasingly difficult to ignore. Last but not least, we noted that its medical efficacy is now not even taken seriously by fictional characters playing roles in cinematic blockbusters that are far removed indeed from ancient tragedies, yet convey informed diagnostic principles nonetheless. Given these heterogeneous facts, it is legitimate to wonder: why does the medical interpretation of catharsis still tend to be uncritically accepted, echoed, and disseminated not only in the sphere of media and popular culture but also in the academic sphere of high theory and culture?

We noted the role of psychoanalysis as a literary or philosophical theory (more than as a therapy) in shaping the critical imagination concerning

149

cathartic matters in the twentieth century. There is no doubt that the shadow of Oedipal dramas that find in a specific tragedy a paradigmatic example, or model of the unconscious, based on incestuous and murderous desires, continues to titillate the popular imagination. This is especially true since such familial dramas have had an enormous success in cultural industries like Hollywood, informing directors from Alfred Hitchcock to Woody Allen, David Lynch to David Cronenberg, among many others. Perhaps against their directorial intentions, film contributed to turning Oedipal fantasies into second nature among generations of postwar globalized viewers.[1] And yet, no matter how popular this theory of the unconscious became as a cultural force in the past century, blaming psychoanalysis alone for the success of the catharsis hypothesis will not be sufficient for new generations of theorists currently engaged in rethinking the powers of the unconscious to face the multiple challenges of the present century.

As Nietzsche would put it, an attempt at self-criticism is in order.

A Mirror for Academic Patho(-)Logies

My suspicion is that an increasing academic demand in the humanities and social sciences for what the French transdisciplinary thinker Edgar Morin calls academic "hyperspecialization," which mimetically follows the model of the hard sciences, is equally responsible for this state of affairs. As Morin defines it, "hyperspecialization" is a dominant and widely disseminated academic practice "that is closed upon itself and blocks an integration of the object of study within a global problematic, or a unifying conception [*conception d'ensemble*]; instead, it considers only one aspect or part of the object of inquiry."[2] As a trained sociologist; pioneer of film studies; privileged interlocutor of major figures in transdisciplinary fields like semiotics (Roland Barthes), cybernetics (Norbert Wiener), media studies (Jean Baudrillard), philosophy (Cornelius Castoriadis), among others; lifelong director of research at a prestigious French institution like the CNRS; and author of landmark studies on topics as diverse as death and cinematic stars, ethics and aesthetics, Morin does not dispute that a degree of specialization is undoubtedly necessary to make valuable contributions to scientific debates. Similarly, as my endnotes indicate, I am not only subjected to the weight of a long genealogy of scholarly work; I also gratefully relied on specialized scholarship in order to cast light on a concept like catharsis that would otherwise have required a lifetime of research in order to be adequately framed. It should go without saying that no progress is possible without specialized research. The latter is the necessary base on which transdisciplinary approaches rely—in order to go further.

A call for a transdisciplinary, problem-oriented rather than discipline-oriented approach to the patho(-)logical interplay of violence and the unconscious via the Janus-faced problematic of catharsis and affective contagion does not intend to dispute the value of specialized academic knowledge that has been accumulated over the centuries. Quite the contrary. It puts it to use to cast a broader and refined net on a slippery and protean problem that tends to be restricted to contemporary theories and quantitative methods in order to bring multiple perspectives to bear on a complex problematic. In theory, then, there should be no tension, antagonism, or agonism between these two complementary approaches. Discipline-based and transdisciplinary perspectives complement and supplement each other in productive ways that this study aims to foster. And yet, in academic practice, genealogical lenses also reveal that a unilateral excess of specialization, or hyperspecialization, in contemporary academia delimits territories that are simply too narrow to adequately frame, contextualize, and disentangle complex, interwoven problems that, by definition, do not fit a singular disciplinary frame. Hyperspecialization also sets up arbitrary fences that all too often prevent nomadically inclined scholars from tracing experimental connections between different fields, periods, and disciplinary traditions—generating what Nietzsche calls "amicable and fruitful exchanges" with researchers in different fields, rather than mimetic rivalries within the same field. Hence the importance of a methodological attempt at self-critique at the end of this volume—in order to go further in the subsequent volume.

If we look into this self-critical mirror, common symptoms that structure the very organization of academic knowledge and practices begin to appear. It is tempting to look away for the image is not all that flattering. Still, if we overcome this automatic reflex, we might see the following tendencies appear repeatedly, which does not mean that minor academic voices do not seek to oppose them. But to go beyond them, it is important to recognize these territorial drives first. Without the aim of being exhaustive, they include: a life commitment to a single discipline of inquiry; an uncritical belief in the intrinsic superiority of one's own field; antagonistic relations with neighboring fields; rivalrous relations with divergent schools within the same field; hiring practices confined to increasingly specialized areas; one-sided privileging of human rationality, individualism, and autonomy characteristic of *Homo sapiens* or *economicus* over disinterested forms of relational, aesthetic, and potentially irrational activities constitutive of *homo ludens* or *mimeticus*; a general tendency to overestimate the importance of one's area of inquiry, scholarly outputs, and academic status (not to speak of the ego); and clear-cut alignment on one front of the "two cultures" (science/humanities) divide that, in a mirroring ironic reflection, plagues both academic cultures alike, among other territorial tendencies.

Such self-reflective critiques are necessary in all fields of inquiry, but they are particularly urgent for the humanities, and for at least two reasons: first, because those complex protean creatures that are humans are both the subjects and objects of inquiry; and second, because hyperspecialization is particularly privileged in humanistic fields in ways that are detrimental to its object of inquiry. As Morin puts it: "Paradoxically, the human sciences currently offer the weakest contribution to the study of the human condition, precisely because they are so disjointed, fragmented and compartmentalized."[3] This claim might sound excessive to a non-academic readership unfamiliar with the thick barriers of academic corridors and buildings, but to those inside those buildings it reflects an all too real concern. Hyperspecialization entails symptomatic tendencies humanistic scholars working in a university are all too familiar with. Again, important exceptions to these tendencies, especially among younger generations but not only, naturally exist, and tend to work underground generating secret passages and relay stations. They operate often in covert, unofficial ways, via extra-curricular reading groups, informal interfaculty seminars, targeted dialogues with transdisciplinary thinkers who paved the way, collaborations with the city (museums, libraries, high schools, etc.), use of alternative media of dissemination, and other voluntary-based communal gatherings, assemblages, and conversations, that may not be officially inscribed in the academic curriculum, let alone "the canon," but play a vital function within universities: they contribute to shaping new generations of students with an eye to the present and future.

If we do not let go of our self-reflective mirror and continue to resist the temptation to look away, symptoms of hyperspecialization that infect the humanities in particular and set up hurdles to transdisciplinary genealogical investigations tend to include, again with underground exceptions working against them: a tendency to value the past over and against the present, let alone the future; an antiquarian relation to canonical authors and texts that comes uncomfortably close to a form of religious devotion; a narrow delimitation of the scope of investigation to a historical period, school of thought, author, or even text; a nostalgic attachment to hierarchical distinctions between "high" and "low" cultures after such binaries have long been deconstructed; accumulation of knowledge for its own sake deposited in self-contained silos; a more than justified and critically vital propensity to denounce ideological biases in authors of the past, most notably in terms of race, class, gender, and sexuality, coupled with an unjustifiable and increasingly anachronistic reluctance to apply the same standards to the present in terms of consumerist practice, materialist greed, environmental pollution, species extermination, and a general disregard for the survival of future generations who are inheriting a damaged planet; an inherent suspicion of problems that are directly relevant for life and inevitably transgress the field; a delight in relying on an obscure rhetoric or jargon that is unintelligible outside one's discipline, let alone field; a mimetic tendency to adopt the latest theoretical jargon every time a "new" turn promises to revolutionize the field; a hypermimetic tendency to abandon it once a newer, often antithetical turn comes along; obsession to travel across the world to read a twenty-minute paper to small audiences of scholars concerned with their own paper—among other embarrassing symptoms that tend to be tacitly accepted as legitimately constitutive of the academic "profession."

Within the universities, first steps for the creation of transdisciplinary centers are beginning to be taken, but these are difficult times for the humanities. Hence, other influential centers, like the Humanities Center at Johns Hopkins University that set the stage for the structuralist controversy that shook the foundations of the humanities opening it up to the outside under the rubric of theory in the 1970s and 1980s, are now hastily dismantled. Overall I think it is fair to say that despite the growing awareness that interdisciplinary, multidisciplinary, or transdisciplinary innovations are vital for future generations, the fundamental academic structures still dominant today in the humanities tend to favor the opposite. Increasingly under pressure to demonstrate their relevance in a precarious world oriented toward an even more precarious future, the humanities, as Morin points out, still continue to fold back on defensively narrow turfs, favoring, encouraging, and ultimately promoting a past-oriented hyperspecialization in practice—while often paradoxically masking it under a thin varnish of interdisciplinary rhetoric.

In a self-reflective critical mood, a theory of homo mimeticus has a role to play in the future to foster transdisciplinary alternatives via a problem-oriented approach. Since education and scholarship are based on tacitly accepted, and little discussed or theorized, imitative practices that remain powerful, formative, and transformative forces in the constitution of every academic identity, mimesis cannot be avoided, for both good and ill. If only because imitation is the very medium of education. As Samuel IJsseling points out in *Mimesis*, also in a self-critical mood, "philosophers imitate other philosophers, even if only by quoting them both implicitly and explicitly,"[4] and this mimetic principle applies beyond philosophy as well. What we add is that this imitation is at least double: it can be done in a passive spirit of mechanical reproduction of a past logos restricted to the logic of the same or in an agonistic spirit of creative re-*production* of logoi in view of addressing problems located at the juncture of sameness and difference. While the transdisciplinary dynamic of the mimetic agon led me to devote a considerable amount of energy to go beyond the confines of one single discipline, period, or department, by training and profession, I have also been complicit with some of the above, simply in order to continue to swim in the academic current. As noted, this is not only a critique but an attempt at self-critique. If I acknowledge my partial complicity with widely diffused scholarly pathologies, I do so in an attempt to put them to patho-*logical* use. Academic hyperspecialization might, in fact, serve as a sort of a scholarly patho(-)logy that cuts both ways in the end: it simultaneously offers the logoi to solve academic riddles in theory while at the same time promoting academic pathologies in practice.

At first sight the mirroring picture is not flattering, but at second sight it looks in opposed directions. What we have learned from our genealogy of homo mimeticus in the past applies to the present as well. A critical evaluation can never be unilateral, for pathologies generate their balancing patho-*logies* that are already underway. Productive encounters often emerge from the empty spaces between disciplines that can happen at conferences over coffee breaks, for instance; via underground exchanges and dialogues within and across faculties; during transdisciplinary in-person seminars; and, increasingly, during pandemic crises via transnational online seminars that are based on problems or questions more than disciplines and territories. In Europe, for instance, such an incentive is supported by competitive but generous public funding schemes that promote problem-oriented, bottom-up approaches. At the macro-level there are also growing incentives to promote future-oriented institutes or centers for research to keep up with the transdisciplinary problems characteristic of our fast-changing times. In addition to the inherently transdisciplinary nature of what I propose to call mimetic studies theory, emerging fields like environmental humanities, digital humanities, gender and critical race studies, posthuman studies, among other burgeoning perspectives provide new impetus to the humanities from the bottom up. Morin's monumental but still untranslated *La Méthode*[5] provides new epistemic principles for these developments, which resonate with the patho-*logies* proposed in this study. Together, a focus on the complexity of problems that leads researchers to draw selectively from different disciplinary discourses or logoi can be put in productive dialogues with more recent calls for multi-, post-, trans-, and interdisciplinary approaches, without setting up clear borders between these emerging perspectives.[6]

As the active dynamic of agonistic intellectual confrontations makes clear, and the passive dimension of reproduction of ideas confirms, the transmission of knowledge central to education is implicated in mimetic practices that can be double. On the one hand, our genealogy of the specific, even specialistic, yet wide-ranging hypothesis of catharsis revealed how in the case of ambitious and exemplary figures, mimetic agonism can be productive and patho-*logical*. Time and again, we have seen that influential figures across the ages open up innovative lines of inquiry with and against heterogeneous predecessors who are creative in nature, going as far as inaugurating new fields of inquiry altogether. This deterritorializing tendency is constitutive of the genealogy of the agon. The Greeks were, in fact, quick to understand that a plurality of competitors belonging to different geographical territories was essential to push excellence further; and this applies to cultural territories as well. As Jacob Burckhardt noted: "It was altogether the nature of the agon to transcend territorial boundaries, because its interest diminished if the same individuals were always involved" (*GGC* 168). These deterritorializing forces not only ensured a high level in contests that went from chariot racing to dramatic and philosophical contests; they were also "decisive in breaking down enmity between tribes" (168). Perhaps, then, what was true of geographical and cultural boundaries for Greek tribes continues to apply to disciplinary boundaries that still divide academic tribes—a division mimetic agonism aims to overcome. On the other hand, in a less agonistic age, the imitative practices internal to increasingly corporate-driven, applied, and profit-oriented forms of education risk being simply mechanical, reproductive, and territorial. Territorial or tribal specialization can be cognitively pathological in the sense that it tends to ignore research in other fields of inquiry, but also to favor the application of ready-made disciplinary grids or structures in the same field. Paradoxically, these territorializing tendencies internal to hyper-specialization also risk to performatively produce "realities" that confirm the dominant theory at hand, in a spiral of hypermimetic mirroring reciprocity that is easy to denounce in competing or rivalrous fields but is difficult to take hold of in our own field.

As a skilled practitioner of mimetic agonism, Nietzsche helps us deepen our attempt at self-critique in view of going beyond disciplinary binaries. An introspective genealogist of knowledge once trained within the strict walls of the academia, who was relatively quick in entering but also breaking free of that world, he was among the first to register and diagnose the paradoxical effects of academic hyperspecialization in the humanities as they retroact on the all too human subject of investigation. In *Gay Science*, for instance, Nietzsche makes the following diagnostic, autobiographical, and thus confessional observation: "You see the friends of your youth again after they have taken possession of their specialty—and always the opposite has happened, too! Always they themselves are now possessed by it and obsessed with it."[7] The scholar who works himself or herself up, step by step, the steep ladder of humanist knowledge might have the following subjective agentic feeling: namely, of taking active possession of the rational tools needed for the mastery of a disciplinary logos vital to freely developing specialized accounts of academic objects in view of finding a position in a highly competitive and rivalrous job market. This feeling is truly experienced, freely lived, and thus considered true. And yet, over time, an inversion of perspective risks to occur under the gravitational weight of disciplinary practices that, Nietzsche specifies, "press down upon the soul": this active possession of a specialty spirals back against the scholar's body and soul, turning into an insidious form of academic dispossession that generates visible physio-psychological pathologies. To be sure, Nietzsche himself was not a model of health, yet his pathologies only sharpened his diagnostic patho-*logies* as he noted: "Every specialist has his hunched back. Every scholarly book also mirrors a soul that has become crooked" (*GS* V; 322). According to this patho-*logical* perspective, scholarly books might not always set up a transparent mirror to the outside world. Instead, they might set up a self-reflecting mirror to a human, all too human soul that can indeed be imprisoned in the mirroring networks of power-knowledge, as Michel Foucault's archaeology of knowledge will famously confirm—also on the shoulders of Nietzsche.[8]

Attention to a genealogy of discursive formation of Nietzschean inspiration, then, cautions us against restricting such a diagnostic to personal pathologies that affect and infect only few philological scholars. The constraining forces that "press down" upon the scholar—be it Nietzsche's friends, Nietzsche himself, contemporary scholars, or ourselves—are internal to the very logoi that inform academic practices in the humanities. In the process, they generate paradoxes in which the production of knowledge, which aspires to provide the solution to specific problems, can actually contribute to a type of academic blindness that is part of the creation of more general educative problems as well. Broadening the scope of Nietzsche's diagnostic beyond personal academic pathologies to account for the hyperspecialism that continued to increase in the twentieth century, Morin outlines the following "paradox": "The twentieth century has produced an enormous progress in all domains of scientific knowledge, as well as in all technical domains"; but then he adds, in a mirroring move: "at the same time, it has also produced a new blindness concerning global, fundamental and complex problems, and this blindness could generate a innumerable errors and illusions, primarily among scientists, technicians, and specialists."[9]

In sum, the mirror of self-critique points to a blind spot in specialized scholarly practices that needs to be looked into in order to be overcome: disciplinary lenses and the rational discourses they promote are not only the source of new patho-*logical* insights; they can also cast a spell on the researcher and take possession of an ability to think beyond boundaries that, over time and repetition, generates pathological blindness with respect to the complexity of homo mimeticus.[10] Hence the need for a self-critical mirror to see more clearly into a complex, transdisciplinary subject.

Homo Mimeticus, a Complex Subject

The paradox of knowledge Morin identifies for the twentieth century is real and is aggravated by the increasing interconnectedness of systemic objects of study in the twenty-first century. It should urgently generate institutional changes in the very organization of the university at the macro-level from the top down. At the same time, it should encourage attempts at self-critiques by individual researchers working on specific problems that call for transdisciplinary lenses at the micro-level from the bottom up. This concluding section is an effort at the micro-level that aims to join forces with other researchers to promote changes at the macro-level as well. Together, both micro and macro transformations would give researchers of the future a chance to move beyond the hyperspecialistic fallacy—a move vital to facing the increasingly complex and thus interwoven challenges of the twenty-first century.

For good and ill, homo mimeticus is entangled in this complexity. We have seen that despite its transdisciplinary scope, mimetic theory is not immune to the blindness internal to epistemic pathologies, especially if it is taken as a transhistorical, universal frame to be mechanically applied on heterogeneous processes of imitation that undergo genealogical transformations. And yet, in a mirroring patho-*logical* reflection, a new theory of homo mimeticus attentive to the metamorphic powers of concepts like catharsis and mimesis over the ages can also contribute to revealing this epistemic blindness internal to the dominant contemporary structures of hyperspecialization.

Could it be, then, that the all too familiar rivalries that plague specialized disciplines are the natural—or, I should rather say, structural—consequence of too many brains reaching for the same contested academic object of inquiry in order to develop an "originally" different solution via highly competitive practices Girard already called our attention to? These include but are not limited to the following: competing in the same and increasingly narrow academic market; fighting to land the same and increasingly territo-rialized job; targeting articles and books in the same and highly competitive and thus coveted journals and presses; developing originally differentiated theories in the context of increasingly homogenized schools, among other practices. In light of Morin's critique of hyperspecialization, Girard's ironic reference to MLA as a breeding territory for mimetic desires, rivalries, and scapegoating mechanisms that should be studied as a new milieu to further a theory of mimesis in the twenty-first century turns out not to have been a joke, after all; it had real patho-*logical* value for mimetic studies of the future. In sum, attempts at self-critique attentive to reevaluating the value of theo-ries set up a mirror to scholars to reevaluate the knowledge of our specialized knowledge, including that self-reflective knowledge par excellence that is mimetic knowledge.

Such a rivalrous hyperspecialism characteristic of academic practices in the humanities is certainly detrimental to the general understanding of a major transdisciplinary concept like catharsis, a concept that (not unlike mimesis), the same specialized scholars agree, requires transdisciplinary lenses to be properly understood, framed, and reevaluated in its aesthetic, anthropological, moral, religious, psychological, and medical manifesta-tions. As we prepare to leave the catharsis hypothesis behind us in order to look ahead to the affective hypothesis we already glimpsed at but still have to evaluate, let me reiterate the genealogical point with which we started. This theoretical account of the transformations of the cathartic and the affec-tive hypotheses is not a scholarly end in itself geared toward accumulating antiquarian historical knowledge for its own sake; nor does it entail the cel-ebration of a hermeneutic that elevates suspicion to a transcendental value. Just as this book does not promote interdisciplinarity because it is the latest academic meme new generations of scholars need to mime, genealogical lenses are not confined to contemporary academic quarrels that all too often still pit language contra affect, the mind contra the body, the brain against the soul, consciousness against the unconscious, to name just some of the most often invoked reified structural oppositions.

On the contrary, the genealogical perspectivism I practice is rooted in a Nietzschean long-standing tradition in philosophy, aesthetics, and psy-chology, among other disciplines that aim to recuperate past theories and concepts in order to put them to use "for the purpose of *life*."[11] The passage is worth quoting at the end because it has been informing this investigation from the beginning:

> We want to serve history only to the extent that history serves life: for it is possible to value the study of history to such a degree that life becomes stunted and degenerate—a phenomenon we are now forced to acknowledge, painful though this may be, in the face of certain striking symptoms of our age.[12]

These symptoms, I'm afraid, are perhaps even more striking in our age of hyperspecialization. Consequently, the aim of tracing the vicissitudes of the cathartic and contagious hypotheses from their origins in classical antiquity to their modern and contemporary manifestations, is to mobilize different logoi to come to grips with the protean powers of violent pathos in a life-affirmative, transdisciplinary spirit that puts history in the service of life. We have seen that the genealogical method attentive to the emergence of theories led us to cross naturally between different areas of specialization. The focus on the problem of media violence led us to engage with disciplinary traditions that go from ancient philosophy to classical philology, psychoanalysis to anthropology, literary theory to new media studies following connections that emerge directly from the problematic at hand. Thus, conceived transdisciplinarity is not mapped onto the problem; on the contrary, it is the problem and the genealogy of thinkers that addressed it that call for a plurality of logoi in order to be understood. In the processes, it aims to reevaluate the patho(-)logical relevance of these competing hypotheses for contemporary hypermediatized generations under the spell of violent spectacles in the digital age, a hypermimetic age that, no matter how immaterial and ideal the representations, casts a dark material shadow on present and future generations.

The problematic of mimesis that serves as our Ariadne's thread in the labyrinth of theories of violence and the unconscious, which we access via the revolving doors of catharsis and contagion, provides a particularly interesting transdisciplinary perspective to set up a self-critical mirror to dominant methodological practices. Since humans imitate at radically different levels of experience that go from the neurological to the psychological, the sociological to the anthropological, the aesthetic to the political, the ethical to

the ontological, among different discourses, it inevitably encourages a perspectival, transdisciplinary, and qualitative approach that multiplies logoi
to account for the complex dynamic of mimetic pathos, be it cathartic or
contagious. At the same time, it is the transmission of these theoretical logoi
themselves that rely on *mimetic* practices in the sense that knowledge is not
produced in a vacuum. On the contrary, it is reproduced via textbooks, theories, methods, and, last but not least, teachers that, for good and ill, serve
as examples for students and play a decisive role in the formation of new
scholars, scholarly knowledge, and professional identities.

Girard's theory contributed significantly to establishing bridges between
humanistic disciplines as diverse as literary criticism, anthropology, philosophy, and psychoanalysis. So did the linguistic turn by opening up discussions
traditionally confined to literary and philosophy departments to the human
and social sciences more generally in the age of the so-called theory wars
that dominated the humanities in the 1970s and 1980s.[13] Today, the war is
apparently over for theory has been proclaimed dead—at least in theory. But
in critical practice, recent turns to affect, embodied, cognition, new material-
ism, digital humanities, and the neurosciences open up exciting new lines of
inquiry that benefit from being inscribed in a longer genealogy in order to
be evaluated and furthered. It is now crucial for new generations of theorists
of mimesis and its contemporary avatars (identification, influence, simulation, mirror neurons, algorithmic contagion, etc.) not to rest content with
original turns, and to realize that these new turns entail a *re*-turn to a minor
but long-standing conception of mimesis attentive from the very beginning
of philosophy to affective contagion, bodily mimicry, and protean meta-
morphoses. A mimetic re-turn inevitably entails increasing transdisciplinary
connections that cut across the "two cultures" divide, but also self-critically
reflecting on the mimetic processes that informs the very constitution of
humans and posthumans.

If I retain the concept of the human in homo mimeticus after it has
been decentered, deconstructed, and deterritorialized, and so on, it is thus
certainly not to erect it as a transcendental, universal, and ahistorical ideal.
Nor is it to divide human animals from nonhuman animals, for the latter
can be imitative as well—often in ways that far exceed human mimetism.
On the contrary, the telos of the mimetic turn is to root the human back
in evolutionary forms of nonlinguistic affective communication that are

constitutive of the genealogy of homo mimeticus and are partially shared with nonhuman animals as well.[14] Moreover, revisiting the mimetic faculty reloaded in the digital age opens up the porous, relational, and eminently plastic concept of the human to nonhuman technologies constitutive of the posthuman turn, which is contributing to the mimetic turn as well. Immersed in a plurality of immanent processes of becoming *other* that shatter any fixed or monolithic idea of what the human is or should be, the re-turn to homo mimeticus opens up humans and nonhuman entanglements constitutive of our becoming posthuman as well.[15]

If we now return to the problem of violence and its contradictory unconscious effects on homo mimeticus in light of this methodological attempt at self-critique, we can confirm that it is a characteristically complex and thus transdisciplinary problem that is impossible to consider from a singular or totalizing disciplinary perspective. The problematic of (new) media violence is a total social phenomenon (Mauss's term) that cuts across the nature/culture binary insofar as it concerns the brain and the psyche, fictional images and real affects, the individual body and the social body. Hence, it urges scholars to mobilize different logoi to account for the cathartic and contagious pathos of violence as diverse psycho-logy and anthropo-logy, philo-logy and socio-logy, but also as neuro-logy and bio-logy, not to speak of ethical, political, and aesthetic perspectives internal to philosophy that are all constitutive of the patho(-)logies of homo mimeticus since the very origins of philosophy with Plato and Aristotle.

In this first volume of a Janus-faced study, we have seen that catharsis plays a central and often marginalized role in the development of a contemporary mimetic theory that reopened the question of the unconscious on the basis of a reframing of an Oedipal myth (Girard). We have equally seen that this reading entails an agonistic relation with modern physicians of the soul (Freud and Bernays) who relied on philological interpretations (Bernays) in order to turn the catharsis hypothesis into a clinical method. The method led to therapeutic failures. Hence, even its main advocate (Freud again) who aspired to develop a science of the unconscious eventually turned away from the cathartic method—without repudiating the mythic model on which his theory of the unconscious was based. This methodological assumption led us to investigate the origins of cathartic theory in a classical figure (Aristotle) who is often mentioned by advocates of the catharsis hypothesis but is rarely studied let alone close read in contemporary debates on (new) media violence. If this genealogical inquiry did not make transparently clear what catharsis means for Aristotle, at least it excluded a medical interpretation that cast a long spell in the past century, (mis)informing the popular opinion that representations of violence themselves can have cathartic effects. It also revealed so far largely unnoticed mechanisms of imitation via new concepts like romantic agonism and mimetic agonism that account for paradoxical movements of writing with and against influential predecessors. That is, agonistic movements, which, as we have seen, are central to the formation, transformation, and dissemination of theories that, to this day, cast a spell on the public imagination. Last, we returned to a figure at the foundations of our theory of homo mimeticus (Nietzsche) who joined his philological and psychological lenses in order to both dispute the moral/medical interpretation of catharsis and introduce an aesthetic/physiological interpretation that is attentive to the affective hypothesis instead.

Relying on a genealogy that is as much past-oriented as it is present- and future-oriented, let us thus return to our initial question. Can catharsis still operate in a hypermediatized world in which spectators are increasingly subjected to representations of violent "actions" that may still be advertised as cathartic by certain dominant theories, yet, as any responsible parent cannot fail to notice, are no longer based on classical formal principles but on formless aesthetic principles, are no longer sacred but profane, are no longer administered in homeopathic doses but in massive doses—reaching the risk of overdoses? The answer was already given by advocates of the catharsis hypothesis with which we started. In guise of conclusion, or coda, let us consider their call for the end of a method.

Coda

The End of a Method

On the shoulders of our genealogy of the catharsis hypothesis, we are now in a position to see much farther than when we started, which also means we can revisit the beginning of our investigation from a more informed critical distance. Let us thus return to the figure who provided us with a starting point in the thorny issue of violence and the unconscious revisited from the angle of catharsis. At the end of his career, Girard—again like Freud before him—eventually lost faith in the unconscious efficacy of the catharsis hypothesis he had initially posited at the origins of culture in order to account for the problem of cultural violence. Instead, his last words on the spiraling vortex that ties violence to the unconscious advocates more forcefully than before, an affective or contagious hypothesis.

This is a revealing turn, or *re*-turn, to an ancient hypothesis we shall have to supplement from a contemporary perspective. The late Girard, in fact, considers it necessary to reevaluate the pathologies of contagion to face a type of reciprocal process of unconscious violence that not only is characteristic of rituals in the past but also threatens to escalate in the present and future. Theories, we have learned, bear the traces of historical vicissitudes. They often reflect preoccupations that are those of the epoch in general and specific thinkers in particular. This applies to mimetic theory as well. The genesis of Girard's theory of violence in the late 1950s is historically close to the most devastating crisis of the twentieth century, which culminated with the threat of nuclear escalation, the bombing of Hiroshima and Nagasaki, and the horror of the Holocaust. These were amongst the darkest times in the history of "civilization" so far. And yet, while Girard's thought came to fruition at the end of the twentieth century, it is not without resonances with a growing chain of contemporary thinkers who consider that we now also live in increasingly precarious, vulnerable, and potentially catastrophic times on multiple human and nonhuman fronts[1]—a realization now confirmed with the Russian invasion of Ukraine in 2022 which destabilizes an already precarious world order.

Since Girard is no longer alone in ringing alarm bells in the twenty-first century, his diagnostic of the escalating powers of mimesis is worth bearing in mind, especially since the shadow of nuclear escalation, better angels of human nature aside, returned to darken the horizon. As he suggests in *Battling to the End* (2007), we live in a world in which violence has not only lost its cathartic power; it may contribute to generating more violence instead. Thinking of the horrors of the twentieth century as well as of the emerging threats of the twenty-first century—terrorism, nuclear escalations, resuscitation of cold wars, and, we should not forget, rapid climate change in the age of the Anthropocene—Girard writes: "Violence, which produced the sacred, no longer produces anything but itself" (*BE* x).[2] At the twilight of his career, Girard acknowledges that cathartic ideas about violence and their representations thereof that go back to the origins of culture might turn out to be a fiction.

Gone is the therapeutic value of violence as an unconscious cure. What remains? The catharsis hypothesis, perhaps? No, that hypothesis proved to be the product of a theoretical illusion. We unmasked it as an idealist speculation on a classical myth that had a solver of riddles as its tragic hero in fiction, but that yielded poor therapeutic results in practice. What remains instead is the contagious reality of a mimetic pathology that continues to require clinical, transdisciplinary, and immanent investigations to be properly assessed. For the late Girard, in fact, what is true for desire turns out to be equally true for violence in the end: they are both caught in reciprocal, escalating, and highly contagious principles that produce more of the same pathos—which does not mean that a critical distance on violent pathologies cannot be developed. On the contrary, therapeutic patho-*logies* are more urgent than ever.

This diagnostic conclusion had been a theoretical possibility from the very beginning. Both desire and violence are, in fact, essentially contagious affects that spread unconsciously, generating sameness in place of difference. Hence, grounding his hypothesis on Carl von Clausewitz's *On War*, but with a broader historical and theoretical perspective in mind, Girard explains that violent actions tend to generate violent reactions that, in turn, escape the control of rational consciousness and threaten to catch self and others, pacifist and warlike subjects, pro-terrorist and anti-terrorist nations in a turbulent spiral of reciprocal violence that, he argues, threatens to "escalate to extremes." As Girard puts it: "Humans cannot control reciprocity because they imitate one another too much and their resemblance to one another increases and accelerates"; and he adds: "Violence looks terribly frightening when we have understood its laws and grasped that it is reciprocal and will thus *return*" (*BE* 19). Girard is talking about contagious mechanisms of escalation of physical violence, which in his view are likely to return in the real world, with catastrophic consequences, a tendency amplified by the rise of (new) fascist and authoritarian leaders who deftly exploit the mechanism of contagion in periods of crisis, including pandemic, economic, migrant, and environmental crises.

The question Girard does not address and leaves open for future theorists of mimesis to investigate is whether representations of violence via (new) media—from film to video games—also have the power to affect subjects in the digital age, contributing to the escalation of violence he predicts in reality. We shall have to return to this question by, once again, avoiding unilateral evaluations and paying attention to the double movement of pathos of distance constitutive of our theory of homo mimeticus. Significantly, after a career spent meditating on the potentially pharmaceutical properties of violence, Girard no longer promotes any cathartic, therapeutic, or purgative solution to the plague of mimetic pathologies. On the contrary, he diagnoses the return of violence—with a vengeance. This, however, does not mean that the unconscious principle that triggers this return rests on a repressive hypothesis—quite the contrary.

Beginning, middle, and end, the general telos of our genealogy has cast a shadow on the catharsis hypothesis that dominated the past, Freudian century.

It also encouraged future-oriented transdisciplinary theorists to develop alternative hypotheses to face the post-Freudian challenges that haunt the twenty-first century. On the subject of violence and the unconscious, these challenges not only overturn an entire tradition concerned with the therapeutic effects of catharsis, in which physicians of the past sought therapies in the very pathologies they set out to diagnose in theory. They also urge theorists concerned with the effects of violent representations in practice to pursue the diagnostic of the entangled relation between violence and the unconscious—and of the theories they gave rise to. We shall do so on the basis of a marginalized tradition of the mimetic unconscious that is no less ancient and influential, and is now returning to the forefront of the theoretical scene. If this mimetic theory has been marginalized in the past century, it is increasingly difficult not to notice the centrality of homo mimeticus to the ethical preoccupations, political challenges, new aesthetic media, and revolutionary scientific discoveries characteristic of the present century.

This change of perspective from an Oedipal to a mimetic unconscious on which this study pivots and turns is urgent for at least two reasons. First, because the science of the unconscious has changed significantly in recent years. Thanks to new developments in the humanities, the social sciences, and the neurosciences, all of which are currently informing and transforming the contours of mimetic studies, the unconscious can no longer be limited to familiar Oedipal dramas or dreams to be interpreted. On the contrary, it is proved to be constitutive of our daily waking lives. This book is both the product of recent transformations in theories of mimesis and of the unconscious and a contribution to a theory of homo mimeticus for generations to come. And second, because our network-based societies, and the new digital media that inform them, and more often disinform them, are rapidly changing as well. They do so at an increasing speed, and with growing intensity and power of ramification, catching subjects in a spiral of what I shall call hypermimetic contagion. This contagious spiral that is controlled not by humans but by algorithms is nested in increasingly ubiquitous portable devices that, for better *and* worse, blur the line between representations and realities, what we see online and how we feel and act offline. After a period of enthusiasm for the progress induced by the digital revolution, its shadow can no longer be ignored—from fake news to conspiracy theories, cyberwars to the rise of (new) fascism. This digital shadow concerns the pathologies of new media violence as well.

In a network society dominated by an increasing fascination for representations of violence that are virtually pervasive; are made available from early childhood; and, via full-immersive participatory forms of "entertainment" that now include interactive social media and video games, infiltrate, affect, and infect the psychic life of the subject, a change of hypothesis is urgently in order. We notice, in fact, that contemporary dramatic actions online are far from operating according to a classical Aristotelian conception of aesthetic mimesis as a carefully crafted rational plot (*muthos*) predicated on reversal of fortune and tragic recognition with philosophical potential. Rather, such digital actions reflected on digital surfaces set up a self-reflective mirror to homo mimeticus that urges us to operate an inversion of perspectives—if only because they tend to generate lasting pathological impressions that operate according to a Platonic conception of affective mimesis understood as irrational, contagious, and violent reaction (or mimetic pathos). It is this return of violence deprived of cathartic efficacy that we turn to diagnose in the sequel to this study under the rubric of the affective hypothesis. We shall do so in the company of Plato, Nietzsche, (new) materialist thinkers, affect theorists, and recent re-turns of attention to mimesis constitutive of what I shall call, in the mirroring sequel to this diptych, the mimetic turn.

Notes

ACKNOWLEDGMENTS

1. Cinematic shadows of some of these dialogic encounters are available on the HOM Videos (ERC Project) channel on YouTube: https://www.youtube.com/channel/UCJQy0y0qCxzP4QImG2YWqpw.

PROLOGUE

1. See Nidesh Lawtoo, *Homo Mimeticus: A New Theory of Imitation* (Leuven: Leuven University Press, 2022).

INTRODUCTION: HOMO MIMETICUS

1. For a representative sample of studies on media violence, see Matthew S. Eastin, ed., *Encyclopedia of Media Violence* (Thousand Oaks, CA: Sage, 2013); W. James Potter, *The 11 Myths of Media Violence* (Thousand Oaks, CA: Sage, 2003); *On Media Violence* (London: Sage Publications, 1999); Jonathan L. Freedman, *Media Violence and Its Effect on Aggression: Assessing the Scientific Evidence*, repr. ed. (Toronto: University of Toronto Press, 2003); and Cynthia Carter and C. Kay Weaver, *Violence and the Media* (New York: Open Univeristy Press, 2003). On the role of gender in the debate, see Karen Boyle, *Media and Violence: Gendering the Debates* (London: Sage, 2004); for a historical account of film violence, see James Kendrick, *Film Violence: History, Ideology,*

Genre (London: Wallflower, 2009); for a study that shifts the debate from film and TV to video games, see Barrie Gunter, *Does Playing Video Games Make Players More Violent?* (London: Palgrave Macmillan, 2016); for a collection on the performative effects of online violence (online shaming, bullying, hate speech) via social media (Twitter, Facebook) that generate offline violence, see Sara Polak and Daniel Trotter, eds., *Violence and Trolling on Social Media* (Amsterdam: Amsterdam University Press, 2020).

2. Chad Mahood, "Cathartic Theory," in Eastin, *Encyclopedia of Media Violence*, 59–62, 59.

3. Mahood, "Cathartic Theory," 59.

4. Potter, *11 Myths*, 39.

5. For an overview of the literature on violent video games, see John L. Sherry, "Violent Video Games and Aggression: Why Can't We Find Effects?," in *Mass Media Effects Research: Advances through Meta-Analysis*, ed. R. W. Presiss, B. M. Gayle, N. Burrell, M. Allen, and J. Byrant (Mahwah, NJ: Erlbaum, 2007), 245–62.

6. After framing the causes of behavioral violence in a larger social context, W. James Potter writes: "Media stories tell us how we should deal with conflict, how we should treat other people, what is risky, and what it means to be powerful. The media need to share the blame for this serious public health problem." Potter, *On Media Violence*, 1, 2.

7. Susan Hurley, "Imitation, Media Violence, and Freedom of Speech," *Philosophical Studies: An International Journal for Philosophy in the Analytic Tradition* 117, no. 1–2 (2004): 165–218, 182.

8. Hurley, "Imitation," 182.

9. Barrie Gunter summarizes the overview of the literature by noting that "there is plenty of empirical evidence in the public domain that has concluded that violent video games can trigger aggressive reactions in players," while at the same time noting that "the research evidence is conflicted." Gunter, *Does Playing*, 271.

10. See Edgar Morin, *On Complexity* (New York: Hampton Press, 2008).

11. See Edgar Morin, *Le paradigme perdu: la nature humaine* (Paris: Seuil, 1973), 107–26.

12. In a video interview, Edgar Morin was pleased to add homo mimeticus to his list; see Nidesh Lawtoo and Edgar Morin, *The Complexity of Mimesis: Edgar Morin*, HOM Videos, Ep. 3, 2019, https://www.youtube.com/watch?v=iSKzMydA5Mw&t=6s. For the written version, see Nidesh Lawtoo, "Coda," in *Homo Mimeticus: A New Theory of Imitation* (Leuven: Leuven University Press, 2022).

13. See Steven Pinker, *The Better Angels of Our Nature: Why Violence Has Declined* (New York: Viking Press, 2011).

14. Terry Eagleton, *Sweet Violence: The Idea of the Tragic* (Oxford: Blackwell Publishing, 2003), x.

15. For a rich new materialist account of fragility in the Anthropocene, see William

E. Connolly, *The Fragility of Things: Self-Organizing Processes, Neoliberal Fantasies, and Democratic Activism* (Durham, NC: Duke University Press, 2013). For a philosophically informed feminist account of the lacerating violence internal to terrorism, or "horrorism," see Adriana Cavarero, *Horrorism: Naming Contemporary Violence* (New York: Columbia University Press, 2011). From a decolonial perspective, Achille Mbembe called attention to a type of "brutalism" characterized by a pathos of demolition that operates at the geological, technological, and neurological level in Achille Mbembe, *Brutalisme* (Paris: La Découverte, 2020), 8. For a comprehensive account of the history of violence from prehistoric to the present times that challenges Pinker's hypothesis on a decrease of violence, see *The Cambridge World History of Violence*, vols. 1–4 (Cambridge: Cambridge University Press, 2020).

16. Lawtoo and Morin, *Complexity of Mimesis*.

17. René Girard, *The Scapegoat*, trans. Yvonne Freccero (Baltimore: Johns Hopkins University Press, 1986).

18. René Girard and Michel Serres, *Le tragique et la pitié* (Paris: Le Pommier, 2007), 78 (my trans.).

19. Michel Serres, *Hominescence* (Paris: Le Pommier, 2014), 21.

20. René Girard, *Violence and the Sacred* (Baltimore: Johns Hopkins University Press, 1972). Hereafter *VS*.

21. Friedrich Nietzsche, *On the Genealogy of Morals: A Polemic*, trans. Douglas Smith (Oxford: Oxford University Press, 1996), 10.

22. Butler gives an account of nonviolence in the public sphere where nonviolent protests are often semantically qualified as violent in order to justify racial, gendered, sexual, and other repressions that are constitutive of structural or systemic violence. The fight is thus different, yet Butler's strategic position speaks to this study as well, as she writes: "we have to accept that 'violence' and 'nonviolence' are used variably and perversely, without pitching into a form of nihilism suffused by the belief that violence and nonviolence are whatever those in power decide they should be." Judith Butler, *The Force of Nonviolence: An Ethico-Political Bind* (London: Verso, 2020).

23. As Lode Lauwaert puts it in an anti-essentialist account of violence: "Can we not expect, precisely because 'violence' is related to many other concepts, that there is an overlap between 'violence' on the one hand and, for example, 'aggression' on the other, in such a way that you cannot draw sharp boundaries between the two?" Lode Lauwaert, "Violence and Essentialism?," in *Violence and Meaning*, ed. Lode Lauwaert, Laura Katherine Smith, and Christian Sternad (New York: Palgrave Macmillan, 2019), 27–37, 30.

24. Potter gives the following definition of violence: "Violence is a violation of a character's physical or emotional well-being. It includes two key elements—intentionality and harm—at least one of which must be present." Potter, *On Media Violence*, 80. The World Health Organization equally stresses intentionality as constitutive of violence as it defines the latter as "'the intentional use of physical force or power, threatened or

actual, against oneself, another person, or against a group or community, that either results in or has a high likelihood of resulting in injury, death, psychological harm, maldevelopment or deprivation'" (qtd. in Eastin, ed., *Encyclopedia*, 10). Similarly, definitions of aggression tend to include the "intent to hurt" (Eastin, ed., *Encyclopedia*, 10) as an essential dimension of violence. Based on an anti-essentialist conception of violence, this study both restricts the protean meanings of violence to the problematic of the effects of (new) media violence and expands its meaning to include *non-intentional*, unconscious actions and reactions that go beyond rationalist accounts of the subject.

25. Nidesh Lawtoo, *The Phantom of the Ego: Modernism and the Mimetic Unconscious* (East Lansing: Michigan State University Press, 2013).

26. E. R. Dodds, *The Greeks and the Irrational* (Berkeley: University of California Press, 1964), 185.

27. On the power of digital computational media in general to affect the unconscious and transform our conception of the human, see also Patricia Ticineto Clough, *The User Unconscious: On Affect, Media, and Measure* (Minneapolis: University of Minnesota Press, 2018).

28. Potter, *On Media Violence*, 7.

29. On mimesis in literature, albeit restricted to realism, see Erich Auerbach, *Mimesis: The Representation of Reality in Western Literature*, trans. Willard R. Trask (Princeton, NJ: Princeton University Press, 2003); for an informed study that traces the shifting meanings of catharsis in theories, from Aristotle to Freud, the new critics to structuralism and reader-response, see Adnan K. Abdulla, *Catharsis in Literature* (Bloomington: Indiana University Press, 1985).

30. For an informed reframing of the history of mimesis that starts in aesthetics and includes sociology and anthropology, see Gunter Gebauer and Christoph Wulf, *Mimesis: Culture-Art-Society*, trans. Don Reneau (Berkeley: University of California Press, 1995); for transdisciplinary essays that take seriously the powers of mimesis, see Susan Hurley and Nick Chater, eds., *Perspectives on Imitations: From Neuroscience to Social Science*, vol. 2, *Imitation, Human Development, and Culture* (Cambridge, MA: MIT Press, 2005); for a collection that opens up Girard's mimetic theory to the neurosciences, see Scott R. Garrels, ed., *Mimesis and Science: Empirical Research on Imitation and the Mimetic Theory of Culture and Religion* (East Lansing: Michigan State University Press, 2011); for a short and clear philosophical reframing of mimesis attentive to mimicry and subject formation, see Samuel IJsseling, *Mimesis: On Appearing and Being* (Kampen, NE: Pharos, 1990); for a rich collection of essays that calls for a return of attention to mimesis and society in different strands of social theory, see Christian Borch, ed., *Imitation, Contagion, Suggestion: On Mimesis and Society* (New York: Routledge, 2019); for a transdisciplinary project that builds on these and other studies to further a mimetic turn, or re-turn of mimesis in the twenty-first century, see the outputs of the ERC-funded project titled *Homo Mimeticus: Theory and Criticism*, http://www.homomimeticus.eu/publications/. See also Lawtoo, *Homo Mimeticus*.

31. On the modernist foundations of my theory of mimesis qua homo mimeticus, see Lawtoo, *Phantom of the Ego*; and *Conrad's Shadow: Catastrophe, Mimesis, Theory* (East Lansing: Michigan State University Press, 2016). On its contemporary political implications, see *(New) Fascism: Contagion, Community, Myth* (East Lansing: Michigan State University Press, 2019). Lawtoo, *Homo Mimeticus*.

32. The classicist Stephen Halliwell writes that the ideas of Greek poetics "are part of the genealogy of arguments and attitudes in whose modern forms some of our own values may still be invested"; and thinking of Aristotle's *Poetics* he says that it has "left lingering traces, if often at the subconscious level, in many areas of literary theory and criticism." Stephen Halliwell, *Between Ecstasy and Truth: Interpretations of Greek Poetics from Homer to Longinus* (Oxford: Oxford University Press, 2011), 5, 220. Adnan Abdulla generalizes this point as he argues that "the history of literary criticism . . . is the history of contested meanings of basic concepts, such as catharsis, mimesis, and the sublime." Abdulla, *Catharsis*, 1. After an informed overview of translations of catharsis as purgation, purification, clarification with "medical, religious, moral, or aesthetic connotations" (13), he sets out to chart the transformations of the concept of catharsis in both its affective and cognitive dimensions in the history of literary criticism until the 1980s. Brining the debate closer to our concerns, Terry Eagleton notices that "the conflict between Plato and Aristotle is thus one familiar today between mimetic and therapeutic theories of pornography or media violence." Eagleton, *Sweet Violence*, 154. We shall go further and stress that this conflict also opens up an alternative conception of the unconscious that does not rest on an Oedipal myth as a *via regia*. For a short and informed genealogy of catharsis and contagion in theatrical spectacles that goes back to Plato and Aristotle and acknowledges these medical foundations, see also Denis Guénon, "Contagion and Purgation," in *Actions et acteurs: Raisons du drame sur scène* (Paris: Belin, 2005), 189–99.

33. Funded by the European Research Council, outputs of *Homo Mimeticus* also include special issues on "Poetics and Politics," *Modern Language Notes* 132, no. 5 (2017); "The Mimetic Condition," *CounterText* 8, no. 1 (2022); and "Posthuman Mimesis," *Journal of Posthumanism* (2022); as well as the monographs *(New) Fascism* (2019) and *Homo Mimeticus*, among other outputs.

34. Friedrich Nietzsche, "On the Uses and Disadvantages of History for Life," in *Untimely Meditations*, ed. Daniel Breazeale, trans. R. J. Hollingdale (Cambridge: Cambridge University Press, 2007), 57–124, 59.

35. Nietzsche, "On the Uses," 59.

36. Nietzsche, "On the Uses," 59.

37. Nietzsche, *Genealogy of Morals*, 3; hereafter in-text citation (*GM*, section number; page number).

38. Nietzsche, "On the Uses," 60.

39. Friedrich Nietzsche, *Daybreak: Thoughts on the Prejudices of Morality*, trans. R. J. Hollingdale (Cambridge: Cambridge University Press, 1982), 31. Michel Foucault's

structuralist lens may have made too much an opposition out of Nietzsche's use of synonymous concepts like *Ursprung* and *Herkunft* constitutive of his genealogical perspective. Still, we agree with Foucault that "where the soul pretends unification or the self fabricates a coherent identity, the genealogist sets out to study the beginning— numberless beginnings whose faint traces and hints of color are readily seen by an historical eye." Michel Foucault, "Nietzsche, Genealogy, History," in *Language, Counter-Memory, Practice: Selected Essays and Interviews*, ed. Donald F. Bouchard (Ithaca, NY: Cornell University Press, 1984), 138–64, 145.

40. See also Lawtoo, *Phantom of the Ego*, 27–52.

41. Walter Kaufmann comments on the semantic richness of πάθος (pathos) as he notes: "Occasion, event, passion, suffering, destiny are among the meanings of this Greek word." Friedrich Nietzsche, *The Will to Power*, trans. Walter Kaufmann, R. J. Hollingdale, ed. Walter Kaufmann (New York: Vintage Books, 1968), 339. Hereafter *WP* (section; page number).

42. I first articulated the differences between Girard's mimetic theory and my theory of mimesis in Lawtoo, "Mimetic Theory Revisited," in *Phantom of the Ego*, 281–305; see also *Conrad's Shadow*, esp. chs. 1, 3, 4, and *(New) Fascism*, ch. 1.

43. Thomas Gould places the contested notion of pathos at the heart of the ancient quarrel between poetry and philosophy, thereby tying the force of pathos to mimesis. He specifies: "It is probable, but not entirely certain, that *pathein*, from which *pathos*, *pathema*, and other new nouns were formed in the fifth century, meant, from the beginning, 'to suffer,' 'to undergo a calamity.' The verb's etymology is obscure." To give this pathos a mythic face, Gould also notes that in addition to Dionysus for the gods, for humans, "Odysseus was the Homeric hero most closely identified with *pathein*." Thomas Gould, *The Ancient Quarrel between Poetry and Philosophy* (Princeton, NJ: Princeton University Press, 1990), xi, 27; see also 22–28. For a study that ties pathos to images of violence in the twentieth century, or "pathos of the real," see Robert Buch, *The Pathos of the Real: On the Aesthetics of Violence in the Twentieth Century* (Baltimore: Johns Hopkins University Press, 2010). If both Gould and Buch adopt a psychoanalytical (Freudian and Lacanian, respectively) lens to account for the unrepresentable violence of the twentieth century (or Real), my study adopts a (Nietzschean) account of representable violence via the catharsis/contagion debate for the twenty-first century.

44. Friedrich Nietzsche, *The Birth of Tragedy*, in *The Birth of Tragedy and The Case of Wagner*, ed. and trans. Walter Kaufmann (New York: Vintage Books, 1967), 38.

45. Addressing the dancers' exclamation to Oedipus's tragic suffering in *Oedipus Rex*, "fearful pathos for men to look on," Thomas Gould notes: "The dancers' aversion and abhorrence at the sight of the blinded Oedipus is almost as strong as their intense fascination. The same is true of the audience. This is very strange: we are taking a grim kind of pleasure in what horrifies us." Gould, *Ancient Quarrel*, x.

46. As Desmond Morris points out in the context of a discussion of the physio-psychology of fighting: "The former is the one that is concerned with preparing the body for

violent activity [pathos]. The latter has the task of preserving and restoring bodily reserves [distance]." Desmond Morris, *The Naked Ape: A Zoologist's Study of the Human Animal* (London: Vintage Books, 2005), 100.

47. Michel Henry, *Généalogie de la psychanalyse: le commencement perdu* (Paris: Presses Universitaires de France, 1985), 328, 5 (my trans.). Hereafter *GP*. For an incisive reevaluation of the significance of Michel Henry's genealogy for a critique of psychoanalysis' disavowal of a non-representational affective mimesis, see Mikkel Borch-Jacobsen, *The Emotional Tie: Psychoanalysis, Mimesis, and Affect* (Stanford, CA: Stanford University Press, 1992), 123–54.

48. What I call patho(-)logy finds in Nietzsche's perspectivism its main source of inspiration and has its ancient origins in Plato's conception of the *pharmakon*. Building on Jacques Derrida, a contemporary philosopher who also furthers this tradition to develop an influential pharmacology of technics is Bernard Stiegler. Stiegler and I share a number of presuppositions on the good/bad nature of media, the necessity to develop a therapeutic approach that is attentive to both pathos and logos, which we both group under the concept of patho(-)logy—a genealogical connection I became aware of after the publication of *The Phantom of the Ego* (2013) and is internal to Stiegler's *What Makes Life Worth Living: On Pharmacology*, trans. Daniel Ross (Cambridge: Polity, 2013). This overlap is less surprising if we consider that we inherit it from a partially shared genealogy: Derrida is the main source for Stiegler's pharmacology of techne; Nietzsche for the present author's diagnostic of the patho(-)logy of mimesis. Our differences touch on the conception of the unconscious on which our respective patho-*logies* rest: while Stiegler remains in line with a (Oedipal) conception of the unconscious that has in Freud's concept of libido its main driving force, the present author, while being informed by the history of this tradition (or perhaps because of that), departs from it in significant ways by furthering a (Nietzschean) conception of the unconscious that has mimesis as its *via regia*. This *différend* shall not prevent productive exchanges between these two exemplary traditions and find in the psychoanalytical notion of identification a productive genealogical bridge. Last, let me note that in August 2020 Stiegler had kindly agreed to engage in a dialogue on mimesis; I regret that his premature death prevented this encounter.

49. On Nietzsche's perspectivism as patho(-)logy see also, Lawtoo, *Phantom of the Ego*, 6–8, 27–81.

50. Walter Benjamin, *Illuminations*, trans. Harry Zohn, ed. Hannah Arendt (New York: Schocken Books, 2007), 257–58.

51. See Lawtoo, *Phantom of the Ego*, and "The Mimetic Unconscious," in Borch, ed., *Imitation, Contagion, Suggestion*, 37–53.

52. See Henri F. Ellenberger, *The Discovery of the Unconscious: The History and Evolution of Dynamic Psychiatry* (New York: Basic Books, Inc., Publishers, 1970); see also, Mikkel Borch-Jacobsen and Sonu Shamdasani, *The Freud Files: An Inquiry into the History of Psychoanalysis* (Cambridge: Cambridge University Press, 2012).

CHAPTER 1. THE "TRUE" UNCONSCIOUS: GIRARD TO FREUD

1. For a recent example of an influential theorist who both echoes and furthers Girard's insights into sacrificial violence, see Terry Eagleton, *Radical Sacrifice* (New Haven, CT: Yale University Press, 2018).

2. René Girard and Michel Serres, *Le tragique et la pitié* (Paris: Le Pommier, 2007), 63 (my transl.).

3. Adnan K. Abdulla, *Catharsis in Literature* (Bloomington: Indiana University Press, 1985), 2. I shall not reiterate discussions of the meaning of catharsis in Hegel, Cassirer, Lukács, the new critics, formalists, and reader response critics already discussed in this informed book. Instead, I start were Abdulla's account ended by taking my genealogy of mimesis beyond traditional literary criticism in view of reconstructing, in a more critical vein than Abdulla does, the theories of the unconscious now animating debates on media violence as well.

4. René Girard, *Evolution and Conversion: Dialogues on the Origins of Culture* (with Pierpaolo Antonello and João Cezar de Castro Rocha) (London: Continuum, 2007), 59. Hereafter *EC*.

5. On Girard's dispensation with the notion of a "collective unconscious," see also William A. Johnsen, *Violence and Modernism: Ibsen, Joyce, and Woolf* (Gainesville: University of Florida Press, 2003), ix.

6. See, respectively, René Girard, *Deceit, Desire and the Novel*, trans. Yvonne Freccero (Baltimore: Johns Hopkins University Press, 1965); René Girard, *Violence and the Sacred* (Baltimore: Johns Hopkins University Press, 1977); and René Girard, *The Scapegoat*, trans. Yvonne Freccero (Baltimore: Johns Hopkins University Press, 1986).

7. For informed introductions to Girard's mimetic theory, see Chris Fleming, *René Girard: Violence and Mimesis* (Cambridge: Polity, 2004); Wolfgang Palaver, *René Girard's Mimetic Theory* (East Lansing: Michigan State University Press, 2013).

8. René Girard, *Battling to the End: Conversations with Benoît Chantre* (East Lansing: Michigan State University Press, 2010), 30. Hereafter *BE*.

9. For an early review that recognized that "the starting point for Girard's argument is to be found in the Hegelian analysis of the development of self-consciousness," see Carl A. Rubino, "Review: *La Violence et le sacré*," *Modern Language Notes* 87, no. 7 (1972): 986–98, 987. For a rigorous philosophical account of Girard's thought that is attentive to the latter's "(paradoxical) refusal to deal directly with Hegel," while being obviously influenced by Hegel, see Philippe Lacoue-Labarthe, *Typography: Mimesis, Philosophy, Politics*, ed. Christopher Fynsk (Stanford, CA: Stanford University Press, 1998), 105, n101; see also 102–21.

10. Konrad Lorenz, *On Aggression*, trans. Marjorie Latzke (London: Routledge, 1966).

11. The added quotation marks around "true" indicate the author's suspicion on a single "truth" concerning the slippery concept of the unconscious.

12. For a phenomenological critique of the Freudian unconscious' entanglement in a philosophy of representation and consciousness, see also Henry, *Généalogie*, 343–86.

13. On Girard's interest in hypnosis and the unconscious, see *Des choses*, 445–56; on Girard's "demythification" and inversion of Freud's take on narcissism and the unconscious dynamic it entails, see "Narcissism: The Freudian Myth Demythified by Proust," in *Psychoanalysis, Creativity, and Literature*, ed. Alan Roland (New York: Columbia University Press, 1978), 293–311. In these and other texts, Girard seems both attracted and repelled by the Freudian unconscious, both intent in uncovering a "true" unconscious and doubtful about retaining what he calls "perhaps too equivocal a term." Girard, *Des choses*, 499 (my trans.). I shall return to this mimetic or, as I shall call it, romantic agonism.

14. On jealousy, see Jean-Pierre Dupuy, *La jalousie: Une géométrie du désir* (Paris: Seuil, 2016).

15. I trace the development of Nietzsche's thought out of a mimetic agonism with main models Schopenhauer, Plato, and Wagner, in Lawtoo, *The Phantom of the Ego: Modernism and the Mimetic Unconscious* (East Lansing: Michigan State University Press, 2013), ch. 1.

16. As Huizinga puts it, "The function of play . . . can largely be derived from the two basic aspects under which we meet it: as a contest *for* something or a representation *of* something. These two functions can unite in such a way that the game 'represents' a contest, or else becomes a contest for the best representation of something." Johan Huizinga, *Homo Ludens: A Study of the Play-Element in Culture* (Kettering, OH: Angelico Press, 2016), 13. On the role of both agon and mimetism in games, see also Roger Caillois, *Man, Play, and Games*, trans. Meyer Barash (New York: The Free Press of Glencone, 1961), 14–23. Mimesis/mimetism and the agon are thus genealogically linked, but what I call mimetic agonism concerns the specific dynamic of contestation internal to intellectual contests, as it will become clear below.

17. Friedrich Nietzsche, "Richard Wagner in Bayreuth," in *The Untimely Meditations*, ed. Daniel Breazeale, trans. R. J. Hollingdale (Cambridge: Cambridge University Press, 2007), 195–294 , 223. For an informed account of the Greek origins of the early Nietzsche's mimetic agonism with Wagner, see also Herman Siemens, "Agonal Configurations in the *Unzeitgemässe Betrachtungen*. Identity, Mimesis and the *Übertragung* of Culture in Nietzsche's Early Thought," *Nietzsche-Studien* 30 (2001): 80–106. For two illuminating studies completely devoted to the role the agon plays in Nietzsche's thought that regrettably appeared too late to be incorporated here, see James S. Pearson, *Nietzsche's Philosophy of Conflict and the Logic of Organizational Struggle* (Cambridge: Cambridge University Press, 2022); and Herman Siemens, *Agonal Perspectives on Nietzsche's Philosophy of Critical Transvaluation* (Berlin: De Gruyter, 2021). What Siemens calls "agonistic mimesis" is extremely close to what I call "mimetic agonism," the only difference being perhaps that the latter stresses the centrality of a mimetic/Dionysian pathos in tying the subject to the model as a necessary affective precondition for the productive logical, or patho-*logical*

contestation to subsequently take place. I am grateful to Herman for inviting me to discuss my version of the mimetic agon in his Nietzsche seminar at Leiden University (where Huizinga first gave his *homo ludens* lectures) and for his warm hospitality during my stay.

18. Harold Bloom sums up his romantic theory of anxiety of influence as follows: since "every poet is belated, . . . every poem is an instance of what Freud called *Nachträglichkeit*"; and specifying the dynamic of "creative misreading" or "misprision" that ensues, he continues: the poet "strives for a selection, through repression, out of the traces of the language of poetry." Harold Bloom, "Poetry, Revisionism, Repression," in *Critical Theory since 1965*, ed. Hazard Adams and Leroy Searle (Tallahassee: Florida State University Press, 1989), 330–43, 332. See also Harold Bloom, *The Anxiety of Influence: A Theory of Poetry*, 2nd ed. (Oxford: Oxford University Press, 1997).

19. See Jacob Burckhardt, *The Greeks and Greek Civilization* (London: HarperCollins, 1998), 160–213. Hereafter *GGC*. As Oswyn Murray puts it, speaking of Burckhardt and Nietzsche's "joint discovery" of the agon: "undoubtedly the most significant specific idea about the Greek world that Burckhardt and Nietzsche shared was the belief in the importance of the 'agonal' aspect of Greek and (in Nietzsche's case) modern culture. . . . Nietzsche seems to have realized the importance of agon or contest, even before he arrived in Basel; but Burckhardt had already formulated it independently and was busy working out in detail the consequences of this discovery for the understanding of every aspect of Greek culture" (xxxii). From a different perspective, Johan Huizinga notes: "Jacob Burckhardt coined the word 'agonal' and described the purport of it as one of the main characteristics of Hellenic culture. Burckhardt, however, was not equipped to perceive the widespread sociological background of the phenomenon." Huizinga, *Homo Ludens*, 71; see also 30–31.

20. For a thorough and wide-ranging discussion of the dynamic of *Wettkampf* in Nietzsche, see Siemens, *Agonal Perspectives*, 42–88.

21. Homer, *The Odyssey*, trans. E. V. Rieu (London: Penguin Books, 1991), 8.133–55, 110. Hereafter *O*.

22. For an informed and groundbreaking theory of art from the Greeks to the present that counters the myth of originality from the angle of art understood as a "craft" and "techne" that, like mimesis, originates in Plato and Aristotle, see Henry Staten, *Techne Theory: A New Language for Art* (London: Bloomsbury, 2019), esp. 47–83.

23. Pseudo-Longinus, "On the Sublime," in *Critical Theory since Plato*, 3rd ed., ed. Hazard Adams and Leroy Searle (Boston: Thomson Wadsworth, 2005), 94–118, 103.

24. Pseudo-Loginus, "On the Sublime," 103.

25. As Murray notes: "The exact relation between the views of Burckhardt and Nietzsche on the agon is obscure, and would repay further investigation." Murray, "Introduction," n55, 369. From the comparison that follows, it is apparent that Nietzsche was much influenced by Burckhardt's account of the Greek agon, but he put it to creative use in his practice of the modernist, mimetic agon.

26. Friedrich Nietzsche, "Homer's Contest," trans. and ed. Christa Davis Acampora, *Nietzscheana* 5 (1996): 1–8. Hereafter HC.

27. See Girard, *Deceit, Desire and the Novel*. Given's Nietzsche's emphásis on "resentment," "jealousy," and other rivalrous passions internal to the bad Eris, it would be interesting to know if Girard was familiar with this early Nietzschean text for two reasons: first, because it serves as precursor to the logic of mimetic rivalry; second, because it provides an alternative to it. Should Girard have been familiar with this text, this would mean he voluntarily turned away from theorizing good Eris.

28. Burckhardt, *Greeks*, 165.

29. I confronted Girard's thought in the spirit of this mimetic agonism qua duel in Nidesh Lawtoo, *Conrad's Shadow: Catastrophe, Mimesis, Theory* (East Lansing: Michigan State University Press, 2016), ch. 1.

30. On how measure, for Nietzsche, is the product of the reciprocal dynamic of the agon, the most insightful account is again Siemens, *Agonal Perspectives*, 23–41.

31. Karl Jaspers, *General Psychopathology vol. I*, trans. J. Hoenig and Marian W. Hamilton (Baltimore: Johns Hopkins University Press, 1997), 310.

32. I first noticed the continuities between Girard and Freud in Lawtoo, *Phantom of the Ego*, 233–47, 284–95. For a precursor that sets up a critical dialogue between Girard's mimetic theory and psychoanalysis, see Mikkel Borch-Jacobsen, *The Freudian Subject*, trans. Catherine Porter (Stanford, CA: Stanford University Press, 1988), esp. 26–52.

33. The original formulation reads: "You *ought to be* like this (like your father) . . . You *may not be* like this (like your father)—that is, you may not do all that he does; some things are his prerogative." Sigmund Freud, *The Ego and the Id*, trans. Joan Rivière, ed. James Strachey (London: W.W. Norton & Company, 1960), 30.

34. René Girard, "Tiresias and the Critic," in *The Structuralist Controversy: The Languages of Criticism and the Sciences of Man*, ed. Richard Macksey and Eugenio Donato (Baltimore: Johns Hopkins University Press, 1972), 15–21, 19.

35. Girard, "Tiresias and the Critic," 17.

36. Girard, "Tiresias and the Critic," 17.

37. Girard, *Deceit*, 2.

38. I am grateful to Richard (Dick) Macksey for inviting me, during my stay at the Humanities Center from 2013 to 2016, to his legendary library and sharing numerous stories about the 1966 symposium and the role Girard played in it. For a biographical account of Girard's role in the 1966 conference, see the chapter "French Invasion" in Cynthia L. Haven, *Evolution of Desire: A Life of René Girard* (East Lansing: Michigan State University Press, 2018), 121–46.

39. Haven, *Evolution of Desire*, 121.

40. Girard qtd. in Haven, *Evolution of Desire*, 124.

41. This does not mean that violence was not a fundamental preoccupation during the linguistic turn. See, for instance, Jacques Derrida, "Violence et métaphysique," in *L'écriture et la différence* (Paris: Seuil, 1967), 117–228.

42. On Girard and Derrida's mimetic agonism via sameness and difference, see Lawtoo, *Homo Mimeticus: A New Theory of Imitation* (Leuven: Leuven University Press, 2022), ch. 3; for a comparative study that considers Girard and Derrida "enemy brothers [*frères ennemies*]," see Andrew J. McKenna, *Violence and Difference: Girard, Derrida, and Deconstruction* (Champaign: University of Illinois Press, 1992).

43. Friedrich Nietzsche, *Beyond Good and Evil*, trans. R. J. Hollingdale (London: Penguin Books, 2003), 37.

44. Benoît Chantre, *Les derniers jours de René Girard* (Paris: Grasset, 2016), 50 (my trans.).

45. For an anecdotal, biographical, but theoretically revealing account of typically academic "friendly rivalry," or mimetic agonism, concerning Girard and his former colleague at Johns Hopkins and major advocate of deconstruction, J. Hillis Miller, see Nidesh Lawtoo, "The Critic and the Mime: J. Hillis Miller in Dialogue with Nidesh Lawtoo," *Minnesota Review* 95 (2020): 93–119, 103–4.

46. On the escalation of violence, see Girard, *Battling to the End*; on the politics of mimesis, see Lawtoo, *(New) Fascism*; on mimesis and economy, see Jean-Pierre Dupuy, *Economy and the Future: A Crisis of Faith*, trans. M. B. DeBevoise (East Lansing: Michigan State University Press, 2014); for an insightful account of mimesis in financial markets explicitly in line with our theory of homo mimeticus, see Christian Borch, *Social Avalanche: Crowds, Cities and Financial Markets* (Cambridge: Cambridge University Press, 2020), 94–95.

47. See Sara Polak and Daniel Trotter, eds., *Violence and Trolling on Social Media* (Amsterdam: Amsterdam University Press, 2020).

48. See the special issue on "Posthuman Mimesis," in *Journal of Posthumanism* 2, no. 2 (2022).

49. Benedict de Spinoza, *Ethics* (including *The Improvement of the Understanding*), trans. R. H. M. Elwes (Amherst, NY: Prometheus Books, 1989), 152, 153. On the basis of this mimetic hypothesis, in Book 3, Spinoza sets out to explain envy, honor, shame, hatred, and other sad affects that diminish a body's power of activity. On Girard and Spinoza, see also Jean-Michel Oughourlian, *The Mimetic Brain*, trans. Trevor Cribben Merrill (East Lansing: Michigan State University Press, 2016), 17–19.

50. On the role of *homo sacer* in Roman law that is not without parallels to mimetic theorists like Girard and Bataille, see Giorgio Agamben, *Homo Sacer: Sovereign Power and Bare Life*, trans. Daniel Heller-Roazen (Stanford, CA: Stanford University Press, 1998).

51. Jacques Lacan, "The Mirror Stage as Formative to the Function of the I as Revealed in Psychoanalytical Experience," in *Écrits: A Selection*, trans. Alan Sheridan (Paris: Seuil, 1977), 1–7, 6.

52. Lacan, "Mirror Stage," 5, 6.

53. René Girard, *Des choses cachées depuis la fondation du monde: Recherches avec Jean-Michel Oughourlian et Guy Lefort* (Paris: Bernard Grasset, 1978), 422–28, 448–56.

54. For a mention to Girard's "praise [of] the imitative aspects of dramatic tragedy that he says lead to a purification of the passions of pity and fear, or the famous Aristotelian 'catharsis,'" see Palaver, *René Girard*, 45.

55. Jean-Pierre Vernant and Pierre Vidal-Naquet, *Myth and Tragedy in Ancient Greece*, trans. Janet Lloyd (New York: Zone Books, 1988), 16, 17.

56. Vernant and Vidal-Naquet immediately add: "If that is so [that representations of sacrifice were condemned], how can the tragedies be regarded as sacrificial crises, as they are by many of René Girard's disciples, or rather, how could they possibly *not* be, given that, thanks to a major distortion, the very idea of a sacrificial crisis is taken from Greek tragedy?" Vernant and Vidal-Naquet, *Myth and Tragedy*, 17.

57. See Georges Bataille, "Hegel, la mort, le sacrifice," in *Œuvres Complètes*, vol. 12 (Paris: Gallimard, 1988), 326–45, 336–37.

58. Friedrich Nietzsche, *The Birth of Tragedy*, in *The Birth of Tragedy and The Case of Wagner*, ed. and trans. Walter Kaufmann (New York: Vintage Books, 1967), 73. Hereafter *BT*.

59. In his overview of the different interpretations of catharsis, Adnan Abdulla puts it thus: "It is not an exaggeration to say that in the history of aesthetics and criticism no other single concept has created such controversy." Abdulla, *Catharsis*, 13.

60. Gerald F. Else, "'Imitation' in the Fifth Century," *Classical Philology* 53, no. 2 (1958): 73–90, 76.

61. On Girard's engagement with Freud's Oedipal and anthropological thesis, see Girard, *Violence and the Sacred*, chs. 7 and 8.

CHAPTER 2. BIRTH OF PSYCHOANALYSIS: OUT OF THE CATHARTIC METHOD

1. See Robert J. James, *Dictionnaire universel de la médecine*, vol. 3, trans. Diderot Eidous et Toussaint (Paris: Rue St. Jacques, 1747), 151.

2. René Girard, "Perilous Balance: A Comic Hypothesis," *Modern Language Notes* 87, no. 7 (1972): 811–26, 813. This idea of purgation of humors, as Adnan Abdulla specifies, originates in "Greek medicine," with Hippocrates's theory of "four humors" and the evacuation assumed to keep them in harmonious balance. Adnan K. Abdulla, *Catharsis in Literature* (Bloomington: Indiana University Press, 1985), 14.

3. Pierre Corneille, "Discours de la tragédie," qtd. in *Dictionary of Untranslatables: A Philosophical Lexicon*, ed. Barbara Cassin, translation ed. Emily Apter, Jacques Lezra, and Michael Wood (Princeton, NJ: Princeton University Press, 2014), 128; see also 127.

4. See M. H. Abrams, *The Mirror and the Lamp: Romantic Theory and the Critical Tradition* (Oxford: Oxford University Press, 1953).

5. As Abrams specifies via romantic figures like John Keble, Byron, and others: "Aristotle's description of the cathartic effect of tragedy upon pity and fear of its auditors was generalized to include all emotions in all forms of poetry, and silently shifted to denote the healing expenditure of feeling in the poet himself." Abrams, *The Mirror and the Lamp*, 138.

6. See also Abdulla, *Catharsis*, 19.

7. Jean-Jacques Rousseau, *Lettre à d'Alambert* (Paris: Flammarion, 2003), 72 (my trans.).

8. Rousseau, *Lettre*, 68.

9. As Michel Henry also recognizes: "To be sure, when Freud comes to Paris, a psychology of the unconscious thought of as the unavoidable condition of the central phenomenon of memory, drags in all philosophical manuals of the time. The concept of the unconscious, which is simultaneously the one of Bergson and Freud [and we should also add of Nietzsche, Janet, Bernheim and many others], was taught in schools before it became their genial discovery in their books." Michel Henry, *Généalogie de la psychanalyse: le commencement perdu* (Paris: Presses Universitaires de France, 1985), 13. For an informed historical account, see Henri F. Ellenberger, *The Discovery of the Unconscious: The History and Evolution of Dynamic Psychiatry* (New York: Basic Books, 1970), 110–417.

10. Foucault, "Nietzsche, Genealogy, History," 156.

11. Frank J. Sulloway, *Freud, Biologist of the Mind: Beyond the Psychoanalytic Legend*, 2nd ed. (Cambridge, MA: Harvard University Press, 1992), 57.

12. Friedrich Nietzsche, *On the Genealogy of Morals: A Polemic*, trans. Douglas Smith (Oxford: Oxford University Press, 1996), 8.

13. Jacob Bernays, "Aristotle on the Effect of Tragedy," trans. Jennifer Barnes, in *Oxford Readings in Ancient Literary Criticism*, ed. Andrew Laird (Oxford: Oxford University Press, 2006), 158–75, 165. Henceforth "AET." The article was later collected in Jacob Bernays, *Zwei Abhandlungen über die Aristotelische Theorie des Drama* (Berlin: Wilhelm Hertz, 1880). I checked the English translation against the original German edition, *Grundzüge der Verlorenen Abhandlung des Aristoteles über Wirkung der Tragödie* (Breslau: Verlag von Eduard Trewendt, 1857).

14. Sulloway, *Freud*, 57.

15. Aristotle, *Politics*, in *The Complete Works of Aristotle*, vol. 2, ed. Jonathan Barnes (Princeton, NJ: Princeton University Press, 1984), 1986–2129. Hereafter *Pol.*

16. Jacques Lacan, *The Ethics of Psychoanalysis 1959–60: The Seminar of Jacques Lacan, Book VII*, ed. Jacques-Alain Miller, trans. Dennis Porter (New York: Routledge, 2008), 303, 304.

17. Lacan, *Ethics*, 304.

18. Historians generally agree that "it is extremely difficult to believe they [Freud and Breuer] were not" familiar with Bernays's cathartic theory; even the first patient on which this method was tested (Anna O.) was apparently informed by it and responded accordingly. See Sulloway, *Freud*, 57, and Ellenberger, *Discovery of the Unconscious*, 484. See also Jacques Le Rieder, "Philologie grecque et formation de la théorie psychanalytique: Sigmund Freud et Theodor Gomperz," *Essaim* 1, no. 7 (2001): 203–17; and Martin Treml, "Zum Verhältnis von Jacob Bernays und Sigmund Freud," *Luzifer-Amor* 19 (1997): 7–38. Mikkel Borch-Jacobsen also informed me that Freud mentions Bernays in a letter to Arnold Zweig on November 27, 1932 (email to the author, May 19, 2016). From the above, it is obvious that Freud had read Bernays.

19. The English translation renders *zurückdrängen* as "subjugate," but the literal meaning is actually "pressing" (*drängen*) "back" (*zurück*) or, more simply, "re-pressing."

20. Abdulla also notes that "the study of catharsis is the study of the development of psychoanalysis" and that "catharsis became the cornerstone of psychoanalysis." Abdulla, *Catharsis*, 30, 118. Accurate at the general level, and right in insisting on both the emotional and cognitive sides of catharsis, Abdulla in our view doesn't push his chapter on "Catharsis in Psychoanalysis" far enough as he uncritically accepts both Bernays's medical interpretation and Freud's and Breuer's cathartic methods. Recent developments in the history of psychoanalysis, without being dismissive of catharsis altogether, call for a more critical reevaluation.

21. Mikkel Borch-Jacobsen notes: "the word *Verdrängung* had already been used by [Johann Friedrich] Herbart in *Psychologie als Wissenschaft* (1824) and in *Lehrbuch zur Psychologie* (1806) and Freud apparently knew of this via [Theodor] Meynert." Borch-Jacobsen specifies: "I always thought that the term 'cathartic method' comes from Breuer rather than Freud who speaks of 'Breuer-method'"; "Freud starts to use the term *verdrängen* in 1893 in conjunction to *unterdrücken*, which he had already used in 1892 in an article titled, 'Un cas de guérison par l'hypnose'" (email to the author, May 19, 2016). Interestingly, the early 1890s also correspond to the period of the development of the cathartic method.

22. Genealogists of psychoanalysis like Michel Henry trace the Freudian theory of repression back to Schopenhauer's metaphysical theory of the "will to refuse to allow a representation contrary to the mind [*esprit*] to penetrate it" (*GP* 227); if this theory is shot through with a number of aporias—for instance, how can a blind will show such discernment? (see *GP* 227–34)—my genealogical hypothesis links repression to a dynamic account of drives embryonic in Bernays's cathartic theory.

23. Michel Foucault, *Histoire de la sexualité I: la volonté de savoir* (Paris: Gallimard, 1976), 74–75.

24. On the iconography of hysterical pantomime, see Georges Didi-Huberman, *L'invention de l'hystérie: Charcot et l'Iconographie photographique de la Salpêtrière* (Paris: Macula, 1982); on the performative effects of psychiatric theories in the construction of mimetic symptoms, see Mikkel Borch-Jacobsen, *Making Madness: From Hysteria to Depression* (Cambridge: Cambridge University Press, 2009).

25. Ellenberger, *Discovery*, 485. Ellenberger also points out that Janet "claimed priority in having discovered the cathartic cure of neurosis brought forth by the clarification of traumatic origins" (*DU* 344).

26. Mikkel Borch-Jacobsen, "Sigmund Freud, Hypnotiseur," in Sigmund Freud, *L'Hypnose: Textes 1886–1993* (Paris: Éditions l'Iconoclaste, 2015), 13–180, 65. On Freud's mimetic relation with Charcot, see 62–113. I am grateful to Mikkel for sending me the typeset manuscript before it was available in print and for numerous friendly and formative discussions on mimesis and hypnosis to which this chapter is indebted.

27. Borch-Jacobsen, "Sigmund Freud, Hypnotiseur," 69.

28. See Mikkel Borch-Jacobsen, *The Freudian Subject*, trans. Catherine Porter (Stanford, CA: Stanford University Press, 1988); *The Emotional Tie: Psychoanalysis, Mimesis, and Affect* (Stanford: Stanford University Press, 1992), esp. 39–61. On the theoretical continuities between hypnosis and psychoanalysis, see Ellenberger, *Discovery of the Unconscious*, 418–500, and Sulloway, *Freud*, ch. 3. On the continuities between hypnosis, psychoanalysis, and mimetic theory, see also Nidesh Lawtoo, *The Phantom of the Ego: Modernism and the Mimetic Unconscious* (East Lansing: Michigan State University Press, 2013), 233–47, 284–95.

29. Sulloway, *Freud*, 57, 56.

30. Sigmund Freud and Joseph Breuer, *Studies on Hysteria*, in *The Standard Edition of the Complete Psychological Works of Sigmund Freud*, vol. 2 (1893–1895), ed. J. Strachey (London: The Hogarth Press and the Institute of Psycho-Analysis, 1955), 7. Hereafter *SH*. Breuer reconstructed the case of Anna O.; Freud added four case histories, those of Emmy von N., Lucie R., Katharina, and Elisabeth von R. Still, Anna O. remained the Ur-patient of the cathartic cure. Borch-Jacobsen expressed skepticism concerning the Breuer-Freud priority claim: "In my view," he wrote, "this is a retrospective construction in order to claim priority over Charcot, Janet, Delboeuf and others" (email to the author, May 19, 2016). This dynamic would be perfectly in line with what I call romantic agonism.

31. Borch-Jacobsen makes this point clearly: "since in true Aristotelian doctrine 'catharsis' refers to dramatic rather than narrative imitation—or as we might say with Plato, to *mimesis* in which the speaker enacts a role, rather than in *diegesis*, in which the speaker recounts events." And he adds: "If Freud and Breuer described the stories of their patients as cathartic, it is because these stories were in fact dramas that were played out, acted, mimed." Borch-Jacobsen, *Emotional Tie*, 45.

32. On catharsis as a method to "forget," rather than remember, see Borch-Jacobsen, "Sigmund Freud, Hypnotiseur," 142–48.

33. Lacan, *Ethics*, 304.

34. Sigmund Freud, "Two Encyclopaedia Articles," in *The Standard Edition of the Complete Psychological Works of Sigmund Freud*, vol. 18 (1920–1922), 233–60, 211.

35. As early as 1897 the philologist Alfred Berger wrote: "The cathartic treatment of hysteria described by the physicians Dr. Josef Breuer and Dr. Sigmund Freud is very

well suited to elucidate the cathartic effect of tragedy." Alfred Berger, "Wahrheit und Irrtum in der Katharsistheorie des Aristoteles," in *Aristoteles' Poetik*, trans. and ed. Theodor Gomperz (Leipzig: Veit, 1897), 69–98, 81.

36. On Freud's later reliance on Aristotle's theory of "catharsis of emotions" understood in terms of "release," "discharge," as well as "sexual stimulation," which inform the spectator's desire to "identify himself with a hero," see Sigmund Freud, "Psychopathic Characters on the Stage," *Psychoanalytical Quarterly* (1942): 459–64, 459.

37. Sigmund Freud, "An Autobiographical Study," in *The Freud Reader*, ed. Peter Gray (London: Vintage, 1995), 3–41, 18.

38. Freud, "Autobiographical Study," 19.

39. Jaspers, *General Psychopathology*, 360.

40. In addition to Ellenberger's and Sulloway's pioneering work, readers can find a detailed unmasking of the Freudian legend in Borch-Jacobsen and Shamdasani, *Freud Files*. For readers curious about the therapeutic efficacy of psychoanalysis from the point of view of Freud's patients, see also Mikkel Borch-Jacobsen, *Freud's Patients: A Book of Lives* (London: Reaktion Books, 2021).

41. Henry, *Généalogie*, 343, 344.

42. Sulloway, *Freud*, 57.

43. See Mikkel Borch-Jacobsen, *Remembering Anna O.: A Century of Mystification*, trans. Kirby Olson (New York: Routledge, 1996).

CHAPTER 3. THE RIDDLE OF CATHARSIS: ARISTOTLE'S *POETICS*

1. Gerald Else writes in his six-hundred-page commentary of *Poetics*: "Even a full survey of the literature on the subject [*katharsis*] would require a book in itself." Gerald F. Else, *Aristotle's Poetics: The Argument* (Cambridge, MA: Harvard University Press, 1967), 439, 225. Stephen Halliwell defines catharsis as "arguably now the most famous/ notorious, as well as enigmatic concept in the entire history of Western poetics." Stephen Halliwell, *Between Ecstasy and Truth: Interpretations of Greek Poetics from Homer to Longinus* (Oxford: Oxford University Press, 2011), 222.

2. Plato, *Republic*, in *The Collected Dialogues of Plato*, trans. P. Shorey, eds. E. Hamilton and H. Cairns (Princeton, NJ: Princeton University Press, 1963), 575–844, 832, 607a. Hereafter *Rep.* followed by page and line number.

3. Aristotle, *The Poetics of Aristotle*, trans. Stephen Halliwell (Chapel Hill: University of North Carolina Press, 1987), 37. Hereafter *P*.

4. Barbara Cassin, ed., *Dictionary of Untranslatables: A Philosophical Lexicon*, trans. and ed. Emily Apter, Jacques Lezra, and Michael Wood (Princeton, NJ: Princeton University Press, 2014), 126–28.

5. Adnan K. Abdulla, *Catharsis in Literature* (Bloomington: Indiana University Press,

1985), 13; for a survey of interpretations of catharsis, see also 12–25. For a recent account of catharsis that stresses the centrality of "vicarious" emotions such as fear, which I call mimetic, see also Bence Nanay, "Catharsis and Vicarious Fear," *European Journal of Philosophy* 26 (2018): 1371–80.

6. Barbara Cassin, Jacqueline Lichtenstein, Elisabete Thamer, "Catharsis," in *Dictionary of Untranslatables*, 126.

7. Cassin, ed., *Dictionary of Untranslatables*, 126–27.

8. Jean-Pierre Vernant and Pierre Vidal-Naquet, *Myth and Tragedy in Ancient Greece*, trans. Janet Lloyd (New York: Zone Books, 1988), 131.

9. Jean-Pierre Vernant, "Greek Tragedy: Problems of Interpretation," in *Structuralist Controversy*, 273–95, 293.

10. For a first step on the genealogical importance of the Symposium for mimetic theory, see Nidesh Lawtoo, "The Shadow of the Symposium: Sameness and Difference Replayed," *Modern Language Notes* 134, no. 5 (2019): 898–909.

11. Jacques Derrida, "Plato's Pharmacy," in *Dissemination*, trans. Barbara Johnson (Chicago: University of Chicago Press, 1981), 61–171.

12. See also Nidesh Lawtoo, "The Classical World: Sacrifice, Philosophy, and Religion," in *Handbook of Mimetic Theory and Religion*, ed. James Alison and Wolfgang Palaver (London: Palgrave Macmillan, 2018), 119–26.

13. Plato, *The Sophist*, trans. F. M. Cornford, in *The Collected Dialogues of Plato*, 957–1016, 969–70, 226d, 227a, 227c.

14. Plato, *Laws*, trans. A. E. Taylor, in *Collected Dialogues of Plato*, 1225–1513, 1230, 628d. Hereafter *Laws*.

15. Plato, *Laws*, 648b.

16. Elizabeth Belfiore, "Wine and Catharsis of the Emotions in Plato's *Laws*," *Classical Quarterly* 36, no. 2 (1986): 421–37, 437.

17. Aristotle, *Politics*, in *The Complete Works of Aristotle*, vol. 2, ed. Jonathan Barnes (Princeton, NJ: Princeton University Press, 1984), 1986–2129, 2128, 1342a-5-15.

18. Lacan's overview of Aristotle's different focus of catharsis in *Politics* and the *Poetics* is correct at the general level and follows Erwin Rohde's "admirable work" in *Psyche* on Dionysian rituals (hence the proximity to Nietzsche). Where Lacan goes astray is as he follows Bernays's medical interpretation, which he considers "excellent," but few philologists take seriously these days; see Jacques Lacan, *The Ethics of Psychoanalysis 1959–60: The Seminar of Jacques Lacan, Book VII*, ed. Jacques-Alain Miller, trans. Dennis Porter. New York: Routledge, 2008), 300–304.

19. The ethnomusicologist Gilbert Rouget, with this passage in mind, rightly notices that "the *katharsis* that occurs in possession rituals, as a result of 'enthusiastic' harmonies and 'sacred melodies,' is presented as being of the same order as that which is at work in the theater." Gilbert Rouget, *Music and Trance: A Theory of the Relations between*

Music and Possession, trans. Brunhilde Biebuyck (Chicago: University of Chicago Press, 1985), 224.

20. Aristotle is here clearly referring to Plato's discussion of mimesis in terms of enthusiasm, frenzy, and madness in dialogues like *Ion*, *Republic* III, and *Phaedrus*.

21. Cynthia Carter and C. Kay Weaver, *Violence and the Media* (New York: Open Univeristy Press, 2003), 84.

22. As Jean-Pierre Vernant and Pierre Vidal-Naquet point out: "for the student of myth, all myths, whether rich or poor, belong to the same level and are of equal value from a heuristic point of view. No single one has the right to be given preference over the others and the only reason for the interpreter to single it out is that, for reasons of convenience, he has chosen it as the model or reference point to be used in his inquiry." Vernant and Vidal-Naquet, *Myth and Tragedy*, 8. For a collection of essays on the case of Oedipus and its links to mimetic theory, see Mark R. Anspach, ed., *The Oedipus Casebook: Reading Sophocles' Oedipus the King* (East Lansing: Michigan State University Press, 2020).

23. Terry Eagleton, *Sweet Violence: The Idea of the Tragic* (Oxford: Blackwell Publishing, 2003), 43.

24. Eagleton, *Sweet Violence*, 14.

25. Bruno Latour, "The Enlightenment without the Critique: A Word on the Philosophy of Michel Serres," in *Contemporary French Philosophy*, ed. A. Phillips Griffiths (Cambridge: Cambridge University Press, 1987), 83–97, 86.

26. Else, *Aristotle's Poetics*, 440.

27. Else, *Aristotle's Poetics*, 440. As Pier Luigi Donini also notices, Bernays's "analogy with a medical cure entails the assumption that fear and pity are pathological conditions to be completely removed, while even a hasty reading of *Poetics* tells us immediately that Aristotle conceives of these passions in this work as the right, correct, and even dutiful [*doverosa*] reaction for the spectator in front of the acts represented." Pier Luigi Donini, *La tragedia e a la vita: Saggi sulla* Poetica *di Aristotele* (Alessandria: Edizioni dell'Orso, 2004), 55 (my trans.). I thank my colleague Jan Opsomer for this reference.

28. Halliwell, *Between Ecstasy and Truth*, 237, 245.

29. Philippe Lacoue-Labarthe, "*Katharsis et Mathésis*," *Europe* 88, no. 973 (2010): 72–93, 82; my emphasis and trans. Else confirms this point when he says that, for Aristotle, "we can speak of rational aspects of feeling or emotional employments of reasons." Else, *Aristotle's Poetics*, 435.

30. Abdulla equally stresses that catharsis is based on "two elements: 1) emotional arousal that leads to 2) intellectual understanding," but his dialectical lens leads him to stress that "the cathartic experience presupposes the harmony, and not the dichotomy, of emotions and reason." Abdulla, *Catharsis*, 119. While far from being a dualist and agreeing on the necessity of both pathos and logos, I do not posit an harmonious synthesis at play in patho-logy. Thomas Gould articulates the interplay between pathos

and distance for Aristotle's take on tragedy as follows: "the pathos has a function, but it needs to be balanced by an awareness of a genuine justice in the events depicted." Thomas Gould, *The Ancient Quarrel between Poetry and Philosophy* (Princeton, NJ: Princeton University Press, 1990), xxiii.

31. Halliwell, *Between Ecstasy and Truth*, 30.

32. The analogies with Nietzsche's notion of "pathos of distance" are profound, perhaps unsurprisingly given Nietzsche's philological training in classics. See Nidesh Lawtoo, *Phantom of the Ego: Modernism and the Mimetic Unconscious* (East Lansing: Michigan State University Press, 2013), 3–6; see also ch. 1. That Nietzsche considers both the Apollonian and the Dionysian as mimetic principles is equally made philologically clear as he states, for instance: "every artist is an 'imitator' [*Nachahmer*], that is to say, either an Apollinian artist in dreams, or a Dionysian artist in ecstasies, or finally—as for example in Greek tragedy—at once artist in both dreams and ecstasies." Friedrich Nietzsche, *The Birth of Tragedy*, in *The Birth of Tragedy and The Case of Wagner*, ed. and trans. Walter Kaufmann (New York: Vintage Books, 1967), 38.

33. Philippe Lacoue-Labarthe and Jean-Luc Nancy, *Scène* (Paris: Christian Bourgois, 2013), 19 (my trans.).

34. Lacoue-Labarthe and Nancy, *Scène*, 20.

35. Lacoue-Labarthe and Nancy, *Scène*, 22.

36. Donini, *La tragedia*, 56.

37. Halliwell, *Between Ecstasy and Truth*, 31.

38. As Terry Eagleton also puts it, summarizing a number of modern theories of tragic emotions: "Pity, roughly speaking, is a matter of intimacy, while fear is a reaction to otherness." Eagleton *Sweet Violence*, 161; see also 153–77.

39. For the early Nietzsche, of course, this interplay between pathos and distance is mediated by the "tragic chorus of primitive tragedy"; or, as he puts it, echoing Schiller, "the chorus as living wall that tragedy constructs around itself in order to close itself off from the world of reality" (*BT* 7:58).

40. Edmund Burke, *A Philosophical Enquiry into the Origin of Our Ideas of the Sublime and Beautiful*, ed. Adam Phillips (Oxford: Oxford University Press, 1990), 42; see also 41–46.

41. Hannah Chapelle Wojciehowski, "Interview with Vittorio Gallese," *California Italian Studies* (2011), https://escholarship.org/uc/item/56f8v9bv (no pagination).

42. Pier Luigi Donini offers an interesting and daring account of catharsis that confirms Halliwell's point that tragic pleasure triggers "emotions of pity and fear that will be balanced by the understanding of the action's rationality." Donini goes even further by making catharsis marginal to the *Poetics*. He notices that tragedy, in *Poetics*, does not generate catharsis itself but rather the "effecting," or "completion," of a catharsis that remains ritual in origins. This allows Donini to reconcile *Poetics* with *Politics*, while at the same time stressing the difference between ritual and aesthetic cathartic

experiences. As he puts it: "the catharsis to which the *Poetics* alludes is indeed the one that is discussed in *Politics*, a medical-musical fact that concerns human irrationality and Bernays was right with respect to *Politics*; but this catharsis is not at all the proper function of tragedy; it's only one of its presuppositions. With respect to the irrational musical catharsis, tragedy has thus the function of bringing it to completion and crowning it in the mode of rationality; and this is possible thanks to its mimetic procedure and its consequences (intellectual pleasure, reasoning, understanding)." Donini, *La tragedia*, 65 (my trans.).

43. As Else puts it, "There are in fact *pathê* which are bloody or painful enough but which do not arouse either pity or fear." Else, *Aristotle's Poetics*, 229; see also 231, 443.

44. Paul Ricoeur, *Temps et récit*, vol. 1., *L'intrigue et le récit historique* (Paris: Seuil, 1983), 89 (my trans.).

45. What Robert Buch notes for the pathos of violence in the twentieth century, equally applies for the twenty-first century: passions "provide no cathartic relief or soothing sentiment of compassion." Robert Buch, *The Pathos of the Real: On the Aesthetics of Violence in the Twentieth Century* (Baltimore: Johns Hopkins University Press, 2010), 23. And Gould, while retaining Bernays's "medical" interpretation, scales back the importance of catharsis for Aristotle as follows: "the benefit to be expected from the pleasurable 'cleansing' of tragedy is really quite minor, according to Aristotle: potentially troublesome emotions are flushed out so that viewers can get back to more important things—philosophy for instance." Gould, *Ancient Quarrel*, n1, 49, xxiii.

CHAPTER 4. BEYOND THE CATHARTIC PRINCIPLE: NIETZSCHE ON INFLUENCE

1. See especially Nidesh Lawtoo, *The Phantom of the Ego: Modernism and the Mimetic Unconscious* (East Lansing: Michigan State University Press, 2013), 1–83; "and "Birth of *Homo Mimeticus*: Nietzsche, Genealogy, Communication," *CounterText* 8, no. 1 (2022): 61–87.

2. Robert Pippin, *Nietzsche, Psychology, and First Philosophy* (Chicago: University of Chicago Press, 2010), 3.

3. Paul Ricoeur, *Freud and Philosophy: An Essay on Interpretation*, trans. Denis Savage (New Haven, CT: Yale University Press, 1970), 33.

4. As Ellenberger puts it: "Ludwig Klages has characterized Nietzsche as an eminent representative of a trend that was prevalent in the 1880s, the 'uncovering' or 'unmasking' psychology, which Dostoevsky and Ibsen developed in other directions" (*DU* 273). Ricoeur famously added Freud and Marx to the list.

5. In *Thus Spoke Zarathustra*, Nietzsche distinguished between the "ego" or "I" (*Ich*) confined to consciousness and the "self" (*Selbst*) or "it" (*es*) that finds in the body the "great reason" (*große Vernunft*). Friedrich Nietzsche, *Thus Spoke Zarathustra*, trans. Graham Parkes (Oxford: Oxford University Press, 2008), 30–31.

6. Friedrich Nietzsche, *The Gay Science*, trans. Walter Kaufman (New York: Vintage, 1974), 262.

7. Henri F. Ellenberger already noted that the Freudian legend "attributes to Freud much of what belongs, notably, to Herbart, Fechner, Nietzsche, Meynert, Benedikt, and Janet, and overlooks the work of previous explores of the unconscious." *The Discovery of the Unconscious: The History and Evolution of Dynamic Psychiatry* (New York: Basic Books, 1970, 548; see also 271–78. For a recent historical study, see Mikkel Borch-Jacobsen and Sonu Shamdasani, *The Freud Files: An Inquiry into the History of Psychoanalysis* (Cambridge: Cambridge University Press, 2012). What follows relies on the logic of romantic agonism to supplement these rich historical studies via a specific focus on Freud's unacknowledged debt to Nietzsche.

8. Karl Jaspers, *General Psychopathology*, vol.1., trans. J. Hoenig and Marian W. Hamilton (Baltimore: Johns Hopkins University Press, 1997), 315. For a recent insightful study on Kierkegaard that promotes a mimetic turn in line with our theory of homo mimeticus, see also Wojciech Kaftanski, *Kierkegaard's Existential Mimesis: A Study of Imitation, Existence, and Affect* (New York: Routledge, 2021).

9. Jaspers, *General Psychopathology*, 360.

10. Jaspers, *General Psychopathology*, 360; see also 359–63.

11. In addition to the sources already discussed (Ellenberger, Sulloway, Borch-Jacobsen, and Shamdasani), see also Mikkel Borch-Jacobsen, *Apprendre à philosopher avec Freud* (Paris: Ellipses, 2018).

12. Ellenberger also broadens the scope of Nietzsche's influence as he writes that in the 1890s "an entire generation was permeated with Nietzschean thinking—whatever interpretation was given to it—in the same way as the former generation had been under the spell of Darwinism. It is also impossible to overestimate Nietzsche's influence on dynamic psychiatry. More so even than Bachofen, Nietzsche may be considered the common source of Freud, Adler, and Jung" (*DU* 276).

13. Ronald Lehrer, *Nietzsche's Presence in Freud's Life and Thought: On the Origins of a Psychology of Dynamic Unconscious Mental Functioning* (Albany: State University of New York Press, 1995). Lehrer's evidence includes Freud's mention of Nietzsche in his correspondence with Eduard Silberstein as early as of 1875, the intellectual prominence of Nietzsche in fin de siècle Vienna, not to speak of evidence from the minutes of the Vienna Psychanalytical Society from April 1908 where *On the Genealogy of Morals* was studied—and read aloud—and the analogies discussed, among other shared genealogical connections. (Lou Andreas-Salomé, who met Nietzsche in the early 1880s, published a perceptive study of his psychology in 1894, and became part of the Psychoanalytic Association in the early 1910s where she ended up on Freud's couch.)

14. See Lehrer, *Nietzsche's Presence*, 4.

15. Michel Foucault, "Discussion," in *Nietzsche: Colloque de Royaumont* (Paris: Les Éditions de Minuit, 1967), 193–200, 198.

16. Sigmund Freud, *On the History of the Psycho-Analytic Movement*, in *Collected Papers*, vol.1, trans. Joan Riviere (New York: Basic Books, 1959), 287–359, 297.

17. Lorin Anderson, "Freud, Nietzsche," *Salmagundi* 47/48 (1980): 3–29, 15.

18. Anderson, "Freud, Nietzsche," 5. The performative efficacy of Freud's move can be gauged by the following interpretative fact: even an informed commentator of Nietzsche's psychology like Robert Pippin, when it comes to a comparison with Freud, sets out to call "Nietzsche's account [of the unconscious] Freudian" rather than Freud's account Nietzschean. Pippin, *Nietzsche*, 96. There is much to admire in this rich study of Nietzsche's psychology, yet when it comes to "pre-reflexive" unconscious activity, the distinction between "somatic" and "psychological" Pippin relies on (93–96) is precisely what Nietzsche's "physio-psychology" of the unconscious encourages us to go beyond. For a more perceptive account of Nietzsche's psychological ideas that recognizes they has a "logic of their own" that resonates with the study at hand, see Graham Parkes, *Composing the Soul: Reaches of Nietzsche's Psychology* (Chicago: University of Chicago Press, 1994).

19. Anderson, "Freud, Nietzsche," 25.

20. Harold Bloom's theory of "anxiety of influence" is shadowed by a romantic concern with originality. Still Bloom agrees with our diagnostic as he points out, with Shakespeare as a model, that "Freud suffered from a Hamlet complex (the true name of the Oedipus Complex) or an anxiety of influence in regard to Shakespeare." Harold Bloom, *The Anxiety of Influence: A Theory of Poetry*, 2nd ed. (Oxford: Oxford University Press, 1997), xxii. Whether this anxiety of influence Freud displays is toward Shakespeare or Nietzsche, finds a mimetic reproduction in Bloom's anxiety of influence toward Freud, on whose concepts (repression, identification, defense mechanism, *Nachträglichkeit*, among others) he heavily relied while at the same time denying the Oedipal origins of his theory ("I never meant with 'anxiety of influence' a Freudian Oedipal rivalry" [xxii]) is a legitimate question worth asking. The models change, the mimetic agonism remains the same.

21. This is a genealogical fallacy internal to Bloom's account of anxiety of influence. "Nietzsche and Freud are, as far as I can tell, the prime influences upon the theory of influence" he presents, and Nietzschean traces are present in his notion of "strong" misreadings characteristic of the "Over-reader" and "Over-poet." Bloom, *Anxiety*, 8; Harold Bloom, "Poetry, Revisionism, Repression," in *Critical Theory since 1965*, ed. Hazard Adams and Leroy Searle (Tallahassee: Florida State University Press, 1989), 333. This conflation of Freud and Nietzsche leads Bloom to claim that his theory is "un-Nietzschean in its deliberate literalism" (8) and to critique Nietzsche because he "over-idealized the imagination" (9). The move from literal to symbolic interpretation based on the idealization of the imagination are romantic fallacies that apply to Freud but not Nietzsche. Nietzsche opens up an anti-Oedipal genealogy of the unconscious that privileges the body over the imagination. In the process, he also accounts for an agonistic confrontation that does not hinge on a repressive but on a mimetic hypothesis.

22. Michel Foucault, "Nietzsche, Freud, Marx," in *Transforming the Hermeneutic Context: From Nietzsche to Nancy*, ed. Gayle L. Ormiston and Alan D. Schrift (Albany: State University of New York Press, 1990), 59–67, 62.

23. Friedrich Nietzsche, *On the Genealogy of Morals*, in *The Portable Nietzsche*, trans. and ed. Walter Kaufmann (New York: Penguin Books, 1982), 8.

24. For an informed essay that shows continuities between Nietzsche's and Bernays's take on catharsis, specifically with respect to the issue of "discharge" (*Entladung*), while also inscribing the former in a critical dialogue with Schopenhauer, see James Pearson, "On Catharsis, Conflict, and the Coherence of Nietzsche's Agonism," *Nietzsche-Studien* 45, no. 1 (2016): 3–32. On Nietzsche's antagonistic relation to Bernays, see also Le Rieder, "Philologie grecque et formation de la théorie psychanalytique: Sigmund Freud et Theodor Gomperz," *Essaim* 1, no. 7 (2001): 203–10.

25. Friedrich Nietzsche, *The Antichrist* in *The Portable Nietzsche*, trans. and ed. Walter Kaufmann (New York: Penguin Books, 1982), 565–656, 574. Hereafter *A*.

26. Oscar Wilde, an early modernist writer qua philologist with strong affinities with Nietzsche, also privileges an aesthetic over a moral interpretation of catharsis as he writes: "That purification and spiritualization of the nature which he [Aristotle] calls κάθαρσις is, as Goethe saw, essentially aesthetic, and is not moral, as Lessing fancied." Oscar Wilde, "The Critic as Artist," in *The Complete Works of Oscar Wilde*, vol. 4, ed. Josephine M. Guy (Oxford: Oxford University Press, 2007), 124–61, 140.

27. Friedrich Nietzsche, *Human, All Too Human I*, trans. Gary Handwerk (Stanford, CA: Stanford University Press, 1995), 212;141. Hereafter *HH*.

28. For a special issue that joins the mimetic turn with the post-literary turn, see "The Mimetic Condition," ed. Nidesh Lawtoo, *CounterText* 8, no. 1 (2022).

29. As Graham Parkes notes in his informed study of Nietzsche's psychology: "It is the main trait of the genealogical method to take what appears to be a unitary phenomenon and disclose its multiple origins, showing it to be generated by a plurality of drives." Parkes, *Composing the Soul*, 277. For an informed genealogy of Nietzsche's theory of drives attentive to mimesis, see also 251–318.

30. Terry Eagleton, *Sweet Violence: The Idea of the Tragic* (Oxford: Blackwell Publishing, 2003), 154.

31. I thank William (Bill) Connolly for reminding me of this passage in one of our numerous Nietzschean chats during my stay at Johns Hopkins University back in 2015–16.

32. James Person belongs to a younger generation of Nietzsche scholars attentive to Nietzsche's engagement with science as he rightly notices: "We might also add that Nietzsche's thought aligns with current empirical research, which tends to contest the idea that physically destructive tendencies can be adequately explained by a hydraulic drive theory, such as one finds in the thought of Freud and Lorenz, for example." Pearson, "On Catharsis," 18. On the physio-psychology of "sensation" [*Empfindung*] in Nietzsche, the most informed overview I know is Herman Siemens, "Empfindung,"

in *Nietzsche-Wörterbuch Online*, ed. Paul van Tongeren, Gerd Schank, and Herman Siemens (Berlin: Walter de Gruyter, 2011), n.p.

33. Georges Bataille, "Collège de sociologie" in *Œuvres Complètes*, vol. 2 (Paris: Gallimard, 1988), 291–376, 331.

34. Plato, *Phaedo*, 50, 67c. On catharsis as "purification," see also *Cratylus* in *The Collected Dialogues of Plato*, ed. Edith Hamilton and Huntington Cairns (New York: Pantheon Books, 1963), 421–23, 441–42, 405a–c.

CHAPTER 5. AN ATTEMPT AT SELF-CRITIQUE: CONTRA HYPERSPECIALIZATION

1. See Janet Bergstrom, ed., *Endless Night: Cinema and Psychoanalysis, Parallel Histories* (Berkeley: University of California Press, 1999). Given these parallel histories it is no wonder that, in a spiraling loop, film can in turn serve as an introduction to psychoanalysis and its Freudian and Lacanian manifestations. See *The Pervert's Guide to Cinema* (Dir. Sophie Finnes, written by Slavoj Žižek, 2006).

2. Edgar Morin, *Les sept savoirs nécessaires à l'éducation du futur* (Paris: Seuil, 2000), 46 (my trans.).

3. Edgar Morin, *La tête bien faite* (Paris: Seuil, 1999), 44 (my trans.).

4. Samuel IJsseling, *Mimesis: On Appearing and Being* (Kampen, NE: Pharos, 1990), 32.

5. See the six volumes of Edgar Morin, *La Méthode* (Paris: Seuil, 2008), esp. vols. 3, 4, 5, 6.

6. For a recent wide-ranging collection recognizing that "in response to new conditions, the research processes of interdisciplinarity foster the particular space of ideation as limen, as threshold, or as interstice, then they also function like nodes in a network, as spaces inter or in-between," see Celia Lury et al., eds., *The Routledge Handbook for Interdisciplinary Research Methods* (London: Routledge, 2018), 31.

7. Friedrich Nietzsche, *The Gay Science*, trans. Walter Kaufman (New York: Vintage, 1974), 322.

8. For an influential discussion of this mirroring reflection, see Foucault's diagnostic of "Las Meninas," in Michel Foucault, *The Order of Things: An Archaeology of the Human Sciences* (New York: Vintage Books, 1973), 3–16.

9. Morin, *Les sept savoirs*, 51.

10. For a dialogue with Edgar Morin on the complexity of homo mimeticus, see Nidesh Lawtoo, *The Complexity of Mimesis: Edgar Morin*, HOM Videos, Ep. 2, https://www.youtube.com/watch?v=iSKzMydA5Mw&t=2292s.

11. Friedrich Nietzsche, "On the Uses and Disadvantages of History for Life," in *Untimely Meditations*, ed. Daniel Breazeale, trans. R. J. Hollingdale (Cambridge: Cambridge University Press, 2007), 57–123, 66.

12. Nietzsche, "On the Uses," 59.

13. On the role of mimesis in the linguistic turn, see Nidesh Lawtoo and Jean-Luc Nancy, "The *CounterText* Interview: Jean-Luc Nancy Mimesis: A Singular-Plural Concept," *CounterText* 8, no. 1 (2022): 23–45. This whole issue on "The Mimetic Condition" is devoted to furthering the mimetic turn.

14. I trace this genealogy in more detail in Nidesh Lawtoo, *Homo Mimeticus: A New Theory of Imitation* (Leuven: Leuven University Press, 2022).

15. For a first step toward a mimetic turn in posthuman studies see the special issue on "Posthuman Mimesis," ed. Nidesh Lawtoo, *Journal of Posthumanism* 2, no. 2 (2022).

CODA: THE END OF A METHOD

1. See, for instance, Noam Chomsky, *Nuclear War and Environmental Catastrophe* (New York: Seven Stories Press, 2013); Slavoj Žižek, *Living in the End Times* (London: Verso Books, 2010); Brecht Volders and Tom Sauer, eds., *Nuclear Terrorism: Countering the Threat* (London: Routledge, 2016).

2. See also Nidesh Lawtoo, "Dueling to the End/Ending 'The Duel': Girard *avec* Conrad," *Contagion* 22 (2015): 153–84.

Bibliography

Abdulla, Adnan K. *Catharsis in Literature*. Bloomington: Indiana University Press, 1985.

Abrams, M. H. *The Mirror and the Lamp: Romantic Theory and the Critical Tradition*. Oxford: Oxford University Press, 1953.

Agamben, Giorgio. *Homo Sacer: Sovereign Power and Bare Life*. Translated by Daniel Heller-Roazen. Stanford, CA: Stanford University Press, 1998.

Anderson, Lorin. "Freud, Nietzsche." *Salmagundi* 47/48 (1980): 3–29.

Anspach, Mark R. *The Oedipus Casebook: Reading Sophocles' Oedipus the King*. East Lansing: Michigan State University Press, 2020.

Aristotle. *The Poetics of Aristotle*. Translated by Stephen Halliwell. Chapel Hill: University of North Carolina Press, 1987.

———. *Politics*. In *The Complete Works of Aristotle*, vol. 2, edited by Jonathan Barnes, 1986–2129. Princeton, NJ: Princeton University Press, 1984.

Auerbach, Erich. *Mimesis: The Representation of Reality in Western Literature*. Translated by Willard R. Trask. Princeton, NJ: Princeton University Press, 2003.

Bataille, Georges. "Hegel, la mort, le sacrifice." In *Œuvres Complètes*, vol. 12, 326–45. Paris: Gallimard, 1988.

Belfiore, Elizabeth. "Wine and Catharsis of the Emotions in Plato's *Laws*." *Classical Quarterly* 36, no. 2 (1986): 421–37.

Benjamin, Walter. *Illuminations*. Edited by Hannah Arendt, translated by Harry Zohn. New York: Schocken Books, 2007.

Berger, Alfred. "Wahrheit und Irrtum in der Katharsistheorie des Aristoteles." In *Aristoteles' Poetik*, edited and translated by Theodor Gomperz, 69–98. Leipzig: Veit, 1897.

Bergstrom, Janet, ed. *Endless Night: Cinema and Psychoanalysis, Parallel Histories*. Berkeley: University of California Press, 1999.

Bernays, Jacob. "Aristotle on the Effect of Tragedy." Translated by Jennifer Barnes. In *Oxford Readings in Ancient Literary Criticism*, edited by Andrew Laird, 158–75. Oxford: Oxford University Press, 2006.

——. *Grundzüge der Verlorenen Abhandlung des Aristoteles über Wirkung der Tragödie*. Breslau: Verlag von Eduard Trewendt, 1857.

——. *Zwei Abhandlungen über die Aristotelische Theorie des Drama*. Berlin: Wilhelm Hertz, 1880.

Bloom, Harold. *The Anxiety of Influence: A Theory of Poetry*, 2nd ed. Oxford: Oxford University Press, 1997.

——. "Poetry, Revisionism, Repression." In *Critical Theory since 1965*, edited by Hazard Adams and Leroy Searle, 331–44. Tallahassee: Florida State University Press, 1989.

Borch, Christian., ed. *Imitation, Contagion, Suggestion: On Mimesis and Society*. New York: Routledge, 2019.

——. *Social Avalanche: Crowds, Cities and Financial Markets*. Cambridge: Cambridge University Press, 2020.

Borch-Jacobsen, Mikkel. *Apprendre à philosopher avec Freud*. Paris: Ellipses, 2018.

——. *The Emotional Tie: Psychoanalysis, Mimesis, and Affect*. Stanford, CA: Stanford University Press, 1992.

——. *The Freudian Subject*. Translated by Catherine Porter. Stanford, CA: Stanford University Press, 1988.

——. *Freud's Patients: A Book of Lives*. London: Reaktion Books, 2021.

——. *Making Madness: From Hysteria to Depression*. Cambridge: Cambridge University Press, 2009.

——. *Remembering Anna O.: A Century of Mystification*. Translated by Kirby Olson. New York: Routledge, 1996.

——. "Sigmund Freud, Hypnotiseur." In Sigmund Freud, *L'Hypnose: Textes 1886–1993*. Paris: Éditions l'Iconoclaste, 2015.

Borch-Jacobsen, Mikkel, and Sonu Shamdasani. *The Freud Files: An Inquiry into the History of Psychoanalysis*. Cambridge: Cambridge University Press, 2012.

Boyle, Karen. *Media and Violence: Gendering the Debates*. London: Sage, 2004.

Buch, Robert. *The Pathos of the Real: On the Aesthetics of Violence in the Twentieth Century.* Baltimore: Johns Hopkins University Press, 2010.

Burckhardt, Jacob. *The Greeks and Greek Civilization.* London: HarperCollins, 1998.

Burke, Edmund. *A Philosophical Enquiry into the Origin of Our Ideas of the Sublime and Beautiful,* edited by Adam Phillips. Oxford: Oxford University Press, 1990.

Butler, Judith. *The Force of Nonviolence: An Ethico-Political Bind.* London: Verso, 2020.

Carter, Cynthia, and C. Kay Weaver. *Violence and the Media.* New York: Open Univeristy Press, 2003.

Cassin, Barbara, ed. *Dictionary of Untranslatables: A Philosophical Lexicon.* Translation edited by Emily Apter, Jacques Lezra, and Michael Wood. Princeton, NJ: Princeton University Press, 2014.

Cavarero, Adriana. *Horrorism: Naming Contemporary Violence.* New York: Columbia University Press, 2011.

Chantre, Benoît. *Les derniers jours de René Girard.* Paris: Grasset, 2016.

Chater, Nick, and Susan Hurley, eds. *Perspectives on Imitations: From Neuroscience to Social Science.* Vol. 2, *Imitation, Human Development, and Culture.* Cambridge, MA: MIT Press, 2005.

Chomsky, Noam. *Nuclear War and Environmental Catastrophe.* New York: Seven Stories Press, 2013.

Connolly, William E. *The Fragility of Things: Self-Organizing Processes, Neoliberal Fantasies, and Democratic Activism.* Durham, NC: Duke University Press, 2013.

Derrida, Jacques. "Plato's Pharmacy." In *Dissemination.* Translated by Barbara Johnson, 61–171. Chicago: University of Chicago Press, 1981.

———. "Violence et métaphysique." In *L'écriture et la différence,* 117–228. Paris: Seuil, 1967.

Didi-Huberman, Georges. *L'invention de l'hystérie: Charcot et l'iconographie photographique de la Salpêtrière.* Paris: Macula, 1982.

Dodds, E. R. *The Greeks and the Irrational.* Berkeley: University of California Press, 1964.

Donini, Pier Luigi. *La tragedia e la vita: Saggi sulla Poetica di Aristotele.* Alessandria: Edizioni dell'Orso, 2004.

Dupuy, Jean-Pierre. *Economy and the Future: A Crisis of Faith.* Translated by M. B. DeBevoise. East Lansing: Michigan State University Press, 2014.

———. *La jalousie: Une géométrie du désir.* Paris: Seuil, 2016.

Eagleton, Terry. *Radical Sacrifice.* New Haven, CT: Yale University Press, 2018.

———. *Sweet Violence: The Idea of the Tragic.* Oxford: Blackwell Publishing, 2003.

Eastin, Matthew S., ed. *Encyclopedia of Media Violence.* Thousand Oaks, CA: Sage, 2013.

Ellenberger, Henri F. *The Discovery of the Unconscious: The History and Evolution of Dynamic Psychiatry*. New York: Basic Books, 1970.

Else, Gerald F. *Aristotle's Poetics: The Argument*. Cambridge, MA: Harvard University Press, 1967.

———. "'Imitation' in the Fifth Century." *Classical Philology* 53, no. 2 (1958): 73–90.

Fleming, Chris. *René Girard: Violence and Mimesis*. Cambridge: Polity, 2004.

Foucault, Michel. "Discussion." In *Nietzsche: Colloque de Royaumont*, 193–200. Paris: Les Éditions de Minuit, 1967.

———. *Histoire de la sexualité I: la volonté de savoir*. Paris: Gallimard, 1976.

———. "Nietzsche, Freud, Marx." In *Transforming the Hermeneutic Context: From Nietzsche to Nancy*, edited by Gayle L. Ormiston and Alan D. Schrift, 59–67. Albany: State University of New York Press, 1990.

———. "Nietzsche, Genealogy, History." In *Language, Counter-Memory, Practice: Selected Essays and Interviews*, edited by Donald F. Bouchard, 138–64. Ithaca, NY: Cornell University Press, 1984.

———. *The Order of Things: An Archaeology of the Human Sciences*. New York: Vintage Books, 1973.

Freedman, Jonathan L. *Media Violence and Its Effect on Aggression: Assessing the Scientific Evidence*. Reprint, Toronto: University of Toronto Press, 2003.

Freud, Sigmund. "An Autobiographical Study." In *The Freud Reader*, edited by Peter Gray, 3–41. London: Vintage, 1995.

———. *The Ego and the Id*. Edited by James Strachey, translated by Joan Rivière. London: W.W. Norton & Company, 1960.

———. *On the History of the Psycho-Analytic Movement*. In *Collected Papers*. Vol. 1, translated by Joan Riviere, 287–359. New York: Basic Books, 1959.

———. "Psychopathic Characters on the Stage." *Psychoanalytical Quarterly* (1942): 459–64.

———. "Two Encyclopaedia Articles." In *The Standard Edition of the Complete Psychological Works of Sigmund Freud*, vol. 18, *(1920–1922)*, edited by J. Strachey, 233–60. London: The Hogarth Press and the Institute of Psycho-Analysis, 1999.

Freud, Sigmund, and Joseph Breuer. *Studies on Hysteria*. In *The Standard Edition of the Complete Psychological Works of Sigmund Freud*, vol. 2, *(1893–1895)*, edited by J. Strachey. London: The Hogarth Press and the Institute of Psycho-Analysis, 1955.

Garrels, Scott, ed. *Mimesis and Science: Empirical Research on Imitation and the Mimetic Theory of Culture and Religion*. East Lansing: Michigan State University Press, 2011.

Gebauer, Gunter, and Christoph Wulf. *Mimesis: Culture-Art-Society*. Translated by Don Reneau. Berkeley: University of California Press, 1995.

Girard, René. *Battling to the End: Conversations with Benoît Chantre*. East Lansing: Michigan State University Press, 2010.

———. *Deceit, Desire and the Novel*. Translated by Yvonne Freccero. Baltimore: Johns Hopkins University Press, 1965.

———. *Des choses cachées depuis la fondation du monde: Recherches avec Jean-Michel Oughourlian et Guy Lefort*. Paris: Bernard Grasset, 1978.

———. *Evolution and Conversion: Dialogues on the Origins of Culture* (with Pierpaolo Antonello and João Cezar de Castro Rocha). London: Continuum, 2007.

———. "Narcissism: The Freudian Myth Demythified by Proust." In *Psychoanalysis, Creativity, and Literature*, edited by Alan Roland, 293–311. New York: Columbia University Press, 1978.

———. "Perilous Balance: A Comic Hypothesis." *Modern Language Notes* 87, no. 7 (1972): 811–26.

———. *The Scapegoat*. Translated by Yvonne Freccero. Baltimore: Johns Hopkins University Press, 1986.

———. "Tiresias and the Critic." In *The Structural Controversy: The Languages of Criticism and the Sciences of Man*, edited by Richard Macksey and Eugenio Donato, 15–21. Baltimore: Johns Hopkins University Press, 1972.

———. *Violence and the Sacred*. Baltimore: Johns Hopkins University Press, 1972.

Girard, René, and Michel Serres. *Le tragique et la pitié*. Paris: Le Pommier, 2007.

Gould, Thomas. *The Ancient Quarrel between Poetry and Philosophy*. Princeton, NJ: Princeton University Press, 1990.

Guénon, Denis. "Contagion and Purgation." In *Actions et acteurs: Raisons du drame sur scène*, 189–99. Paris: Belin, 2005.

Gunter, Barrie. *Does Playing Video Games Make Players More Violent?* London: Palgrave Macmillan, 2016.

Halliwell, Stephen. *Between Ecstasy and Truth: Interpretations of Greek Poetics from Homer to Longinus*. Oxford: Oxford University Press, 2011.

Haven, Cynthia L. *Evolution of Desire: A Life of René Girard*. East Lansing: Michigan State University Press, 2018.

Henry, Michel. *Généalogie de la psychanalyse: le commencement perdu*. Paris: Presses Universitaires de France, 1985.

Huizinga, Johan. *Homo Ludens: A Study of the Play-Element in Culture*. Kettering, OH: Angelico Press, 2016.

Hurley, Susan. "Imitation, Media Violence, and Freedom of Speech." *Philosophical Studies: An International Journal for Philosophy in the Analytic Tradition* 117, no. 1–2 (2004): 165–218.

IJsseling, Samuel. *Mimesis: On Appearing and Being*. Kampen, NE: Pharos, 1990.

James, Robert J. *Dictionnaire universel de la médecine*. Vol. 3. Translated by Diderot Eidous et Toussaint. Paris: Rue St. Jacques, 1747.

Jaspers, Karl. *General Psychopathology*. Vol.1. Translated by J. Hoenig and Marian W. Hamilton. Baltimore: Johns Hopkins University Press, 1997.

Johnsen, William A. *Violence and Modernism: Ibsen, Joyce, and Woolf*. Gainesville: University of Florida Press, 2003.

Kaftanski, Wojciech. *Kierkegaard's Existential Mimesis: A Study of Imitation, Existence, and Affect*. New York: Routledge, 2021.

Kendrick, James. *Film Violence: History, Ideology, Genre*. London: Wallflower, 2009.

Lacan, Jacques. *The Ethics of Psychoanalysis 1959–60: The Seminar of Jacques Lacan, Book VII*. Edited by Jacques-Alain Miller, translated by Dennis Porter. New York: Routledge, 2008.

———. "The Mirror Stage as Formative to the Function of the I as Revealed in Psychoanalytical Experience," in *Écrits: A Selection*, trans. Alan Sheridan, 1–7. Paris: Seuil, 1977.

Lacoue-Labarthe, Philippe. "*Katharsis* et *Mathésis*." *Europe* 88, no. 973 (2010): 72–93.

———. *Typography: Mimesis, Philosophy, Politics*. Edited by Christopher Fynsk. Stanford, CA: Stanford University Press, 1998.

Lacoue-Labarthe, Philippe, and Jean-Luc Nancy. *Scène*. Paris: Christian Bourgois, 2013.

Latour, Bruno. "The Enlightenment without the Critique: A Word on the Philosophy of Michel Serres." In *Contemporary French Philosophy*, edited by A. Phillips Griffiths, 83–97. Cambridge: Cambridge University Press, 1987.

Lauwaert, Lode. "Violence and Essentialism?" In *Violence and Meaning*, edited by Lode Lauwaert, Laura Katherine Smith, and Christian Sternad, 27–37. New York: Palgrave Macmillan, 2019.

Lawtoo, Nidesh. "Birth of *Homo Mimeticus*: Nietzsche, Genealogy, Communication." *CounterText* 8, no. 1 (2022): 61–87.

———. "The Classical World: Sacrifice, Philosophy, and Religion." In *Handbook of Mimetic Theory and Religion*, edited by James Alison and Wolfgang Palaver, 119–26. London: Palgrave Macmillan, 2018.

———. *The Complexity of Mimesis: Edgar Morin*, HOM Videos, Ep. 3, 2019. January 3, 2021, https://www.youtube.com/watch?v=iSKzMydA5Mw&t=6s.

———. *Conrad's Shadow: Catastrophe, Mimesis, Theory*. East Lansing: Michigan State University Press, 2016.

———. "The Critic and the Mime: J. Hillis Miller in Dialogue with Nidesh Lawtoo." *Minnesota Review* 95 (2020): 93–119.

———. "The Critic as Mime: Wilde's Theoretical Performance," *Symplokē* 26, no. 1–2 (2018): 317–28.

———. "Dueling to the End/Ending 'The Duel': Girard *avec* Conrad." *Contagion* 22 (2015): 153–84.

———. *Homo Mimeticus: A New Theory of Imitation*. Leuven: Leuven University Press, 2022.

———, ed. "The Mimetic Condition." Special issue, *CounterText* 8, no.1 (2022).

———. "The Mimetic Condition: Theory and Concepts," *CounterText* 8, no. 1 (2022): 1–22.

———. *(New) Fascism: Contagion, Communication, Myth*. East Lansing: Michigan State University Press, 2019.

———. *The Phantom of the Ego: Modernism and the Mimetic Unconscious*. East Lansing: Michigan State University Press, 2013.

———, ed. "Posthuman Mimesis." Special issue, *Journal of Posthumanism* 2, no. 2 (2022).

———. "The Shadow of the Symposium: Difference and Sameness Replayed." *Modern Language Notes* 134, no. 5 (2019): 898–909.

Lawtoo, Nidesh, and Jean-Luc Nancy. "The *CounterText* Interview: Jean-Luc Nancy Mimesis: A Singular-Plural Concept." *CounterText* 8, no. 1 (2022): 23–45.

Lehrer, Ronald. *Nietzsche's Presence in Freud's Life and Thought: On the Origins of a Psychology of Dynamic Unconscious Mental Functioning*. Albany: State University of New York Press, 1995.

Le Rieder, Jacques. "Philologie grecque et formation de la théorie psychanalytique: Sigmund Freud et Theodor Gomperz." *Essaim* 1, no. 7 (2001): 203–17.

Lorenz, Konrad. *On Aggression*. Translated by Marjorie Latzke. London: Routledge, 1966.

Lury, Celia, Rachel Fensham, Alexandra Heller-Nicholas, Sybille Lammes, Angela Last, Mike Michael, and Emma Uprichard, eds. *The Routledge Handbook for Interdisciplinary Research Methods*. London: Routledge, 2018.

Mahood, Chad. "Cathartic Theory." In *Encyclopedia of Media Violence*, edited by Matthew S. Eastin, 59–62. Thousand Oaks, CA: Sage, 2013.

Mbembe, Achille. *Brutalisme*. Paris: La Découverte, 2020.

McKenna, Andrew J. *Violence and Difference: Girard, Derrida, and Deconstruction*. Champaign: University of Illinois Press, 1992.

Morin, Edgar. *La Méthode*. Vol. 1 and 2. Paris: Seuil, 2008.

———. *On Complexity*. New York: Hampton Press, 2008.

———. *Le paradigme perdu: la nature humaine*. Paris: Seuil, 1973.

———. *Les sept savoirs nécessaires à l'éducation du futur*. Paris: Seuil, 2000.

———. *La tête bien faite*. Paris: Seuil, 1999.

Morris, Desmond. *The Naked Ape: A Zoologist's Study of the Human Animal*. London: Vintage Books, 2005.

Nanay, Bence. "Catharsis and Vicarious Fear." *European Journal of Philosophy* 26 (2018): 1371–80.

Nietzsche, Friedrich. *The Antichrist*. In *The Portable Nietzsche*. Translated and edited by Walter Kaufmann, 565–656. New York: Penguin Books, 1982.

———. *Beyond Good and Evil*. Translated by R. J. Hollingdale. London: Penguin Books, 2003.

———. *The Birth of Tragedy*. In *The Birth of Tragedy and The Case of Wagner*, edited and translated by Walter Kaufmann, 15–144. New York: Vintage Books, 1967.

———. *Daybreak: Thoughts on the Prejudices of Morality*. Translated by R. J. Hollingdale. Cambridge: Cambridge University Press, 1982.

———. *The Gay Science*. Translated by Walter Kaufman. New York: Vintage, 1974.

———. "Homer's Contest." Translated and edited by Christa Davis Acampora. *Nietzscheana* 5 (1996): 1–8.

———. *Human, All Too Human I*. Translated by Gary Handwerk. Stanford, CA: Stanford University Press, 1995.

———. *On the Genealogy of Morals: A Polemic*. Translated by Douglas Smith. Oxford: Oxford University Press, 1996.

———. "On the Uses and Disadvantages of History for Life." In *Untimely Meditations*, edited by Daniel Breazeale, translated by R. J. Hollingdale, 57–124. Cambridge: Cambridge University Press, 2007.

———. "Richard Wagner in Bayreuth." In *Untimely Meditations*, edited by Daniel Breazeale, translated by R. J. Hollingdale, 195–294. Cambridge: Cambridge University Press, 2007.

———. *Sämtliche Werke: Kritische Studienausgabe*. 15 vols. Edited by Giorgio Colli and Mazzino Montinari. Berlin: Walter de Gruyter, 1967–77.

———. *Thus Spoke Zarathustra*. Translated by Graham Parkes. Oxford: Oxford University Press, 2008.

———. *The Will to Power*. Edited by Walter Kaufmann, translated by Walter Kaufmann and R. J. Hollingdale. New York: Vintage Books, 1968.

Oughourlian, Jean-Michel. *The Mimetic Brain*. Translated by Trevor Cribben Merrill. East Lansing: Michigan State University Press, 2016.

Palaver, Wolfgang. *René Girard's Mimetic Theory*. East Lansing: Michigan State University Press, 2013.

Parkes, Graham. *Composing the Soul: Reaches of Nietzsche's Psychology*. Chicago: University of Chicago Press, 1994.

Pearson, James S. *Nietzsche's Philosophy of Conflict and the Logic of Organizational Struggle*. Cambridge: Cambridge University Press, 2022.

———. "On Catharsis, Conflict, and the Coherence of Nietzsche's Agonism." *Nietzsche-Studien* 45, no. 1 (2016): 3–32.

Pinker, Steven. *The Better Angels of Our Nature: Why Violence Has Declined*. New York: Viking Press, 2011.

Pippin, Robert. *Nietzsche, Psychology, and First Philosophy*. Chicago: University of Chicago Press, 2010.

Plato. *Laws*. In *The Collected Dialogues of Plato*, translated by A. E. Taylor, edited by E. Hamilton and H. Cairns, 1225–513. Princeton, NJ: Princeton University Press, 1963.

———. *Republic*. In *The Collected Dialogues of Plato*, translated by P. Shorey, edited by E. Hamilton and H. Cairns, 575–844. Princeton, NJ: Princeton University Press, 1963.

———. *The Sophist*. In *The Collected Dialogues of Plato*, translated by F. M. Cornford, edited by E. Hamilton and H. Cairns, 957–1016. Princeton, NJ: Princeton University Press, 1963.

Polak, Sara, and Daniel Trotter, eds. *Violence and Trolling on Social Media*. Amsterdam: Amsterdam University Press, 2020.

Potter, W. James. *The 11 Myths of Media Violence*. Thousand Oaks, CA: Sage, 2003.

Pseudo-Longinus. "On the Sublime." In *Critical Theory since Plato*, 3rd ed., edited by Hazard Adams and Leroy Searle, 95–118. Boston: Thomson Wadsworth, 2005.

Ricoeur, Paul. *Freud and Philosophy: An Essay on Interpretation*. Translated by Denis Savage. New Haven, CT: Yale University Press, 1970.

———. *Temps et récit*. Vol 1., *L'intrigue et le récit historique*. Paris: Seuil, 1983.

Rubino, Carl A. "Review: *La Violence et le sacré*." *Modern Language Notes* 87, no. 7 (1972): 986–98.

Rouget, Gilbert. *Music and Trance: A Theory of the Relations between Music and Possession*. Translated by Brunhilde Biebuyck. Chicago: University of Chicago Press, 1985.

Rousseau, Jean-Jacques. *Lettre à d'Alambert*. Paris: Flammarion, 2003.

Serres, Michel. *Hominescene*. Paris: Le Pommier, 2014.

Sherry, John L. "Violent Video Games and Aggression: Why Can't We Find Effects?" In *Mass Media Effects Research: Advances through Meta-Analysis*, edited by R. W. Presiss, B. M. Gayle, N. Burrell, M. Allen, and J. Byrant, 245–62. Mahwah, NJ: Erlbaum, 2007.

Siemens, Herman. "Agonal Configurations in the *Unzeitgemässe Betrachtungen*. Identity, Mimesis and the *Übertragung* of Culture in Nietzsche's Early Thought." *Nietzsche-Studien* 30 (2001): 80–106.

———. *Agonal Perspectives on Nietzsche's Philosophy of Critical Transvaluation*. Berlin: De Gruyter, 2021.

Spinoza, Benedict. *Ethics* (including *The Improvement of the Understanding*). Translated by R. H. M. Elwes. Amherst, NY: Prometheus Books, 1989.

Staten, Henry. *Techne Theory: A New Language for Art*. London: Bloomsbury, 2019.

Stiegler, Bernard. *What Makes Life Worth Living: On Pharmacology*. Translated by Daniel Ross. Cambridge: Polity, 2013.

Sulloway, Frank J. *Freud, Biologist of the Mind: Beyond the Psychoanalytic Legend*, 2nd ed. Cambridge, MA: Harvard University Press, 1992.

Ticineto, Patricia Clough. *The User Unconscious: On Affect, Media, and Measure*. Minneapolis: University of Minnesota Press, 2018.

Treml, Martin. "Zum Verhältnis von Jacob Bernays und Sigmund Freud." *Luzifer-Amor* 19 (1997): 7–38.

Vernant, Jean-Pierre, and Pierre Vidal-Naquet. *Myth and Tragedy in Ancient Greece*. Translated by Janet Lloyd. New York: Zone Books, 1988.

Volders, Brecht, and Tom Sauer, eds. *Nuclear Terrorism: Countering the Threat*. London: Routledge, 2016.Wilde, Oscar. "The Critic as Artist." In *The Complete Works of Oscar Wilde*, vol. 4, edited by Josephine M. Guy, 124–61. Oxford: Oxford University Press, 2007.

Wojciehowski, Hannah Chapelle. "Interview with Vittorio Gallese." *California Italian Studies* (2011). https://escholarship.org/uc/item/56f8v9bv.

Žižek, Slavoj. *Living in the End Times*. London: Verso Books, 2010.

———. *The Pervert's Guide to Cinema*. Directed by Sophie Finnes, P Guide Ltd. ICA Projects, 2006.

Index

Index

violence
Sophocles, 79, 98, 113, 136–37, 143. *See also*
    Oedipus
sparagmos, 75
spectacle (*opsis*), 119–20
Spinoza, Baruch, 68–69
Staten, Henry, 48
Stiegler, Bernard, 177n48
structuralism, 57, 59
structuralist controversy, 57–58, 105, 153
subject, xviii, 15, 21, 23, 26, 56, 65, 127, 156;
    of *Aufklärung*, 25; mimetic, 37–39,
    44; Oedipal, 41. *See also* phantom of
    the ego
sublimation, 130, 142–43
sublime, the, 48–49. *See also* Longinus
Sulloway, Frank, 85–86, 93

T

Thargelia, 104–5. See also *pharmakos*
tragic sympathy, 130, 142. *See also* pity
transdisciplinarity. *See* hyperspecialization;
    interdisciplinarity

U

Ukraine, 30, 166
unconscious, the, xiv, ix, xx–xxiii, 7–8, 12,
    16, 18–19; Freudian, 24–25, 35–45;
    genealogy of, 24–25, 53; Girardian,
    35–45; Nietzschean, 129–37; Oedipal,
    5, 8, 35, 40, 78–80, 91, 123; Oedipal vs.
    mimetic, 15–16, 35. *See also* cathartic
    method; mimetic unconscious

V

Vernant, Jean-Pierre, 73, 105, 189n22
Vidal-Naquet, Pierre, 73, 189n22
violence, xiv–xix; aesthetic, 76, 124; and
    cathartic method, 84–95; cinema,
    xxi–xxii; complexity of, 9–18; decrease
    or increase, 9–10; digital media,
    xvi, 2, 168–69; essentialism or anti-
    essentialism, 12–14; fiction, xiv–xvii;
    in film, xiv–xvii, 1–2, 111–12, 150;
    genealogy of, xxi, xxiii, 3, 7–8, 17, 80;

in Greek tragedy, 100–104, 113–27;
    intentionality, 15; interpretation of, 14;
    misogyny, xiv–xv, xviii, 3; and reality,
    xxi–xxiii, 1–3, 6; ritual, 76; simulation
    of, xvi–xvii, xxii, 1–3; social factors,
    10; video games, xix, xxi, 1–2, 32, 67,
    112, 125, 144, 167, 169. *See also* Greek
    tragedy; sacrifice; social media
vita mimetica, 31

W

Wagner, Richard, 45
Wilde, Oscar, 194n26
Willis, Bruce, xiv–xvi, xviii; *Vice*, xiv–xvi,
    xviii, 4, 111–12